Approaches to Teaching the Works of Cormac McCarthy

Approaches to Teaching the Works of Cormac McCarthy

Edited by

Stacey Peebles

and

Benjamin West

Modern Language Association of America

New York 2022

Library of Congress Cataloging-in-Publication Data

Names: Peebles, Stacey L. (Stacey Lyn), 1976- editor. | West, Benjamin S., 1979- editor.
Title: Approaches to teaching the works of Cormac McCarthy / edited by Stacey Peebles and Benjamin West.
Description: New York : Modern Language Association of America, 2022. |
Series: Approaches to teaching world literature, 1059-1133 ; 167 | Includes bibliographical references. | Summary: "Offers pedagogical techniques for teaching Cormac McCarthy's works, including considerations of their depiction of violence and dystopia, distinctive prose style, and relation to film. Contextualizes the works as regional literature of the South and West. Gives syllabus suggestions for high school, undergraduate, and graduate courses in American literature"—Provided by publisher.
Identifiers: LCCN 2021017779 (print) | LCCN 2021017780 (ebook) | ISBN 9781603294812 (hardcover) | ISBN 9781603294829 (paperback) | ISBN 9781603294836 (EPUB)
Subjects: LCSH: McCarthy, Cormac, 1933—Study and teaching. | McCarthy, Cormac, 1933—Criticism and interpretation.
Classification: LCC PS3563.C337 Z55 2022 (print) | LCC PS3563.C337 (ebook) | DDC 813/.54—dc23
LC record available at https://lccn.loc.gov/2021017779
LC ebook record available at https://lccn.loc.gov/2021017780

Approaches to Teaching World Literature 167
ISSN 1059-1133

Published by The Modern Language Association of America
85 Broad Street, Suite 500, New York, New York 10004-2434
www.mla.org

CONTENTS

ACKNOWLEDGMENTS

In 2013, at a Cormac McCarthy conference held at Berea College, we had a conversation with Nell Sullivan that was the genesis of this book. We're grateful that she gave us the encouragement we needed to get this project started. Our thanks also go to the Cormac McCarthy Society, which organized that conference as well as many others where friends and colleagues have traded ideas about how best to teach these works we all love so much. Our gratitude goes to the students who have gone with us on this adventure. And finally, we thank our families for serving variously as sounding boards, patient listeners, and inspiration.

Part One

MATERIALS

Works

Novels

The Orchard Keeper. Random House, 1965. Reprinted by Vintage Books, 1993.

Outer Dark. Random House, 1968. Reprinted by Vintage Books, 1993.

Child of God. Random House, 1974. Reprinted by Vintage Books, 1993.

Suttree. Random House, 1979. Reprinted by Vintage Books, 1992.

Blood Meridian; or, The Evening Redness in the West. Random House, 1985. Reprinted by Vintage Books, 1992.

All the Pretty Horses. Alfred A. Knopf, 1992. Reprinted by Vintage Books, 1993.

The Crossing. Alfred A. Knopf, 1994. Reprinted by Vintage Books, 1995.

Cities of the Plain. Alfred A. Knopf, 1998. Reprinted by Vintage Books, 1999.

No Country for Old Men. Alfred A. Knopf, 2005. Reprinted by Vintage Books, 2006.

The Road. Alfred A. Knopf, 2006. Reprinted by Vintage Books, 2006.

Published Plays and Screenplays

The Stonemason: A Play in Five Acts. Ecco Press, 1994. Reprinted by Vintage Books, 1995.

The Gardener's Son: A Screenplay. Ecco Press, 1996.

The Sunset Limited: A Novel in Dramatic Form. Vintage Books, 2006.

The Counselor: A Screenplay. Vintage Books, 2013.

Unpublished Screenplays

Cities of the Plain. 1984. Cormac McCarthy Papers, box 70, folder 3, Southwestern Writers Collection, Wittliff Collections, Texas State University, San Marcos. Shooting script.

No Country for Old Men. Cormac McCarthy Papers, box 79, folder 5, Southwestern Writers Collection, Wittliff Collections, Texas State University, San Marcos. Screenplay.

Whales and Men. Cormac McCarthy Papers, box 97, folder 5, Southwestern Writers Collection, Wittliff Collections, Texas State University, San Marcos. Uncorrected screenplay.

Film Adaptations

The Gardener's Son. Directed by Richard Pearce, performances by Brad Douriff and Ned Beatty, PBS, 1977.

All the Pretty Horses. Directed by Billy Bob Thornton, performances by Matt Damon and Henry Thomas, Columbia Pictures / Miramax, 2000.

No Country for Old Men. Directed by Joel Coen and Ethan Coen, performances by Tommy Lee Jones, Javier Bardem, and Josh Brolin, Paramount Vantage / Miramax Films, 2007.

The Road. Directed by John Hillcoat, performances by Viggo Mortensen and Kodi Smit-McPhee, Dimension Films / 2929 Productions, 2009.

The Sunset Limited. Directed by Tommy Lee Jones, performances by Tommy Lee Jones and Samuel L. Jackson, HBO Films, 2011.

Child of God. Directed by James Franco, performances by Scott Haze and Tim Blake Nelson, RabbitBandini Productions, 2013.

The Counselor. Directed by Ridley Scott, performances by Michael Fassbender, Javier Bardem, and Cameron Diaz, Fox 2000 Pictures, 2014.

Other Works

While a student at Knoxville Catholic High School, Cormac McCarthy published a few short pieces in the school paper, *The Gold and Blue*. In November 1948, his sophomore year, he contributed a poem titled "Sportsman's Wish," and in November 1950, his senior year, he published a poem titled "Autumn's Magic" and a short, humorous piece of journalism titled "Two Hour Scholar Loses His Dollar," about his trip to an annual fair. Dianne Luce and Wes Morgan have written articles about "Autumn's Wish" and McCarthy's high school years generally. The pieces themselves are housed in the Knoxville Catholic High School archives and have not been republished elsewhere.

In college at the University of Tennessee, Knoxville, McCarthy published two short stories that are more widely known: "Wake for Susan," from 1959, and "A Drowning Incident," from 1960. Both appeared in the college literary magazine *The Phoenix* and were reprinted in the magazine's fiftieth anniversary edition in 2010.

McCarthy's recent essay "The Kekulé Problem" is the author's only nonfiction work, and it explores the relation of language and consciousness. It was published in the spring 2017 issue of the popular science magazine *Nautilus*.

Translations

McCarthy's work has been translated widely. Bibliographies have been compiled of translations of McCarthy's works into different languages or of related reviews and criticism in those languages, which include French (Trotignon, "Cormac"), German (Guillemin, "Cormac"), Chinese (Jianran), and Italian (Nasi and Fioretto). By far the most comprehensive resource, however, is Béatrice Trotignon's 2019 bibliography of the first published translations of each of McCarthy's works into any language ("Bibliography"). Beginning with McCarthy's short story "A Wake for Susan" and including every work up through *The Counselor*, Trotignon notes the date, translator, and ISBN of each translation. The twenty-page bibliography indicates a great deal about McCarthy's global appeal—for instance, *The Road* has been translated into more than forty languages, and *Child of God* is the most translated of McCarthy's southern novels.

Interviews

McCarthy is often described as reluctant to give interviews or even as reclusive, though the latter designation is more myth than fact. Substantial, one-on-one interviews with the author have indeed been infrequent, but he gave a smattering of short interviews early in his career and has often paired up with filmmakers for conversations about the adaptations of his work. Early interviews include two with Knoxville newspapers in 1968 (McCarthy, "Author Lives in Blount" and "Knox Native"), one with the University of Tennessee's *Daily Beacon* in 1969 ("'Just Write'"), and another with a different Tennessee newspaper in 1971 ("McCarthy").

By far the most well-known interview given by McCarthy is in the 1992 *New York Times* article "Cormac McCarthy's Venomous Fiction"; the interview was conducted by Richard Woodward and includes oft-quoted statements from McCarthy about his favorite authors, his interest in violence and in the American West, and his reluctance to talk about his own writing process. Also in 1992, Gary Wallace published an account of his interactions and conversations with the author titled "Meeting McCarthy," though this wasn't conducted as a formal interview (Wallace).

McCarthy didn't agree to another interview until he spoke with Woodward again in 2005, this time for *Vanity Fair*, on the occasion of the release of his novel *No Country for Old Men* (McCarthy, "Cormac Country"). Over the next several years, he granted several additional interviews of substance: with Oprah Winfrey in 2007 to discuss his novel *The Road*, which won the Pulitzer Prize for Fiction and was chosen for Oprah's Book Club (Interview); with David Kushner, writing for *Rolling Stone*, in 2007, in which McCarthy talks about his interest in science and his work at the Santa Fe Institute ("Cormac McCarthy's Apocalypse"); and with John Jurgensen, writing for the *Wall Street Journal*, in 2009 ("Hollywood's Favorite Cowboy"). The interview with Jurgensen covers, in part, some of the film adaptations of McCarthy's novels, most particularly *The Road*, which was directed by John Hillcoat and released that same year.

Though the interview primarily features McCarthy, Hillcoat also joins in the conversation. McCarthy has also engaged in briefer collaborative interviews, with the filmmakers Joel Coen and Ethan Coen, about their adaptation of *No Country for Old Men* (McCarthy et al., "Conversation"); with the filmmaker Tommy Lee Jones and the actor Samuel L. Jackson, about the adaptation of *The Sunset Limited* (McCarthy et al., "'Tis"); and with the filmmaker Werner Herzog and the physicist Lawrence Krauss, on a radio program titled "Connecting Science and Art" (McCarthy et al.).

Biography

As of this writing, a book-length biography of McCarthy has not been written. The introduction to the 1999 revised edition of *Perspectives on Cormac McCarthy*, edited by Edwin Arnold and Dianne Luce, includes a biographical overview of McCarthy's life. In 2007 the Wittliff Collections at Texas State University, San Marcos, acquired the Cormac McCarthy Papers, which includes manuscript notes and drafts, correspondence, and other materials and provides a great deal of information about McCarthy's life and creative process that has since been incorporated into a number of scholarly works. *The Cambridge Companion to Cormac McCarthy*, edited by Steven Frye, features a detailed chronology of McCarthy's life and work, and the lead essay of Cambridge's *Cormac McCarthy in Context*, also edited by Frye, is Frye's "Cormac McCarthy's Life and Career." Luce writes more specifically about McCarthy's work with the editor Albert Erskine in "Cormac McCarthy and Albert Erskine: Evolution of a Working Relationship," and Stacey Peebles writes about McCarthy's work with theater, screenplays, and film in *Cormac McCarthy and Performance: Page, Stage, Screen*. Both Luce and Wesley Morgan have published articles in *The Cormac McCarthy Journal* about McCarthy's high school years: "Cormac McCarthy in High School: 1951" (Luce) and "McCarthy's High School Years" (Morgan). Morgan has further unearthed the historical or biographical bases for a number of details in McCarthy's works; see, for example, his "The Route and Roots of *The Road*," "Suttree's Dead Acquaintances and McCarthy's Dead Friends," "Red Callahan: The Actual and the Fictitious," and "Cormac McCarthy and *The Yearling*." Finally, additional archival materials relating to McCarthy's life and career can be found in the Albert Erskine Random House Editorial Files at the University of Virginia; the Howard Woolmer Collection of Cormac McCarthy and the Robert Cumbow Collection, both at Texas State University, San Marcos; the Richard Inman Pearce Collection at the University of South Carolina, which has materials relating to *The Gardener's Son*; and the Robert Coles Papers at the University of North Carolina, Chapel Hill.

Critical Reception

When Vereen Bell published the first monograph devoted to McCarthy, *The Achievement of Cormac McCarthy*, in 1988, the author had yet to receive the widespread acclaim and popularity that he would eventually earn in 1992 with *All the Pretty Horses*. But Bell's book makes the case, as the title suggests, that McCarthy's work is indeed worthy of scholarly discussion, and its appearance drew the attention of other critics interested in McCarthy and effectively created the field of McCarthy studies.[1] That field was codified in 1993, when the Cormac McCarthy Society was created at a conference devoted to the author and held at Bellarmine College. Since that time, regular conferences have been held in the United States and abroad, and Marty Priola's Web site www.cormacmccarthy.com has hosted a robust online conversation about the author. In 1998, a selection of scholarly articles appeared on the site, and in 2001, the society began publishing a hard-copy journal; since 2015, the *Cormac McCarthy Journal* has been published by Penn State University Press and indexed in online databases such as *JSTOR*, the *MLA International Bibliography*, and *Project MUSE*. The initial trickle of scholarly interest quickly became a flood, resulting in a field that is robust and many-faceted and that changes as McCarthy's own interests change. Frye has produced some of the best introductions to McCarthy for those seeking a broad overview. His short monograph *Understanding Cormac McCarthy* succinctly lays out the major backgrounds and themes of his work, and his two edited collections, *The Cambridge Companion to Cormac McCarthy* and *Cormac McCarthy in Context*, provide accessible discussions of the major avenues in McCarthy studies.

Much of the first wave of scholarship sought to make sense in moral (or amoral) terms of the frequent and often taboo-breaking violence in works by McCarthy, in addition to focusing on matters of McCarthy's style, influences, use of genre, and engagement with regional and historical context. Since the Wittliff Collections at Texas State University, San Marcos, acquired McCarthy's papers in 2007, scholarship has focused on different aspects of his creative process, in addition to reflecting other recent critical trends that address matters of ecology, economics, and art's connection to the sciences.

Bell's monograph was significant not only because it was the first but also because it staked out a lasting claim. As Frye puts it in a recent assessment of the field, Bell "established a critical perspective on McCarthy's themes that has remained a part of the academic debate down to the current moment"—namely, that McCarthy's created worlds are nihilistic, without an undergirding metaphysic ("Prospects" 3). They have "no first principles, no foundational truth, Heraclitus without Logos," as Bell puts it (9). Bell covers McCarthy's southern novels as well as *Blood Meridian*, and his thesis was persuasive to many scholars—at least until the publication of the Border Trilogy, which led some to reassess their understanding of McCarthy's style and aims. Since that time, scholars have debated the presence or character of a moral system in McCarthy's oeuvre, and Arnold's 1992 article "Naming, Knowing and Nothingness: McCarthy's Moral Parables" was one of the first palpable hits from the opposing side.

The question has been a central one and other book-length arguments that engage with the moral, philosophical, or theological implications of McCarthy's work include Lydia Cooper's *No More Heroes: Narrative Perspective and Morality in Cormac McCarthy*, Matthew Potts's *Cormac McCarthy and the Signs of Sacrament: Literature, Theology, and the Moral of Stories*, Petra Mundik's *A Bloody and Barbarous God: The Metaphysics of Cormac McCarthy*, Ty Hawkins's *Cormac McCarthy's Philosophy*, and Russell Hillier's *Morality in Cormac McCarthy's Fiction: Souls at Hazard*.

McCarthy has been known as an author of both the South and the Southwest, and a great deal of criticism has explored how his work deals with region, history, and associated literary traditions. Luce's book *Reading the World: Cormac McCarthy's Tennessee Period* is the definitive resource for McCarthy's works set in the South, because she explains a wealth of historical details and context: for instance, the significance of the Tennessee Valley Authority for the region and for some of McCarthy's characters, the real-life murder at the heart of *The Gardener's Son*, and the meticulous recreation of 1950s Knoxville in *Suttree*. "Read with a knowledge of place," Luce argues, "the works open out in unexpected ways, and what may seem like merely a realistic detail relegated to the hazy background of McCarthy's fiction—the displacement of a small landowner, a temperance parade, a flooded river, a passing reference to White Caps, a comically corrupt justice of the peace—comes into focus as a newly perceived foreground, one that was always there to be recognized" (vii–viii). Unlike *Reading the World*, John Sepich's *Notes on* Blood Meridian is not structured as a book-length argument, but it is nonetheless invaluable for an understanding of the numerous and often obscure historical sources McCarthy made use of in writing his most thoroughly researched novel. *Notes on* Blood Meridian was first published by Bellarmine College Press and had been long out of print—though much sought-after by scholars—when the University of Texas Press published a revised and expanded edition in 2008.

Morgan has also taken a historical approach to McCarthy's work, authoring a series of articles uncovering the sources for details of character and place in *The Orchard Keeper*, *Suttree*, and *The Road* ("'Government Tank,'" "Suttree's Dead Acquaintances," and "Route"). John Wegner's article "'Mexico para los mexicanos': Revolution, Mexico, and Cormac McCarthy's Border Trilogy" unpacks the importance of the Mexican Revolution to those three novels, while other scholars have analyzed McCarthy's approach to history more generally, often beyond specific regions: such scholars include David Holloway, in *The Late Modernism of Cormac McCarthy*; John Cant, in *Cormac McCarthy and the Myth of American Exceptionalism*; and Nicholas Monk, in *A True and Living Prophet of Destruction: Cormac McCarthy and Modernity*.

Other critics have engaged McCarthy's depictions of place in different ways. Georg Guillemin's 2004 *The Pastoral Vision of Cormac McCarthy* builds on John Grammer's 1992 essay "'A Thing against Which Time Will Not Prevail': Pastoral and History in Cormac McCarthy's South" in order to apply Grammer's ideas to McCarthy's southern and western works and was one of the first ecocritical readings of McCarthy's works. Jay Ellis's *No Place for Home: Spatial Constraint and Character Flight in the Novels of Cormac McCarthy* addresses the domestic and natural spaces through which characters move—figures who are so often on the run, on the road, without the idea of home as a stabilizing force. Julius Greve undertakes one of the more philosophically in-depth explorations of McCarthy's uses of nature in his 2018 *Shreds of Matter: Cormac McCarthy and the Concept of Nature*. Greve ultimately argues that given the complexity of the subject matter "McCarthy's project is to think nature by literary means, or, in other words, to present nature as thinking itself in literature" (9).[2] In taking this approach, Greve argues against those who would find a humanist ethics at the heart of McCarthy's work, thus circling back to the debate that Bell opened up thirty years before.

The availability of more archival material has made possible a number of fresh critical approaches, and though many scholars have used McCarthy's notes, draft manuscripts, and correspondence to supplement their arguments, several have made McCarthy's creative process a central focus. Luce has published a series of articles in this vein on the working relationship of McCarthy and his editor, Erskine ("Cormac McCarthy and Albert Erskine"); on the ways that McCarthy's writing of *Outer Dark* was influenced by the breakup of his first marriage ("Projecting Interiority: Psychogenesis and the Composition of *Outer Dark*"); on what McCarthy chose not to include in his novel *Suttree* ("Tall Tales and Raw Realities: Late-Stage Deletions from Cormac McCarthy's *Suttree*"); and how unused material from *Outer Dark* made its way into *Child of God* ("Ballard Rising in *Outer Dark*: The Genesis and Early Composition of *Child of God*"). In his *Books Are Made out of Books: A Guide to Cormac McCarthy's Literary Influences*, Michael Crews explicates all the references to other writers that can be found in McCarthy's notes, drafts, and correspondence, providing an encyclopedia of sorts for the building blocks of McCarthy's allusions. Finally, Peebles uses archival material in *Cormac McCarthy and Performance* to tell the story of McCarthy's engagement with film and theater and to provide the reasons behind and implications of McCarthy's movements between different storytelling formats.

Scholarship on McCarthy also includes many edited collections as well as individual articles that now number in the thousands. The early collection *Perspectives on Cormac McCarthy*, first published as a special edition of *Southern Quarterly* in 1992 and edited by Arnold and Luce, two of the field's most esteemed scholars, remains a touchstone and was reissued as a revised edition in 1999. *Perspectives on Cormac McCarthy* includes commonly cited pieces such as John Grammer's on the pastoral, Steven Shaviro's on *Blood Meridian* and the "very life of the darkness," and Leo Daugherty's on *Blood Meridian* as a Gnostic tragedy. Wade Hall and Rick Wallach's collection *Sacred Violence*, published first in 1995 and then in 2002 in an expanded, two-volume edition, is similarly central. James Lilley's collection *Cormac McCarthy: New Directions* reprints a number of influential articles that appeared previously in academic journals, including Daniel Cooper Alarcón's "All the Pretty Mexicos: Cormac McCarthy's Mexican Representations," Wallach's "From *Beowulf* to *Blood Meridian*: Cormac McCarthy's Demystification of the Martial Code," and one of the most frequently cited articles on McCarthy, Dana Phillips's "History and the Ugly Facts of *Blood Meridian*, in which Phillips uses McCarthy's term "optical democracy" to describe the novel's style and metaphysics (444). Nell Sullivan has published several articles dealing with McCarthy's representation of gender that, taken together, provide a definitive look at that subject: "Boys Will Be Boys and Girls Will Be Gone: The Circuit of Male Desire in Cormac McCarthy's Border Trilogy"; "The Evolution of the Dead Girlfriend Motif in *Outer Dark* and *Child of God*"; and "The Good Guys: McCarthy's *The Road* as Post-9/11 Male Sentimental Novel."

At present, *Blood Meridian* and *The Road* have received the most critical attention, and the latter has inspired work on a wide variety of topics: its moral and religious implications, the post-apocalyptic genre, environmental disaster, and the connection of cannibalism to concepts of taboo, consumerism, and capitalism. Given McCarthy's involvement with the Santa Fe Institute and the author's recent essay, "The Kekulé Problem," new explorations of McCarthy's interest in science and of the relevance of complexity theory are currently being undertaken, notably by Bryan Giemza and by Cooper in her forthcoming *Cormac McCarthy: A Complexity Theory of Literature*.

NOTES

[1] For a more detailed and chronological account of the development of McCarthy studies, see Frye, "Prospects," and Peebles, "Cormac."

[2] Here Greve borrows the term *penser* from French philosophy from the last few decades to suggest that an author's work can not only represent or reflect a topic but also "think" it.

Part Two

APPROACHES

Introduction

Stacey Peebles and Benjamin West

In early 1992, few people had heard of Cormac McCarthy. His first four novels were out of print and none of them had sold more than five thousand copies in hardback, despite his quietly winning accolades like a Guggenheim Fellowship in 1969 and the MacArthur Foundation Fellowship in 1981. But in May of 1992, everything changed. Alfred A. Knopf published *All the Pretty Horses*, the first novel in McCarthy's Border Trilogy, and the novel became a best seller and won the National Book Award. Since then his popularity and acclaim have only increased. His 2005 novel, *No Country for Old Men*, was adapted by Joel Coen and Ethan Coen, and the film won Academy Awards for Best Picture, Best Director, Best Adapted Screenplay, and Best Supporting Actor; his 2006 novel, *The Road*, won the Pulitzer Prize for Fiction; and all of his work, which currently constitutes ten novels, two plays, two published screenplays, and a nonfiction essay, has inspired substantial and growing popular and scholarly attention in addition to seven films or film adaptations.

McCarthy was born in Rhode Island in 1933 and moved to Knoxville, Tennessee, with his family just a few years later. His father worked as an attorney for the Tennessee Valley Authority, and many have noted that the authority's influence on the region is significant historical context for McCarthy's early novels set in the South (also known as his Appalachian or Tennessee novels). He attended Knoxville Catholic High School, publishing two poems in the school newspaper *The Gold and Blue*, and later enrolled at the University of Tennessee, Knoxville. While there, he wrote two short stories that appeared in the literary magazine *The Phoenix*, "Wake for Susan" and "A Drowning Incident." McCarthy left the university in 1960 without a degree and was already working on the novels that would eventually become *The Orchard Keeper* and *Suttree*. He submitted the manuscript for *The Orchard Keeper* to Random House in 1962 and, after working briefly with the editor Lawrence Bensky, began corresponding with Albert Erskine. Erskine had worked with prominent authors such as William Faulkner, James Michener, Eudora Welty, and Ralph Ellison, and he and McCarthy enjoyed a productive working relationship until it was curtailed by the illness that led to Erskine's death in 1993.

Between 1965 and 1979 McCarthy published four novels set in the South—*The Orchard Keeper*, *Outer Dark*, *Child of God*, and *Suttree*—to critical praise but very little popular readership. During this period he researched and wrote a screenplay, *The Gardener's Son*, a story also set in the South, working with director Richard Pearce on both the narrative and some aspects of the filmmaking. The film aired on PBS in 1977. In the mid- to late-1970s, McCarthy became interested in the American West, spending extended time in Tucson, Arizona, and El Paso, Texas, and immersing himself in historical research. The product of much of that research, *Blood Meridian*, appeared in 1985. In the 1980s he also completed a number of projects in different formats: a play, *The Stonemason*, and three screenplays, *Cities of the Plain* (which was initially titled "El Paso/Juarez"), *Whales and Men*, and *No Country for Old Men*.

After McCarthy became widely known for *All the Pretty Horses* in 1992, critical and popular attention steadily increased. He followed *All the Pretty Horses* with the next two novels of the Border Trilogy, *The Crossing*, in 1994, and *Cities of the Plain*, in 1998, all of which he built out of plot and character elements that he had explored in the earlier screenplay *Cities of the Plain*. Similarly, he used the basic premise of his screenplay *No Country for Old Men* as the basis for his 2005 novel of the same name, though he made dramatic changes to the story elements and the overall tone. In 2006, McCarthy's second play, *The Sunset Limited*, premiered at Steppenwolf Theatre in Chicago and was also published by Knopf. But most of the attention that year went to *The Road*, his tenth and, at this writing, most recent novel.

McCarthy followed *The Road* with a 2013 screenplay, *The Counselor*, the film of which was directed by Ridley Scott and released that same year, and a nonfiction essay, "The Kekulé Problem," published in 2017 in the popular science magazine *Nautilus*. The essay explores the origins of language and the unconscious, and McCarthy frames his inquiry around his conversations at the Santa Fe Institute, a research and education center for those studying complex systems science. McCarthy has been a fellow at the institute and wrote a version of its mission statement in 2014. Archival sources suggest that McCarthy has been working on a manuscript for a novel called *The Passenger* since 1980, and the Santa Fe Institute hosted an event featuring readings from the manuscript in 2015. David Krakauer, the president of the institute, said at the time that after McCarthy's southern and western phases, the new book would be "full-blown Cormac 3.0, a mathematical-analytical novel" (qtd. in Duhm).

McCarthy is now widely considered one of the greatest contemporary American authors. *Blood Meridian* appears on top-novels lists by *The New York Times* and *Time* magazine, while *The Road* has been cited as the best book of its decade by *The Times* of London. It's no surprise, then, that McCarthy's work has been showing up in classrooms for some time now. His novels have become staples of literature and American studies curricula; *All the Pretty Horses* and *The Road* are taught in a variety of contexts (high schools, first-year-experience college courses, and at all other levels of undergraduate and graduate education); *Blood Meridian* has inspired extensive critical debate as well as conference papers on how best to teach it at the undergraduate level; his Appalachian novels are often taught in courses on southern literature; and McCarthy's engagement with literary genre, philosophy, history, theater, and film has made it possible to approach his work in a wide range of pedagogical, interdisciplinary contexts. Single-author courses on McCarthy are also becoming more common at both the undergraduate and graduate levels.

Indeed, McCarthy's popularity offers significant pedagogical opportunities, both in terms of name recognition and the ways that contemporary students at any level gravitate toward the writer's work. For example, recent McCarthy novels such as *No Country for Old Men* and *The Road* have been best sellers in large part because of their engagement with the crime thriller and post-apocalyptic genres, respectively, categories of narrative that promise fast-paced action and resourceful heroes (in the former) and survivalist tactics coupled with life-or-death decisions (in the latter). McCarthy, however, is simultaneously working within and exploding the conventions of these genres. In *No Country for Old Men*, his complex treatment of the crime thriller is resonant with national debates about immigration policy and drug trafficking; *The Road* evinces similarities with other popular post-apocalyptic narratives, such as the television series *The Walking Dead* and recent films like *The Book of Eli* and *World War Z*, while it also prompts considerations of post-9/11 paranoia, fears of environmental damage and outright catastrophe, the effects of unchecked consumerism, and the day-to-day struggle for survival faced by the underprivileged. The genre conventions that *No Country for Old Men* and *The Road* draw on are familiar, but in both cases the narrative execution is surprising, and the implications of the narrative are far-reaching. This is one way, at least, to account for the considerable popularity of these books, and the explanation applies to the Border Trilogy as well. The trilogy consists of western novels and, in the case of *All the Pretty Horses* and *Cities of the Plain* (1998), romances that push the boundaries of those genres while raising questions about the effects of a globalized economy, changes in labor practices and economic opportunity, gender norms, and American historical and cultural identity, among other topics. Although McCarthy's southern novels and *Blood Meridian* were not popular when initially released, they can be approached as unconventional genre narratives in order to yield similarly productive readings.

Presenting McCarthy as an author who engages with genre in unconventional and layered ways can be a good way for teachers to introduce his work to students, though certainly challenges are common when addressing his work. For instance, McCarthy's use of archaic language and his intensely lyric style can present problems for any reader, but especially for students who are more comfortable with the relatively straightforward and brief textual discourse of social media and other electronic communication. Contemporary students may also find McCarthy's honest but jarring portrayals of racism and sexism to be troubling, and those lacking in historical knowledge may need additional instruction in order to interpret McCarthy's historical and regional fiction. Fortunately, teachers and scholars have been addressing such challenges for some time. The Cormac McCarthy Society has regularly hosted conferences devoted to the author since 1993, and panels that focus on teaching are consistently well attended and receive positive responses. With this volume, we hope to expand the conversation about McCarthy and pedagogy for a wider audience, particularly for those who are considering integrating McCarthy's writing into a course or creating a course around his work. This ongoing conversation has given rise to a number of common questions:

To what extent should McCarthy be considered a regional writer, of both the South and the West, and how is he engaging with those literary and historical traditions?

Those regions are often rendered in detailed descriptions of the natural world, and so which critical or philosophical frameworks can be helpful in unpacking those descriptions and their function in his narratives?

All of McCarthy's fiction, from the short stories he wrote in college to his most recent screenplay, is violent, sometimes gruesomely so—how can that violence be addressed in the classroom in such a way that it becomes generative rather than disruptive?

McCarthy's style is idiosyncratic, given his decisions to eschew quotation marks around dialogue and avoid apostrophes in many contractions in addition to his use of nonstandard capitalization and hyphenation—how can these idiosyncrasies be used to teach students about narrative affect, the modernist tradition, or even basic rhetoric and composition?

And finally, what are some ways to help students navigate these richly allusive texts, which make use of such broad and esoteric realms of knowledge?

We have organized this volume to address questions like these in three major areas (that of course overlap): the historical and cultural context of McCarthy's work; the literary context of the work, including considerations of different literary traditions and comparisons between McCarthy and other authors; and particular classroom situations, from high school through graduate school.

Historical and Cultural Context

The world that McCarthy's characters move through is hardly one characterized by comfort, universal good will, or quiet, peaceful relationships. Much to the contrary, violence erupts across McCarthy's oeuvre in almost every conceivable way and often serves as a catalyst for considerations of human nature, fate, historical change, politics, cross-cultural contact, and the relation of humans to animals and to the natural world. "There's no such thing as life without bloodshed," McCarthy once told the *New York Times* reporter Richard Woodward (McCarthy, "Cormac McCarthy's Venomous Fiction"), and certainly his writing reflects that view. Considering McCarthy's representation of violence both in terms of style and in relation to other themes and issues raised by McCarthy's narratives is an important part of teaching these texts, whether it's Lester Ballard's homicidal necrophilia in *Child of God*, the massacre scenes in *Blood Meridian*, the cannibalism in *The Road*, or the overwhelming sweep of historical violence alluded to in *The Sunset Limited*. Framing this violence by addressing genre, historical context, allusions, narrative structure, and even vocabulary choice can help generate discussion and reflection in the classroom on subjects that can sometimes stop readers cold—the literary critic Harold Bloom, who has championed *Blood Meridian* as a superlative American novel, famously said that it took him three tries just to read it for the first time (Introduction 1). For these reasons, our volume begins with a consideration of McCarthy's representation of violence, which naturally leads into other lines of critical and pedagogical inquiry.

McCarthy engages directly with contemporary social issues and the changing constructs of free will, identity, nation, and border, often portraying social inequities while challenging traditional understandings of race, class, and gender. McCarthy's protagonists are typically—though not exclusively—White and male. Encounters with difference, however, often call those categories and the underlying assumptions of privilege into question. The critical conversation about McCarthy's representations of race and gender is a substantial one, though addressing these issues in the classroom can prove difficult. It's not always easy to navigate a discussion of gender, for example, based on the necrophiliac and ultimately cross-dressing protagonist in *Child of God*, or a discussion of race based on the two characters in *The Sunset Limited*, who are known only as Black and White. Lydia Cooper and Rafael Acosta Morales offer ways for teachers to make these discussions nuanced and productive.

Because of the growing interest in addressing McCarthy in a curriculum devoted to ecocriticism or environmental studies, we include two essays on these topics: one, by Kevin Trumpeter, that provides an overview of ecocriticism and ways that different texts by McCarthy can work within it, and another, by Benjamin Mangrum, that focuses on southern environmental and urban history as they come together in one of McCarthy's more challenging texts, *Suttree*, the author's fourth novel set in the South. Given the longtime affiliation of McCarthy with the Santa Fe Institute, a nonprofit multidisciplinary research institute; his friendship with the Nobel Prize–winning physicist Murray Gell-Mann; and his engagement with fields such as geology and cosmology, scholars and teachers of McCarthy's work are often interested in the scientific elements of his texts, an interest explored here in Morales's essay on the concept of deep time and in the ecocritical approaches of Trumpeter and Mangrum.

Literary Pairings and Context

The first two essays of this section address the two most common ways of situating McCarthy in literary history: first as a southern writer and second as a writer who engages the genre of the western and the history of the American West. McCarthy's first four novels are set in and around Knoxville, Tennessee, and his first editor, Albert Erskine, was also William Faulkner's editor. McCarthy began his career, then, as a southern writer fully engaged with this tradition while seeking, of course, to distinguish himself within it. Then he moved west and published his first of five novels set in that region in 1985. In all of these works McCarthy evidences a meticulous attention to landscape, ecology, and humans' place in the environment, which critics have interpreted in varying ways.[1] Thus McCarthy can be taught as a southern or western writer who shapes those traditions and genres to his own ends, and more broadly as a writer who interrogates notions of region, space, and place—interrogations that have political, cultural, and environmental implications. As Nell Sullivan and Alex Harmon both explain, McCarthy's relations to those genres and historical traditions are hardly straightforward, which only increases the potential for the considerations of McCarthy's work to be richly productive ones. The other essays in this section offer possibilities for approaching the work of McCarthy from a variety of cultural contexts, including that of the border between Mexico and the United States and the musical form of the corrido, nineteenth-century literary and metaphysical movements, McCarthy's interest in film and the film adaptations of his work, and the idea of apocalypse, understood not only as a popular contemporary genre but also as one indebted to early Jewish, Christian, and Islamic texts.

Classroom Contexts

This section offers some ways to calibrate a consideration of McCarthy's work for a variety of pedagogical contexts: a high school class, an American literature survey course, a curriculum that focuses on enduring questions, and a graduate course devoted entirely to McCarthy. Lauren Maxwell's description of using McCarthy's novels to teach ethics and leadership at a military academy is useful for those teaching in other contexts as well, and the guide by Delys Snyder, Phillip Snyder, and Jeremy Browne to their digital humanities initiative *The Cormac McCarthy Corpus Project* introduces readers to an online resource for exploring McCarthy's syntax, diction, and structure. One of the most ubiquitous English classes is the American literature survey course, and Scott Yarbrough explains how to introduce *The Road* to students as the culmination of an ongoing conversation about consumerism and consumption in oft-taught works by Benjamin Franklin, Harriet Jacobs, and Henry David Thoreau. Jay Watson took his graduate students on a semester-long journey through McCarthy's entire oeuvre and, as we note below, found the experience to be intense but uniquely generative.

As this brief overview demonstrates and the essays that follow describe in detail, there are any number of ways to address students' most common questions about McCarthy's work. To address why McCarthy doesn't use standard punctuation, one could talk about the influence of William Faulkner and James Joyce or about the choices McCarthy makes in rendering regionally specific dialect, or one could go to *The Cormac McCarthy Corpus Project* to explore which contractions he renders without apostrophes, which could in turn fuel a discussion about the effects of those choices. To address why he so often uses arcane or esoteric language, one could pick a word—*adipocere* in *Child of God*, perhaps, or *thrapple* in *Blood Meridian*, or *salitter* in *The Road*—and discuss what kind of historical, philosophical, or scientific traditions might have informed those authorial decisions. To explore why McCarthy's characters talk, behave, and interact the way they do, a class could unpack the historical or regional context of the narrative; begin a conversation about motivation, free will, and determinism; or talk about racial and gender norms.

One of the challenges in teaching McCarthy's works at any level is deciding how much of the stylistic, historical, and philosophical elements or allusions to explain for students—and indeed recognizing this often quite obscure or specialized material oneself. Will a detailed discussion of the purpose and use of tarot cards open up a productive interpretive window for students reading *Blood Meridian*, for instance, or will it simply add to the confusion often felt by readers when they first confront this dense and difficult novel? Does recognizing *Suttree*'s historically accurate rendering of Knoxville in the 1950s add or detract from an attempt to parse the title character's actions and motivations? If John Grady Cole thinks of himself as a cowboy hero in *All the Pretty Horses*, does knowing which figures he might be imitating help students think about why Dueña Alfonsa doesn't think he's a good romantic match for Alejandra—or about why he might be entirely too appropriate? In the following essays, teachers offer a variety of ideas about what can work and in which contexts, and how to make these coverage choices so that students can best engage with McCarthy's work in a way that is intellectually satisfying but that also suggests the other avenues of inquiry that are available to them if they choose to keep reading deeply on their own.[2]

Each of McCarthy's ten novels as well as his two plays (*The Stonemason* and *The Sunset Limited*) and his two published screenplays (*The Gardener's Son* and *The Counselor*) are covered in at least one essay, and the books receiving the most attention here—*Blood Meridian* and *The Road*—are also the ones that are most often taught.[3] Teachers who have already chosen a McCarthy text for their classes might do well to seek out essays that address that text in particular, while those teaching in set curricular contexts (e.g., first-year-experience courses, survey courses, or writing courses) can find essays devoted to the demands of those formats. Readers interested in simply paging through the volume for ideas will note that we begin with violence, gender, and race—general but nonetheless significant elements in almost any consideration of Cormac McCarthy's works—and end with a selection of the online conversations that Watson had with his graduate students in a course devoted entirely to the author. Watson explains the efficacy of the public journaling assignment that he gave to his students, but the student entries included in the essay—by Robert Briggs, Andrew Thomas, and Josh-Wade Ferguson—coupled with Watson's responses, also provide a fascinating tour through the various points of engagement that are possible when reading texts by McCarthy.[4]

We have found that when great literature is on the classroom table, we teach the students, but the students teach us, too. That's what we both love about McCarthy's work—it's not always easy reading, but its difficulties make the moments of shared understanding and discovery all the more exciting. We hope this volume allows more teachers to have this challenging, provocative, and rewarding adventure.

NOTES

[1] McCarthy's most recent novel, *The Road*, is a post-apocalyptic narrative set in the South, and its representation of region and space is additionally overlaid with the imagination of ecological disaster.

[2] Uniform editions of McCarthy's novels have been used in this volume except in the essay by Snyder, Snyder, and Browne, which uses e-book as well as print editions.

[3] We chose not to include extended discussions of McCarthy's unpublished screenplay *Whales and Men*, though that work has received some attention by scholars, or the early short stories that McCarthy published in his university's literary magazine, as none of those texts are widely available.

[4] The essay by Watson, Briggs, Thomas, and Ferguson also includes exchanges covering some of McCarthy's texts that are less often taught but that are nonetheless potentially rewarding: *Cities of the Plain*, *The Stonemason*, *The Sunset Limited*, and *The Counselor*.

HISTORICAL AND CULTURAL CONTEXT

McCarthy and the Question of Violence

Stacey Peebles

In 2004, the Honors College at the University of Houston wanted more people to help teach a required course for first-year students: a two-semester, team-taught, interdisciplinary course called The Human Situation. I interviewed for this teaching position, which would be my first job after graduate school, and for my job talk, I wanted to cover something that I knew backward and forward. That was Cormac McCarthy. And if you're trying to look impressive, *Blood Meridian* is a good book to use for that purpose. I talked about McCarthy's representation of violence, using material from my dissertation and some more recent work, and I quoted a few of the novel's more infamous passages—the Comanche attack, the massacre of the Tiguas, the tree hung with dead babies. Afterward, I fielded some questions about the western genre and McCarthy's connections to other writers. Then one faculty member asked a question that floored me: "So, how would you teach this in our required first-year course?"

I was trying my best to be a good candidate—after all, the course sounded great, and I wanted the job—but I just couldn't edit myself. "You want to teach this book to first-year students?" I was incredulous. After all, this was the novel that Harold Bloom had quit reading twice before he finally managed to finish it, blanching at the "overwhelming carnage," even as he would later deem it "a canonical imaginative achievement" (viii). The faculty member said yes, and others in the room nodded; my knowledge of McCarthy's work was one of the reasons they had decided to interview me. I didn't give a very good answer—I talked about the need to lay out the historical context, which isn't well known even to educated adults, and about opportunities for addressing the book's stylistic choices like esoteric vocabulary and the use of chapter headings. "And then you'd need to frame the violence somehow," I said and left it at that.

Teaching McCarthy's work indeed necessitates some thinking about how to address his use of violence—and this is true at any level, from the high school classroom to the graduate seminar. That first year I taught *Blood Meridian* at the University of Houston, I approached it as a revisionist western, working alongside colleagues who were eager to draw out the novel's philosophical and political implications. The lectures and discussions on the novel went fairly well, though admittedly getting through the book's violence proved less of a challenge for students than reading its three-hundred-plus pages in late April.

Since that time, I've taught almost all of McCarthy's novels, as well as the screenplay *The Sunset Limited*, in a variety of undergraduate classes at both large public and small private institutions. In what follows, I focus on the works for which the representation of violence was central to my teaching, whether because of the nature of that violence or its frequency or both. I begin with more detail about *Blood Meridian* and then turn to the taboos of necrophilia and cannibalism that figure prominently in *Child of God* and *The Road*, respectively. And finally, I explain why I don't teach *The Counselor*.

Much has been made of the need for trigger warnings in recent years—warnings provided by professors that alert students to potentially upsetting or triggering representations in the course material, such as a novel that includes scenes of sexual assault or race-related violence. In the case of *Blood Meridian*, however, the potentially troubling material isn't confined to a small number of scenes—it appears throughout the book and is arguably its raison d'être. I tell students that the novel's very subject matter is violence, and that they should be ready for it to be overwhelming. Emotional reactions to violent scenes are certainly possible, but *Blood Meridian* also defies the narrative conventions that students might expect. The Comanche attack on Captain White's expedition, after all, reads like an over-the-top climax, but it's only fifty pages into the book. The body of scholarship on *Blood Meridian* is robust and still growing, and nearly all of it addresses the representation of violence in some fashion. For upper-level undergraduates and for graduate students, there's a great deal of excellent scholarship that demonstrates the process of choosing a critical angle and using it to illuminate aspects of the text—Dana Phillips's article on "optical democracy" (444) and Leo Daugherty's on Gnosticism are both classics that do just that in a style that's clear and accessible for students, and the two approaches contrast usefully with each other. But scholarship like this isn't likely to give students an initial grip on the text. It works well later, once the reading is complete, but as students are beginning and then working through that reading, they need more immediate guidance.

One challenge is that while characters' motivations and goals are discernible—the men in Glanton's gang are paid money to procure Native American scalps, and they move from place to place for that purpose—violence also erupts for reasons that are hard to parse. In chapter 13, for example, the gang members ride into a village, the name of which they don't know, and encounter a company of mounted troops. The soldiers wear formal uniforms and carry lances and muskets, and their captain "raised his sabre to halt the column." Then mayhem ensues: "The next instant the narrow street was filled with riflesmoke and a dozen of the soldiers lay dead or dying on the ground" (McCarthy, *Blood Meridian* 182). Glanton shoots the captain in the head, most of the rest of the company is killed, and Glanton sends five men to chase down those who fled while the rest loot the bodies lying in the street. They overtake the survivors and kill them, then finally ride back into Chihuahua, "enter[ing] the city haggard and filthy and reeking with the blood of the citizenry for whose protection they had contracted" (185).

So what happened? In one sense, this is another instance of the gang taking and then turning in scalps with dark hair that will pass as Native American. But it's hardly the best opportunity to do so—if the survivors had managed to get to Chihuahua or another city, the gang could have been up against a much bigger force and worse odds. The gang fires on the troops, rather, as a preemptive strike, not only because it tends not to follow what mounted soldiers might consider standard rules of engagement, but also because Glanton likely expects the soldiers to arrest them for their massacre of citizens in Nacori, which McCarthy describes just a few pages earlier. Glanton has no intention of submitting to arrest; and so rather than halt and parley, the gang simply surprises the soldiers with lethal gunfire. It's up to the reader, however, to put all this together.

And this is just one violent event (or string of events) among many—including large-scale massacres, the murder of puppies, and an abduction by bear. Small wonder, then, that when I last taught the novel in an upper-level undergraduate seminar, my students asked me to give them reading guidelines in advance of our classes so that they would have some idea of what to focus on in each section of the text. This was most helpful for them in the novel's long middle—chapters 13 through 18, when the Glanton gang has been introduced and begins an extended sequence of traveling and fighting. I tried to write a guide that would explain some of the trickier details, like the way that Glanton cheats a group of Apache out of their barrel of whiskey in chapter 17, and that would direct students to figure out other aspects of the plot on their own. Here are three excerpts from my guide for this section of the text:

> Chapter 15. The Glanton gang has a new contract, this one with the state of Sonora, for Apache scalps. Ironically, a Sonoran army encounters them in the countryside and fights them. (The army has probably heard what happened in Chihuahua or is reacting to the gang's indiscriminate slaughter of others along the way. In either case, the gang members are just murderers now, no longer government-sanctioned bounty hunters.) Note what the kid does when a man named Shelby is injured. The kid is then isolated from the gang for a time.
>
> Chapter 16. The gang wanders on horseback. It parleys with a band of Apaches, but the peaceful encounter nearly goes awry when Glanton's horse bites the chief's horse's ear. The Apache want a barrel of whiskey as recompense. The gang goes to seek it. While doing so, it encounters a caged "idiot" whose brother asks for safe passage for them both with the

> gang. Also, the gang is involved in a dispute in a bar when a barkeep won't serve the gang member known as Black Jackson. Judge Holden lifts and throws a meteorite on a bet.
>
> Chapter 17. Glanton prepares the barrel of whiskey but tricks it out so that it contains mostly water. The judge orates on the nature of the world and then on war and moral law. Finally, the gang reaches the Colorado River, which has a ferry operated by a man named Lincoln. A group belonging to the Yuma tribe lives nearby.

This guide provides a sense of structure that helped the students navigate the reading, and I assigned presentations after our discussion of the novel itself was completed. Selecting and researching one particular topic—for instance, filibustering expeditions, the planet Anareta, or Sarah Borginnis—gave them a sense of mastery over at least one small part of the text, and hearing each other's presentations fleshed out parts of the novel for them that we didn't get to in discussion.

All this enabled the class to better comprehend the novel's plot as it progressed and thus to be less confused or frustrated when episodes of hyperbolic violence took over the narrative. To put it more bluntly—they kept reading. In addition, having some idea of which scenes might be troubling for them allowed them to mentally prepare beforehand. Our final discussions, then, were devoted to understanding the violence on other levels—historical, philosophical, and religious—and were supported by a small selection of relevant scholarship.[1] When I taught *Blood Meridian* that first time at the University of Houston, I framed the novel and its violence rather simplistically as a revisionist western. I ultimately found that approach unsatisfying. Yes, the West was a darker and more violent place than nineteenth-century pulps and early-twentieth-century novels and films would have us believe, but that doesn't quite explain the sprawling, ubiquitous, and cosmically weighty bloodshed that McCarthy gives us. I would have done better to tease out the implications of this violence for an understanding of manifest destiny and, perhaps, human nature, or to guide the students to a more detailed and nuanced investigation of how McCarthy is using history here. When I first taught *Blood Meridian*, McCarthy's papers were not yet available, but now it's possible to use a few copies from the archive at the Wittliff Collections at Texas State University to show students McCarthy's intensive research process and some of the notes he took on historical events, geographic details, and region-specific vocabulary. I also like to show them this comment that McCarthy made in a 1984 letter to his editor Albert Erskine:

> The truth is that the historical material is really—to me—little more than a frame work upon which to hang a dramatic inquiry into the nature of destiny and history and the uses of reason and knowledge & the nature of evil and all these sorts of things which have plagued folks since there were folks. I think the Bard would have agreed with me that that's as proper a use of history as any. (McCarthy, Letter)

What does McCarthy mean here, and what are some of the different arguments one can make about how the violence in *Blood Meridian* functions? That's a topic for at least one full class period, and the discussion can be particularly wide-ranging and illuminating if the class includes students with a variety of majors.

Child of God is a very different book from *Blood Meridian*—it is shorter in length, more minimalist in style, set in the twentieth-century South rather than the nineteenth-century West, and features one-on-one acts of violence rather than large-scale set pieces. *Child of God* is not often taught alongside *Blood Meridian*, except in courses devoted to McCarthy, and the pedagogical challenges of dealing with the violence of *Child of God* are indeed different in scope and character. I tend to associate *Child of God* with *Outer Dark* and *The Road*, given the three novels' use of taboos as central plot points—necrophilia, incest, and cannibalism, respectively.[2]

Child of God may lack the epic sweep of *Blood Meridian*, but as Steven Frye puts it, the novel nonetheless "evokes realms of human degradation striking and rare even in the works of contemporary American authors such as Thomas Pynchon, Toni Morrison, Philip Roth, and Truman Capote" (*Understanding Cormac McCarthy* 39). Yet it is also possible to see the crimes of Lester Ballard, the protagonist in *Child of God*, as the result of his "unhousing"—his eviction from his property—as Jay Ellis has argued, although the absence of family, exile by his community, and even the blows to the head he suffers may have "unhoused" him mentally as well (*No Place* 69, 73). Thus, argues Lydia Cooper, "[a] person as deranged and bizarre as Ballard, the narrator of *Child of God* suggests, is in the end the responsibility of those who condemn him. If he shares common human traits—a desire for love, respect, and a home—with more reasonable humans, then those ordinary folk have a responsibility toward him, if only to recognize him as 'like' themselves" (*No More Heroes* 50).

As comments like this indicate, the novel is something of an exercise in the limits of the reader's sympathy, or at the very least an energetic workshop on its complications. Lester is, the narrator tells us, a "child of God much like yourself perhaps," a claim that's worth spending some time on in the classroom. What does it mean to be a child of God, what kind of similarities between Lester and the reader does this claim imply, and why does McCarthy add that final word, "perhaps"? (*Child of God* 4). What, in turn, are the assessments of Lester by other characters—the auctioneer, the sheriff, and the chorus of unidentified voices who tell stories about the history of Lester's family and the town?

Those discussions can set up a consideration of the subsequent and increasingly violent events that occur. And that progression can be interesting for students, especially if they don't know in advance what to expect from the narrative. If the first reading assignment consists of part 1 of the novel (3–81), then the relationship between Lester and his community (or the lack thereof) can be thoroughly covered before students encounter Lester's first act of necrophilia at the beginning of part 2. Ideally, the section of text that includes that first act, his setting up house with the dead girl, the cabin burning down, and his move to the cave (85–114) would constitute a second reading assignment. However grotesque the act may be, as my students pointed out, it's not described in graphic detail, and Lester's anguish at losing the girl's body in the fire is certainly palpable. Although the dead girl may have family or friends who are suffering in her absence, the novel never tells us about them. Thus we're left to contemplate the actions of this desperately lonely man, and at this point many students are able to do that with some sympathy—the character and limits of which can be rich and productive points of conversation.

The novel changes yet again in the following few pages, when Lester murders a young mother who has rejected his awkward sexual advances, burns down her house with her baby inside, and carries off her body for purposes that we can easily deduce. This, then, becomes a different conversation. Lester fights hunger and cold as he pursues other victims and takes to wearing some of their clothes. In class discussion, I ask students how the acts of violence are described and what the text elides or implies. I also ask them to articulate their reactions to Lester here, and their relation to the text, as the story has progressed from one about a rather put-upon country boy to much darker material.

Part 3 includes a passage that demands, I think, at least thirty minutes of class time:

> He came up flailing and sputtering and began to thrash his way toward the line of willows that marked the submerged creek bank. He could not swim, but how would you drown him? His wrath seemed to buoy him up. Some halt in the way of things seems to work here. See him. You could say that he's sustained by his fellow men, like you. Has peopled the shore with them calling to him. A race that gives suck to the maimed and the crazed, that wants their wrong blood in its history and will have it. But they want this man's life. He has heard them in the night seeking him with lanterns and cries of execration. How then is he borne up? Or rather, why will not these waters take him? (156)

Starting with basic questions—about what precisely is happening and what the definitions are of phrases like "halt in the way of things" and "cries of execration"—I then prompt the class to think about what McCarthy is saying here about the relation between a person who has committed acts of horrific violence and the society around that person. Lester should be drowning, the narrator suggests. But he's not. What's holding him up? In addition to his status as a victimizer, is he also the sacrifice of a community that wishes to define itself against him? Can one be both?

The novel ends, in quick succession, with Lester's institutionalization, pneumonia, death, dissection, and funeral, followed by the discovery and exhumation of Lester's underground mausoleum. That final scene of the corpses of Lester's victims being hauled up, the repressed returning to the surface, parallels nicely with the final shot in Alfred Hitchcock's *Psycho*, of Marion Crane's car being hauled up out of the swamp where Norman Bates sunk it. In her book *Reading the World*, Dianne Luce has explained the connections between *Child of God*, *Psycho*, and the case of the serial killer Ed Gein that served as partial inspiration for both narratives. Pairing *Child of God* with a viewing of *Psycho* and a reading from chapter 3 of Luce's book (134–75) creates a substantial class unit. Luce provides some helpful historical context, and a comparison of the novel and the film can generate discussion about narrative structure and the sympathetic and horrific qualities of each protagonist.[3]

Of all McCarthy's works, I've taught *The Road* most often and in the most number of contexts—as the final novel assigned in two different first-year humanities courses (taught in large public and small private institutions), in an upper-level undergraduate course on contemporary literature, and in an upper-level course devoted solely to texts by McCarthy. I find *The Road* to be the most teachable of McCarthy's works for a number of reasons: it's not overly long, the story is captivating to students, and the post-apocalyptic genre is one that students know at least in passing. Further, its violence is extreme, and central to the plot and setting, but the depictions of violence are parceled out in manageable doses throughout the text. And finally, both the violence and the text as a whole can be understood through a variety of lenses. That point is, in fact, an understatement, as *The Road* has recently surpassed *Blood Meridian* as the McCarthy work with the most entries in the *MLA International Bibliography*. As that body of scholarship shows, the murder and cannibalism that many survivors of an unnamed apocalyptic event choose to practice in *The Road* can be understood in the context of historical instances of cannibalism (Dominy), as the endgame of late capitalism (Jergenson; Malewitz), as recompense for humans' poor ecological stewardship (Chabon), as an innovative twist on the popular post-apocalyptic or zombie genre (Ellis, "*Road*"), and as an evil that must be identified and avoided in order to define the good, in either a generally moral or a specifically Christian sense (Josephs; DeCoste; Wielenberg).

Typically, my opening reading assignment for *The Road* includes the brief description of the cataclysmic event: "The clocks stopped at 1:17. A long shear of light and then a series of low concussions. . . . A dull rose glow in the windowglass" (52). After the usual work of establishing the basics of plot, characters, and setting, I ask students what they understood about the apocalyptic event itself, and how the book's representation compares to other popular representations of apocalypse that they have read or seen.[4] Many are frustrated by the lack of specificity in the novel's description of the ultimate violent event, as McCarthy declines to indicate whether this is a natural disaster (e.g., a meteor strike) or one caused by humans (e.g., a nuclear attack), and that frustration is useful to unpack. Why does it matter what causes the disaster, and what are the implications for engagement with the narrative and characters?

If all the violent events in *Blood Meridian* ultimately lead to one that is hidden from our view—the confrontation between the judge and the kid in the jakes, or outhouse (333)—the violent events in *The Road* all occur as a result of that unnamed catastrophe, one that the characters themselves may not know much about either. In response to the violence around them, the father and son resolve to be the good guys and to not eat people—though the real rub, as critics have noted, would seem to lie with the homicide that usually precedes the eating, at least as enacted by the various marauding groups that the father and son encounter. (Like Lester's necrophilia in *Child of God*, the ethics of cannibalism as a practice separate from murder is a topic worth addressing.) Though I've had several students note that the unrelenting grayness of the environment is the book's most disturbing feature, the scenes with the "roadrat" (*Road* 66, 60–67), the old plantation house with a locked cellar full of naked people (105–12), and the "charred human infant headless and gutted and blackening on the spit" (198) are graphic enough that I typically alert students ahead of time. The encounter with the roadrat makes tangible the son's vulnerability to predators, and the ruthlessness of those predators; the cooked infant, as students and critics often point out, makes less sense, as the energy and resources required to produce a baby far outweigh the sustenance potential of the baby itself.

Of these three scenes, the discovery of the cellar is the most productive for class discussion. Students often don't immediately recognize that the "tall and stately" house with "white doric columns across the front" and a porte cochere is a former plantation house (*Road* 105). McCarthy writes that "[c]hattel slaves had once trod those boards [of the porch] bearing food and drink on silver trays" (90)—the word "chattel" emphasizes that the slaves here were the personal property of the master and that their children would also be his property. The sight of naked people huddled in the cellar, blinking against the light, evokes images from the Holocaust, as does the comment a few pages later that the starved, exhausted son "looked like something out of a deathcamp" (117). If students are used to thinking about post-apocalyptic or dystopian narratives as fantasy, or the violence inherent in them as unrealistic, McCarthy reminds the reader here that treating people as objects or property, even in gruesome ways, has any number of historical precedents.

Rather than ignore or assent to the necessity of horrors like these, as other characters do, the two protagonists instead choose to define themselves against those horrors, as the "good guys" to the innumerable "bad guys" out there (65). For the father, this choice is a righteous response to the suffering that he sees around him as well as to the pain of raising a beloved son in such circumstances, though he is also drawn to his late wife's response, suicide, if the suffering, or potential suffering, grows too great.[5] Eventually, however, he rejects that response as well. When he at last prepares to die from exhaustion and illness, he urges his son to be cautious but to seek out other good guys rather than join him in death. When I teach the end of the novel, I often talk about how I read it differently now—since the novel's publication, I've had a daughter, and I invite students to consider how they view the violence in the world in a different light when they think about a child of theirs navigating that violence.[6]

At the time of this writing, *The Road* is McCarthy's most recent novel, though not his most recent work. McCarthy's screenplay *The Counselor* appeared in 2013, slightly in advance of the film directed by Ridley Scott. When I last taught a course devoted entirely to McCarthy, I had the option of ending it with *The Counselor* but chose not to do so. Its story has a good deal in common with *No Country for Old Men*: both feature a modern setting in Texas and Mexico; the economics of the drug trade; a protagonist trying to get away with some ill-gotten gains, much to the disapproval of a beloved woman; and an ultimately tragic outcome for that protagonist. But while the violence of *No Country for Old Men* is graphic and frequent (in both the novel and Joel Coen and Ethan Coen's film adaptation), the violence of *The Counselor* is more troubling. It's possible to talk about the violent events in *No Country for Old Men* in the context of determinism, capitalism, historical change, the western, and tragedy; in *The Counselor*, McCarthy evokes those same topics but less adeptly. The bigger problem, however, is the representation of the screenplay's two main female characters, one of whom has sex with a car and the other of whom ends up headless in a trash dump. While it's possible to give these characters more nuance in discussion, Scott's film version is overtly sexist, and it's difficult to avoid the conclusion that this project as a whole is a failure or at least pales in comparison to McCarthy's others. I didn't teach *The Counselor* because I didn't want to end the class's deep dive into McCarthy's works with a noseful of sand.[7]

Instead, I find that both *The Road* and *The Sunset Limited*—which are in many ways companion pieces, written at about the same time and with a consideration of suicide as a central plot point—work well as later or final works in a semester, especially if violence has been a main theme or element of the course. They end not with disavowals of the violence of the world but with characters who choose not to participate in the violence, even if those choices don't have the larger effect of making the world "right again" (*Road* 287) or convincing God to answer entreatics (*Sunset Limited* 142–43). In the light of these works, it is possible for students to go back and find the same resistance to violence in *Blood Meridian*'s the kid—whom the judge accuses of clemency, of not "empty[ing] his heart out into the common," which is the deadly and annihilating project of the Glanton gang (307)—and to reconsider established readings of *Blood Meridian*, such as that of Vereen Bell, who argued that the novel shows evidence of its author's nihilism. In this way instructors can use the sometimes overwhelming violence that McCarthy depicts in order to talk about the necessity of acknowledging it, of considering its various causes and vehicles. Some characters, like Lester, are finally taken under—not by the river that somehow won't drown him, but by the isolation that he suffers and then brings on himself by his assent to violence. Others, like the father and son in *The Road*, Black in *The Sunset Limited*, and arguably the kid in *Blood Meridian*, certainly don't save the world, but in resisting, they do save something—maybe themselves, the reader, or McCarthy himself, who binds up these visions of the worst that humans can do to one another in language, in art, that's some of the best.

NOTES

[1] Phillips and Daugherty are helpful here, as are Frye, "*Blood Meridian*"; and Parrish.

[2] For discussions of *Outer Dark*, see the essays by Sullivan and by Lake in this volume.

[3] Colleagues have told me they have had similar success pairing *Child of God* with Faulkner's "Rose for Emily" (*Selected Short Stories* 47–59). I advise against using James Franco's 2014 film adaptation of *Child of God*, however, since I find it to be of uneven cinematic quality at best; see Peebles, *Cormac* (190–200), for more on that point.

[4] For more on representations of apocalypse, see Sheinfeld in this volume.

[5] See lines like "Can you do it? When the time comes?" and "he knew that if he were a good father still it might well be as she had said" (McCarthy, *Road* 29), as well as the father's attempt to teach the boy how to shoot himself: "If they find you you are going to have to do it" (113).

[6] The student populations I've taught have been largely traditional, and very few of my students have been parents themselves; this might be an even richer discussion to have in classes that have more nontraditional students.

[7] See Peebles, *Cormac* 163–90, for more on the screenplay and film of *The Counselor*. For more on teaching gender in McCarthy's work, see Cooper in this volume.

"A Strange Equality": Approaches to Teaching Gender in McCarthy

Lydia R. Cooper

When we teach Cormac McCarthy's works, how do we approach the subject of gender? The first and most obvious problem with the subject is its narrowest category: women. It does not take long for the avid McCarthy reader to notice a striking absence of any nonmasculine characters. This absence in McCarthy's mythic works is eye-catching and exacerbates what appear to be rather regressive depictions of those few women characters who do appear. Nell Sullivan points out that, beginning with the short story "Wake for Susan," McCarthy's narratives are characterized by a general objectification of their women characters, characters who are frequently depicted as doll-like or corpse-like or as actual corpses ("Evolution" 68). Such troubling, objectifying depictions pose an interpretive challenge for McCarthy scholars—but in some ways, they pose a greater obstacle to any attempt to teach McCarthy's works in a university, college, or advanced secondary school classroom. How does one discuss absence in a constructive and meaningful way?

Nor is the absence of women the only challenge posed by an attempt to teach and discuss gender in McCarthy's works. McCarthy's masculine landscapes are constructed with an aesthetic bleakness characteristic of American naturalism, an aesthetic that suggests a deterministic universe in which characters lack any sort of interior life.[1] Incapable of self-reflection, these characters are reduced to action alone. The abjection or complete excision of women, combined with this deterministic, action-dense aesthetic, seems, at first glance, to conjure a prototypical "man's world," a phallocentric fantasy that is apparent in the Appalachian works but that dominates McCarthy's western novels (Kollin 569). These tales, which are light on subjectivity, may seem so overwhelmingly characterized by a hegemonic version of masculine identity that little remains to be said. Yet, perhaps counterintuitively, that very exclusivity creates a provocative challenge to the less obvious but insidious influence of hegemonic masculinity in the culture of the United States. In a culture so fascinated by images of idealized, working-class, heterosexual, White manhood, gender becomes a mechanism by which social power and agency are created or denied.

Two of the most famous works by McCarthy are westerns: his indisputable masterpiece, *Blood Meridian*, and *All the Pretty Horses*, which won the National Book Award and became the author's first bestseller. Westerns are, of course, characterized across the entire genre by heteronormativity and hypermasculine performance. That is, the genre is associated with a form of masculinity characterized by White men who display excessive skill with weapons, perform acts of violence, and dominate the natural world and other characters such as women, children, and racial others. What one can understand, or at least contextualize, in a 1950s John Ford film, however, can present a problem in a twenty-first-century text discussed in a contemporary classroom, particularly in the era of the #MeToo movement, when the challenges faced by women and by sexual and gender minorities are increasingly recognized. Is there any purpose or good to be gained from asking students to analyze these hypermasculine fantasies stripped of realistic or multidimensional feminine characters?

In short, the challenge in teaching gender in works by McCarthy, given his aesthetically hypermasculine prose style and content, is that it seems easy—perhaps inevitable—to reduce discussion of his works to mere commentary on apparent misogyny and misanthropy. A cursory glance at McCarthy's works, after all, strongly suggests that women are objectified or are not there at all and that men, even the good ones, are unreflective sexual aggressors with predilections for violence or predation. Yet literary scholars and teachers persist in teaching McCarthy's works, which are now more popular and prevalent in classrooms than at any previous time in the author's lauded career. There is, I feel, not only merit but something like necessity in teaching his works—and in paying attention to how he depicts gender performances in these quintessentially American narratives. In this essay, I provide an overview of the theoretical approach I used to frame my university course on McCarthy's fiction, briefly describe the interpretive possibilities offered through such an approach, and finally discuss the students' nuanced and complicated analyses of the intersections of agency and political power in McCarthy's hypermasculine fiction.

Recently, I taught an upper-level undergraduate seminar focused exclusively on McCarthy's works. The students were juniors and seniors (and one very bright first-year) at a private university with a liberal arts focus. We read nearly all of McCarthy's published works, including everything intended for a reading audience (thus excepting *The Gardener's Son*, *The Stonemason*, and *The Counselor*, which were written for performance). In that class, we read critical theory that draws attention to the rhetorical, narratological, and stylistic modes of representing gender as a performance of identity and power relative to social constructions that aim to normalize and reproduce existing power structures or to challenge them.[2]

Perhaps the best way to approach gender in McCarthy's works is to start with noting their aesthetic bravura—the dramatic, even biblical cadences of masculine performance. Noting this kind of stylistic emphasis can help facilitate a classroom discussion about McCarthy and gender and avoid a less productive focus on the seeming misogyny of the work. Studying McCarthy's representations of gender can help us isolate and interrogate the influence of hegemonic masculinity in the culture of the United States, and ultimately lead to rich engagement with McCarthy's depictions of gender performances and identities, which tackle head-on the subject of gendered power hierarchies in the culture. Teaching gender in McCarthy's works can actually provide a rich opportunity for complicated engagements with the political power ascribed to certain performances of masculinity precisely because those works are so extreme in their presentation of that particular brand of American hypermasculinity.

In addition to emphasizing the importance of close reading, I chose to frame our discussions in terms of the performativity of gender, as described by scholars such as Judith Butler and R. W. Connell. This approach helped us understand how McCarthy's depictions of gender performances and identities illuminate the nature and limits of power in any culture in which masculinity is both the norm and the fantasy. In addition, I drew on Sara Ahmed's approach to reading agency and subjectivity as expressions of willfulness in spaces of contested power.

For example, in my book *Masculinities*, I draw attention to the constructed nature of gender performance. "All societies have cultural accounts of gender," I argue, "but not all have the concept of 'masculinity' " (L. Cooper 67). That is, masculinity is an idea that codifies certain performances perceived as masculine as opposed to performances perceived as feminine (e.g., being violent rather than peaceable or dominant rather than passive). The notion of masculinity is therefore "inherently relational," always directed against a perceived other who is nonmasculine (68).[3] In *Undoing Gender*, Butler points out that the performativity of gender, even or especially in male-dominated cultures such as that of the United States, means that gender may also be the "apparatus by which such terms [i.e., *masculine* and *feminine*] are deconstructed and denaturalized" (42).

In addition to recognizing the performativity and contingency of gender, we discussed the interconnections of social constructions of gender and power, particularly in the context of human agency. Ahmed's description of "willful subjects" highlights some of the limits of the discourse about gender. Ahmed describes the will as predicating subjecthood—that is, the practice of exercising one's will determines one's status as a subject (23). The subject wills, the object is what is willed (27). The phenomenological aspect of willfulness, in other words, helps readers identify subjectivities in more complex ways than we might if we simply looked at attributions of power or agency. For instance, if we assign acts of willfulness (agency) as key indicators of subjectivity, then the evil, articulate, and active Judge Holden of *Blood Meridian* seems to be the primary subject. Steven Shaviro supports this interpretation, arguing that the kid, the object to the judge's agent, cannot effectively counter the judge because the kid "keeps his distance from the claims both of destiny and of agency" (149). Yet Ahmed would read the kid's willfulness—demonstrated textually in his verbal rejections of the judge's claims and his obdurate refusals to look away from the judge—as evidence of an orientation toward or away from an object, an intellectual willfulness that is the expression of agency when a person's actions are constrained (34–35). Ahmed ascribes willfulness to the agency expressed by women in systems that constrain their outward behavior. Following her theoretical model of reading willfulness, the kid's relative lack of agency renders the kid a feminized (disempowered) character, but careful study of his demonstrations of willfulness provide insight into how the novel permits him the capacity to resist the hegemonic will of the judge—insights that a reading of agency as defined solely by actions might not support.

Ahmed's discussion provides students with particularly helpful language for their analysis of relatively minor yet critical characters, such as Dueña Alfonsa in *All the Pretty Horses*. Alfonsa is an elderly woman socially relegated to certain background roles—she is the mother-in-law whose ancestral property is run by her son-in-law. Yet, conversely, Alfonsa challenges easy claims that McCarthy's women lack subjectivity, willfulness, or agency, as she exhibits all three and the latter two to a remarkable degree, more so than even the novel's protagonist, John Grady Cole. Alfonsa's character is an interpretive lynchpin in that novel, yet scholarly criticism has not spent as much time analyzing her character as it has other, male characters in the novel; this gap in scholarship illuminates the problem with readings that reduce McCarthy's treatment of women characters to essentialized or objectified portrayals of femininity.

In general, the students engaged in energetic discourse—and often disagreed with each other—about the ways in which gender plays out, shapes, and is shaped by the texts' narrative structures. One student, frustrated with several scholars' reductive analyses of the women in *Suttree* as virgins, whores, or witches, chose to write a seminar paper challenging those readings by including the feminine characters in the novel who are infrequently analyzed: Suttree's mother and Trippin through the Dew, Suttree's "androgyne" friend (110). Trippin through the Dew in particular illuminates the problematic nature of marginal characters who operate counter to the dominant social mode of the text. The student notes that Trippin through the Dew is explicitly marginalized by the protagonist as well as the omniscient narrator, yet simply by existing, the "transvestite" friend—characterized by nobility, warmth, and compassion—is ultimately never degraded. On the one hand, the language used to describe Suttree's friend is Victorian, gender-normative, and even more restrictive than the already binary language of 1950s Appalachia, where the novel is set: Trippin through the Dew is called an "invert" (412; a Victorian term used for homosexual men or effeminate-acting men), and the character's doubleness is emphasized sartorially—Trippin's clothes are "harlequin" (467). On the other hand, Trippin is one of the last people with whom Suttree connects—physically and emotionally. This character acts always in love, regardless of Suttree's insistence on misnaming them John. As a character, then, Trippin through the Dew stands outside the gendered paradigm that Suttree creates and inhabits; the character is marginalized by the dominant narrative voices yet pushes back insistently and stands, therefore, as a persistent problem for rejecting the gender binary and refusing to be relegated to the margins of interpretation.

The student's research paper on these other femininities in *Suttree* also includes a complex analysis of Joyce, a woman who engages in sexual relationships for money and who is also dating a woman. The student argues that Suttree's evolving understanding of Joyce's sexual and romantic world, which extends beyond Suttree, and the novel's later revelations of Joyce's self-harm, depression, and insecurity, suggest character growth on Suttree's part that is overlooked in narratives that focus exclusively on Joyce as the prostitute in the virgin-whore-witch triad of stereotypes. In other words, although Suttree resists maturation throughout the novel, the increasing attention that he pays to the compassion, humanity, frailty, and complexity of experience exhibited by these feminine characters suggests that, no matter how he fights it, Suttree may be evolving into a more compassionate person. The novel's imagery focuses on the socially marginalized—images that find their apotheosis in Suttree's fever-vision of the "simmering sinners" who "carry the Logos itself from the tabernacle and bear it through the streets" (458). In the student's reading of *Suttree*, the novel's treatment of gender minorities suggests that, like Suttree, the reader, too, must turn to the marginalized in order to find the realization of God's grace in this world.

This student's paper crystallizes much of the discussion throughout the course. Its approach, in fact, was matched by other students' insistence on troubling the claims of critics who dismiss McCarthy's treatment of women as misogynistic. The class was divided, in the end, between those who felt that McCarthy fails to craft sufficiently complex treatments of women and those who felt persuaded by their own careful readings of gender in his works. But regardless of whether students wished to see more complexity in depictions of gender and sexuality in his works, they all agreed that his depictions of gendered performances demand nuanced and sustained critical attention.

In the course, students had the option of responding to an anonymous survey that asked them to reflect on the readings in the light of our discussions of gender theory and our analysis of McCarthy's corpus as a whole. Samples of these responses illustrate the resistance students felt to any effort to categorize McCarthy's works easily or neatly when it came to gender. One question, for example, asks the following: "Nell Sullivan's claim that women in McCarthy's fiction are absent, dead, dying, or 'doll-like' seems obvious and accurate. Do you agree? If you don't, why? If you do, what is your interpretation of why there are few if any women in McCarthy's fiction and why they are objectified?" All respondents of the survey agreed. Yet they nearly always added a qualifier or challenged that simplistic rendering of Sullivan's claim. This is a characteristic response:

> I wouldn't agree completely based on characters like Alfonsa and her grandmother. These women are given a voice in *All the Pretty Horses* more so than women in the rest of McCarthy's novels. They are allowed to speak their mind in a way that does not seem to be characteristic of the absent, dead, dying, or "doll-like" women from his other novels. The [women] who free the imbecile from his cage in *Blood Meridian* are also noteworthy and do not seem to fit into these categories.

As this example demonstrates, students noted that even minor characters can challenge interpretive claims in interesting ways. Of course, the student who wrote this response does not trouble the larger issue: if indeed all the major women characters fit Sullivan's construction, yet McCarthy is capable of creating characters who defy such labels or stereotypes, then why does McCarthy relegate such comparatively complex women characters to the margins?

Other students, however, attempted to tackle that very problem: the role of agency in crafting the world of the narrative. One student notes that while many characters lack agency, and certainly many women characters do, agency is not, strictly speaking, a gendered concept in McCarthy's work. Instead, certain characters seem to wrest a narratorial power from the omniscient third-person narrator and craft their own exegesis. The student writes,

> Dead and doll-like [women] appear most obviously, and such women are often objects of [White] male desire (hello, Magdalena and Alejandra, and all of [Lester] Ballard's victims). But when I consider *All the Pretty Horses*, *maternal power* is important. It is the lifestyle and morality of [John Grady Cole's] mother that drive him to seek a more codified environment, and it is the matriarch of the ranch that makes [Cole] realize that this environment is not all he believed it would be, and that there are some things that are not available to him (like Alejandra). Female presence is there, [and even if] women themselves are not developed or present as characters . . . their power triggers some kind of loss (whether we believe it is deserved or not) for the male protagonist.

As this comment suggests, reading women characters' roles in isolation suggests that a systematically antifeminist power dynamic is at play in McCarthy's works, even when women exhibit a modicum of power: they tend to act and will in relation to men, while men act and will alone, or with other men, or with men and women.

Because there are so few feminine characters in these works, we focused more of our attention on McCarthy's treatment of masculine performance. One student notes that nearly every depiction of masculinity is troubled by some small detail that feminizes the character, so that regardless of the quality or category of masculinity displayed by a central male character, his attempt at hegemonic masculinity is shown as pastiche, or rendered performative in an explicit way. Thus, for example, the violent masculinity in *Blood Meridian*'s acolyte of war ("War is god," Judge Holden says), is undercut by his daintiness (249, 349). Most obviously, the romantic and chivalric masculinity of John Grady Cole in *All the Pretty Horses* is troubled by both the repression of his femininity and aggressive expressions of power over others (primarily horses). One student notes that John Grady exhibits certain traits that are stereotypically feminine early in the novel; he expresses instincts of nurturing, compassion, and humility. "[John Grady] is [initially] a rather effeminate man," this student writes. "[H]owever, he proves himself by breaking horses (and consequently women even though he doesn't understand them at all)." But when John Grady suppresses these nurturing instincts and pursues glory and a woman to whom his romantic gestures pose a social threat, he is expulsed from his paradise—a reading consistent with, and in certain ways more complex than, Gail Moore Morrison's description of this hero's journey as a "fall from innocence into experience" (179).

Sullivan and Naomi Morgenstern both have written on the father's feminine performance in *The Road*. Sullivan contends that the father represents a return to sentimentality, a form of masculinity that privileges expressions of tenderness, admits weakness, and demonstrates nurture and attachment ("Good

Guys"). For Morgenstern, *The Road* is a male romance that unwrites not only the conflation of the domestic with the feminine and the nation but the role of the patriarchy altogether. The novel ultimately draws into focus "a kind of political origin story" (53)—but in this case, an origin story in which the father, as procreator, is able to "contemplate his own irrelevance" (54). Several students came to similar conclusions without having read these arguments. One student argues persuasively that McCarthy consistently attributes characteristics associated with femininity (nurture, tenderness, sentimentality, and so forth) to "good guy," male-bodied characters (see McCarthy, *Road* 118). She cites the father in *The Road* as one of her main examples: "One way that [feminine] masculinity is performed is via the father in *The Road*. He is charged with caring for his son as a mother would. And later on in the novel he is feminized when he can no longer care for himself [and his son becomes his caretaker]."

Another student addresses the feminizing of other characters in depictions—for instance, in *Child of God*—that could be read as retribution for the characters' treatment of women but that could equally reflect a Freudian relapse to the maternal:

> Lester Ballard is likely the most obvious example of an effeminate man—he dresses as a woman at one point, he dresses the dead women that he collects, and the novel has frequent descriptions of womb-like environments, such as the caves. Lester is a character who never reached his full maturity, he is at stunted growth, and thus really is neither a man nor a woman.

As this student goes on to argue, McCarthy's descriptions of masculinity seem to critique the environment around the men—privation in an apocalyptic culture, for instance, or extreme poverty in rural Appalachia—that renders idealized masculine performance damaging. Damaged men retreat to the feminine, although often without effectively generating the nurture they or their worlds need.

The students tended to read McCarthy's descriptions of gender performance as descriptions (and critiques) of social constraints. For instance, one student writes:

> I believe that McCarthy's view of gender is an inherently social one. It's part of the nature of our heavily divided society, hence it is often placed alongside race in McCarthy's novels. Human actions are not dictated by gender, but can be dictated by gendered societal expectations (i.e. characters such as Alejandra engage in non-gender stereotypical behaviors but are still ultimately dictated by gender expectations in society). Because human society is involved in human nature, gender then has a connection with human nature.

Another student response, while lacking similar explanatory depth, suggests that McCarthy's use of nearly caricatured treatments of gender that are then troubled in subtle ways may be an attempt on the author's part to unwrite the hypermasculinity of American culture: "The femininity of his male characters would seem to portray a lack of worry about typical gendered stereotypes, which could possibly indicate that [McCarthy] doesn't believe in a binary gendered world."

While students demonstrated a consistent eagerness to struggle with their interpretations of McCarthy's treatments of performances of gender as well as depictions of men in a man's world and women who are absent or typed, they also consistently underscored their inability to engage with the topics of gender and sexuality in as complex a fashion as they wanted to given the limitations of the texts themselves. John Cant writes that it "cannot be denied" that the absence of significant women characters in McCarthy's works is notable. While "[f]or feminists this is a serious weakness in McCarthy's vision of the world," Cant notes, for readers who are willing to look past the gendered representation of the American national project, "from the mythoclastic point of view, the absence of the female is consistent with McCarthy's critique of American culture." Cant explains his own interpretation of the feminine-bereft landscapes of McCarthy's fiction by connecting McCarthy's literary worlds to a trope of the "Waste Land"—a realm that "lacks the female principle of fertility." He goes on to explain that sterility and aridity are connected to the hegemonic masculinity of the texts, since "[t]he fact that [McCarthy] very frequently associates the female with water and thus with fertility and the essentials of life itself gives the female a special mythic significance in his texts" (16). For Cant, in other words, McCarthy may be an antifeminist writer, but that should not diminish his larger project.

McCarthy's most phallocentric novel, *Blood Meridian*, certainly offers evidence of Cant's argument. In its mythopoetic tapestry tracing the rise of American imperialism, the novel depicts a world parched and barren. The judge famously tells the kid at the end of the tale that "[t]his desert upon which so many have broken is vast and calls for largeness of heart but it is also ultimately empty" (330). The emptiness of the desert symbolically—and literally—strips potency, agency, and life from even the largest-hearted of men. In this "neuter austerity," humans and the terrain are "bequeathed a strange equality"—albeit a diminished, alien one (258). The students of this class, like Cant, easily recognized the larger social critiques implicit in McCarthy's sterile wastelands. For some, this barrenness enabled them to find sufficient interpretive tools to read back against the grain of feminist interpretations of McCarthy's fiction that would find the fiction lacking. Others, echoing Cant, admitted to an inability to find feminist readings of McCarthy's works that did *not* end in critique.

Certainly, a bleak view of human agency, and of humanity, characterizes McCarthy's fictional terrains, yet there is no way to escape the realization that these nearly agentless worlds are inhabited almost entirely by men. Many students admitted to me that even when they attempted a feminist reading, they had very little textual material to work with in terms of depictions of women or sexual minorities. When this paucity of textual material is read in the context of McCarthy's emphasis on violence as one, if not the central, attribute of human nature, that antifeminist problem is impossible to ignore. And several students refused readings that attempted to reclaim what they felt was missing in the first place.

One student points out that McCarthy cannot so pervasively link violence and masculinity without slipping into misandry: "I think [McCarthy] views male sexuality as naturally predatory and destructive. And when his characters have sex it is a way to establish male dominance. There is very little enjoyment shown in the novels after or during a sexual act for both parties concerned." This student connects depictions of masculinity with the specific sex acts and types of sexuality expressed in McCarthy's fiction and arrives at an undeniable conclusion: men's sexual expression is violent nearly all of the time—John Grady's tender lovemaking with Alejandra notwithstanding, as Alfonsa points out (*All the Pretty Horses* 238–40). Another student echoes this sentiment. "Masculinity is performed through action in McCarthy's novels," the student writes. "The male sex role is always either competitive, covetous, or possessive."

In fact, most of the students noted McCarthy's frequent depictions of or allusions to sexual assault and rape as evidence of an inescapable interpretation: most of McCarthy's characters are men, and those men are mostly violent; they are imperialistic in their quests for power over the natural world, women, and effeminate men. They deny pleasure and give pain. The worlds of these texts are, to a certain degree, clearly misogynistic. I have collected three samples of students' observations of this phenomenon below:

> "[McCarthy] seems to see sexuality as a thing of power and dominance rather than a source of love. Ballard uses sex to completely possess his victims, Rawlins is raped in *All the Pretty Horses* as a form of punishment, and the Judge in *Blood Meridian* sexually abuses children because he is more powerful than them."
>
> "Masculinity is performed largely through violence and the objectification of women in McCarthy's novels. The 'male sex role' is to dominate both other men, through violence and murder, and women, through a complete disregard of their humanity."
>
> "I think McCarthy creates a distinct binary between masculinity and femininity, and he placed men over and above women. This exaggeration, in my opinion, semi works to point out the absurdity of gender and sexuality relations, but I don't think the reader can avoid how misogynistic McCarthy's novels are."

In the first example, the student notes the absence of viable expressions of love through human sexuality in McCarthy's works. The second student identifies the dehumanizing behavior of many male characters as, ultimately, a comment on these fictional worlds' inhumanity and on the inherent violence of men (a worldview that seems to strike the student as misanthropic at best). The final example demonstrates a student's attempts to read into the typified gender performances of characters in McCarthy's novels, before quickly turning to what the student feels is an inevitable conclusion: gender in these works is a problem.

McCarthy's treatment of women characters; the aggression with which the only explicit sexual minority in McCarthy's corpus, in *Suttree*, is treated; and the prevalence of sexual violence and predation are troubling, and students felt compelled to address these thorny issues because they are troubling. More importantly, they felt compelled to address these issues because of the implications of McCarthy's prose style. Violence and hypermasculine performance are rendered with aesthetic mastery in these works. The terrible capacity of art is that it can force our beauty-seeking gaze to contemplate even those things we resist. One student explains that McCarthy's talent as a writer contradicts the problematic inhumanity of the worlds that McCarthy creates. The very degree of artistry in these books, the student writes, McCarthy's "gift for description," renders everything in them valuable. The one necessity underlying any approach to teaching gender in McCarthy's works—or really, any approach to teaching McCarthy's works at all—is to pay attention. That student puts it beautifully (with perhaps an inadvertent riposte to Frank Norris's famous statement about overly decorous realism):[4] "He makes even a broken tea cup handle under a street lamp seem like a tragedy worth recognizing."

At the end of the course, there may not have been a single person in the classroom who felt capable of reading McCarthy's treatment of gender and sexuality as progressive or affirming of the complexities of human experience. But at the same time, not one of us walked out of that classroom into a world in which gender and sexuality are not now and have not historically been contexts of frequent and pervasive brutality, predation, violence, and rage. Many of my students recognized in McCarthy's narratives an exquisite articulation of the brutality and rage experienced by so many women and sexual minorities in patriarchal communities. Ultimately, students welcomed the course as a way to practice analyzing literature of the highest caliber, and in so doing to bear witness to the worst brutality and the most luminous beauty of which humanity is capable. And that feels like a worthy pursuit, no matter how messy or complex it becomes. As one of the students puts it, McCarthy's gift lies in his ability to make the tragedies of our ordinary lives "worth recognizing."

NOTES

[1] McGilchrist reads McCarthy's descriptions of land as "masculine" in style, and she interprets this stylistic choice as rendering the writer's works allegories for the acquisitive nature of American men (186).

[2] Students read Cixous and excerpts from Butler, *Gender Trouble* 3–44; Connell 119–38 and 178–293; and Ahmed 1–57, along with other works.

[3] I have elsewhere explored at greater length the troubling prominence of genital mutilation and the threatened or enacted rape of men, women, and children in *Blood Meridian*. See L. Cooper, *Masculinities* 23–46.

[4] Norris complains that it is the "drama of a broken teacup." See also Walcutt 62.

Multiculturalism, Deep Time, and Judge Holden

Rafael Acosta Morales

Because McCarthy is so keenly aware of Mexican social relationships and worldviews and represents them frankly, a group of Mexican writers that included the northerners Luis Jorge Boone and Julián Herbert, in a panel during the 2015 Guadalajara International Book Fair, went so far as to consider him a Mexican writer (Rodríguez Marcos). I do not know what Cormac McCarthy may think of this, and it is unlikely that I will ever know. Nevertheless, elements of his work seem to resonate powerfully across different cultures, though the elements may not be the same ones, even if both cultures identify with his cultural production.

For a class on McCarthy, I suggest using Wai Chee Dimock's "A Theory of Resonance" as the framework for an inquiry into the meaning of *Blood Meridian*, in particular its reading of the points of contact between Mexico and the United States; such a framework would be especially useful in a multicultural classroom. At first, Dimock's text would appear to point us in a different direction. Describing her concept of resonance as an interpretative tool, Dimock refers to what she calls

> the traveling frequencies of literary texts: frequencies received and amplified across time, moving farther and farther from their points of origin, causing unexpected vibrations in unexpected places. A theory of resonance puts the temporal axis at the center of literary studies. Texts are emerging phenomena, activated and to some extent constituted by the passage of time, by their continual transit through new semantic networks, modifying their tonality as they proceed. (1061)

In this line of thought, literary value is produced through the reconstruction of a message across temporal distance. Most important, value is created by the resonance such a message acquires when it is interpreted through the noise generated by the passage of time. Literature is configured in the resonance of the text's style, the struggle of its characters, and its capturing of a world that can be found in other discourses, and by the conscious project of others, across the depths of time, in claiming it for themselves. This is not, in and of itself, an original proposal. We have long reinterpreted the texts of our forebears to serve our purposes and forgotten those that do not align with the worldviews we peddle. In Dimock's configuration, resonance entails a different understanding of time than that which is dominant in literary studies, where historicism has meant a reconstitution of the context, distant in time as it may be, in which the original was produced.

A central idea in Dimock's notion of resonance is that distance produces noise, whether that distance is temporal or cultural. For a literary text, crossing cultures in this sense is not so different from crossing time, as cultural referents become resignified in the passage from one site of enunciation to the other. What may be most interesting about the use of resonance as a critical tool is that it allows one to see the transformation of texts from one's own culture and time into those of others'. However, while applying the concept of resonance to texts whose origins are distant in time allows us to make those texts our own, it is less likely that we would have an opportunity to observe our own texts or texts from our own time being turned into the texts of a later period. The transformation of texts across cultures is a different matter.

Many interpretations of *Blood Meridian* have focused on the novel as a construction of antinomian or Gnostic origins,[1] where human acts are dislodged from moral judgment, and where salvation is an unnecessary exercise, either because we're saved by divine grace rather than by our actions or because salvation through an evil deity is not worth pursuing. Other interpretations have centered criticism on the relation between McCarthy's work and the myths of the frontier and American exceptionalism.[2] More recently we find contributions from either theories of the posthuman or new materialisms such as object-oriented ontology,[3] which provides a sheer focus on the materiality of the novel.

In my approach to teaching *Blood Meridian*, I guide students toward a different reading of the writer's opus that focuses on the construction of subjectivity while also theorizing the empty spaces within the system of judiciary powers that arise from dialectic subjectivities. This is a mouthful, but such an approach can help students understand the novel in relation to other cultures. The easiest way to think about multiculturalism in *Blood Meridian* would be to think of the multiethnic makeup of the Glanton gang, composed of Delawares, African Americans, and Anglo Americans. Its makeup could be compared to the makeup of the *Pequod*'s crew in Herman Melville's *Moby-Dick*. This is one way to think about multiculturalism, and one that is already prevalent in the United States, where the concept of diversity is favored as the approach to thinking about different ethnic groups. I do not argue against this approach to multiculturalism but point out for students that McCarthy's approach is different, as it focuses more on the limitations of the Anglo American worldview of manifest destiny and domination. Whereas in *Moby-Dick* the limitations of this worldview are coded as the aberrant fixation that Ahab has developed on the white whale, in *Blood Meridian* the actions of the Glanton gang are depicted not as an aberration but as a logical development of a worldview that considers the world as material for domination.

By thinking about the way that McCarthy considers everybody and everything as material objects, students who may have grown accustomed to the feeling of being the subject who observes others, from a position of relative power, can consider what it means to be in a peripheral position. For me, this is key to teaching McCarthy's novel—using the genocidal violence and the philosophical orientation of *Blood Meridian* to allow students to understand the flipside of manifest destiny and other tenets of American political life. This approach is dependent on the use of certain theoretical frameworks, the introduction of which represents a difficulty in the classroom, but not an insurmountable one. Introducing these frameworks is important because the novel does not offer its own hermeneutical tools, leaving open many pathways for interpretation. In order to further students' reading of theoretical background, I bring together views of the novel's approach to materiality and elements from the readings of McCarthy's novel as the fashioning of myths.

It is very difficult to establish an authoritative interpretation of a book like *Blood Meridian*, for as Barcley Owens states, "If we are fishing for critical approaches, we know there may be all sorts of interesting trout in the text, down in there somewhere, but efforts to tease them out, to tie just the right fly, mostly fail" (xiii). Thus, I look not to interpret the novel, but to navigate through its reception, framing its amoral discourse within configurations of the law that the judge, its villain, sutures as he makes decisions. The flattening of morality in the novel allows us to approach the issues it raises from a different perspective. As W. Oliver Baker argues, "While McCarthy's aesthetic form does not privilege human over nonhuman suffering, like Schoenberg's aesthetic, it nonetheless suggests that readers can come to identity with the victims of colonial conquest" (11). Here I relate the morally neutral presentation of violence in the book, its optical democracy of violence (McCarthy, *Blood Meridian* 247), to the construction of political subjectivity and to the possibility of attempting to understand such subjectivity from several viewpoints.

The idea of resonance provides an approach to McCarthy's novel, its concept of others, and the violence that so often develops in the encounter with others. The cultural referents from which the novel's narrative departs and the way in which it arrives at the optical democracy of the West are suggestive of the Hegelian notion of trauma as grounds for cognition. Murderous wanderers such as McCarthy's judge operate from a logic of subjectivity in which a subject's existence is dependent on that subject's freedom. Such freedom is not conceived as something that can be limited, and thus it becomes expansive. This attitude is directly related to knowledge: "Whatever exists, [the judge] said. Whatever in creation exists without my knowledge exists without my consent" (McCarthy, *Blood Meridian* 198). As can be understood from this often-quoted passage, knowledge in this novel is conceived as intrinsically related to domination.

In order to highlight how this quotation is a commentary on the development of American history, we might follow David Willbern's comparison of *Blood Meridian* and Larry McMurtry's *Lonesome Dove*, which emphasizes the idea of domination as represented within the former work:

> *Lonesome Dove* traverses familiar territory. Its characters are sympathetically human, its erotic relations conventionally heterosexual, its actions melodramatic. It is essentially about family: generations and continuity,

> shadowed by mortality. The saga is saddle-soap opera that begs to be made into a television miniseries. It is fun to read and can bring a tear to the eye. *Blood Meridian* can scare the hell out of you. Its characters are almost inhuman, its erotic relations perverse, its violence almost unbearable, its prose soaked in blood. (85)

The same blood soaks both tales, but the tone and plot employed by McMurtry resonate in a way that is already familiar to his American audience. The characters McCrae and Call are not represented as murderous Texas rangers who conspire with landowners to kill and dispossess Mexicans all around south Texas. In this story, their cattle rustling is presented as a game in which they steal cattle from Mexicans and the Mexicans then steal them back, all in good sport. No such thing can be seen in *Blood Meridian*, a novel that aims for a much grimmer version of the events that took place in the West. For Willbern, McCarthy's "version of history is marked by solitude, absence, ignorance, deprivation, violence, and death" (89). These two novels provide two very different concepts of subjectivity. In a sense *Lonesome Dove* might be the more brutal story, portraying as its true tragedy the eventual downfall of McCrae and Call and their replacement by lawyers and other representatives of American settler society. As Willbern states, "Both novels merge geographical and psychological versions of 'frontier.' Larry McMurtry's *Lonesome Dove* understands the advance of civilization as positive achievement; Cormac McCarthy's *Blood Meridian* diagnoses the march of 'civilization' as destruction" (84).

McCarthy's work depicts an optical democracy of slaughter in a world thoroughly configured by violence. The epigraph at the beginning of *Blood Meridian* reflects its approach to history: "Clark, who led last year's expedition to the Afar region of northern Ethiopia, and UC Berkeley colleague Tim D. White, also said that a re-examination of a 300,000-year-old fossil skull found in the same region earlier shows evidence of having been scalped" (i). In *Blood Meridian*, scalping is presented as the ultimate act of violence, in which symbolic import joins literal violence. The scalper is looking not only to kill the victim but also to deny access to the afterlife as well as obtain a trophy. The epigraph, in conjunction with the portrayal of the novel's main antagonist, the judge, can be understood to suggest that violence is the constitutive element of mankind. Even the name of the judge's rifle, "et in Arcadia ego" ("Even in Arcadia I am"; 131), a reference to how death exists even in paradise, points to the pervasiveness of death and violence in McCarthy's universe.

Critics have often sought to find a moral position in *Blood Meridian*, a revisionism that the novel does not offer. Students are likely to share this approach, which is one reason why it is important for teachers to help them understand the novel from a framework that does not render the American genocide acceptable. Displaying an urge for something that justifies the novel's gore is an understandable reaction to the violence. The novel was initially criticized for its optical democracy of violence (James), and as Edwin Arnold and Dianne Luce note, "it has struck many readers initially as devoid of moral or even meaning" (Introduction 7). This reception history can serve for students as a favorable inroad to a deeper analysis of the novel. The proposition that there is no regeneration in the novel's violence is widespread,[4] and it has generally produced a rejection of the work's qualities as a western. The novel has also been read as a revisionist western (Jarrett, *Cormac*), but I would argue that this reading is not accurate. If McCarthy's work is compared to John Wayne's films, where the violence of the cowboy is considered gruesome yet ultimately justified, or to Clint Eastwood's films, where some violence is not justified yet other violence is, I would claim that *Blood Meridian* inhabits a different world. Western epics are almost always allegories, and as such, they are histories whose characters or events often represent a set of political ideas, more often about how to wield violence and how to justify it. The characters represent the danger of diving into primal violence, whether they seek regeneration or not. This allegorical structure is completely absent from *Blood Meridian*. As Susan Kollin notes, "McCarthy's use of violence thus complicates the tradition of the western hero. Rather than allowing the figure to claim redemption through acts of conquest, the novel provides readers with a horrific portrayal of a westerner who offers nothing in the way of heroism" (564). Every character in the novel represents violence unleashed in a story in which every man abandons his community and commits himself to self-defense in a Hobbesian all-out war, in which no quarter is given.

As students seek to understand how McCarthy avoids justifying the violence depicted in *Blood Meridian*, it's helpful to consider the depiction of subjectivity in the novel using the Heideggerian notion of tool-being, as advanced by Graham Harman. Broadly, tool-being is existence not experienced by a subject (Harman 45). According to Daniel Davis Wood, McCarthy writes "fiction in which human beings en masse, regardless of distinguishing features, are displaced to the narrative margins while the dispassionate workings of the inhuman environment obtain narrative centrality" (17). Similarly, Jonathan Pitts argues that "*Blood Meridian* doesn't simply critique frontier myth and symbol in the manner of the revisionary Western. Revisionism often replaces one set of symbols for another, leaving unexamined the underlying claims to greater accuracy of vision and perspective" (9). The novel is not revisionist, because it does not mean to repair an improper use of violence, nor does it offer a path for regeneration, but rather it approaches the issue of violence from the perspective of an optical democracy of subjectivity, where no subject is privileged over another in the development of the maddening display of gore. This is one of the reasons why the novel doesn't develop the character of the kid or allow the narrator to embrace any one character's moral point of view. Dana Phillips writes that in *Blood Meridian*, "the human does not stand out among other beings and objects that make up the world" (43), a perspective that, as Wood notes, has been a productive angle for ecocritics (17).[5] I choose, however, to use these notions to focus on subjectivity and its role as part of a vicious cycle that leads from traumatic experience to states of exception.

I ask students to imagine what would happen if the perspective of the western were applied democratically to everything and everyone under the sky, such that all subjects were reduced to objects of equal violence, every being transformed into equipment. *Blood Meridian*'s discourse embraces the position of chance and the radicalized equality of elements in the novel's narrative. The way in which the novel turns the organic into anorganic[6] and equalizes everything in the sight of the narrator is the novel's take on optical democracy. In the panorama that McCarthy builds, a wide-open desert, goat excrement, stones, shadows, and gods reveal in their blinding appearance under the sun an optical democracy, an equality in which every character is described with the same abandon (with the exception of the judge) and every character is an enshrinement of chance. Life is governed by nothing but luck if the notion of referential subjectivity is removed from the game. The objectivization of the gaze occurs not so much when one vision is overprivileged in order to make one kind of subjectivity objective, but rather when every subject is turned into an object of vision, and all of them are submitted to chance. Baker posits this novel as representing the opposite of the myth of regeneration through violence, where "by representing the frontier less as a place of progress than as one of imperial expansion, economic opportunism, and violent dispossession, the novel serves as what Sara Spurgeon argues is a 'counter-memory' or 'anti-myth' to the narratives of manifest destiny and American exceptionalism" (4).

Blood Meridian thus changes the discourse about the West and offers us a choice of perspectives between the optical democracy of the vast, deserted landscape and the war cult of Judge Holden. But ultimately the novel chooses neither. As for the judge, he proposes contradictory arguments: "War endures. As well ask men what they think of stone. War was always here. Before man was, war waited for him" (248). Then later, the judge claims suzerainty over the world. He is opposed to everyone in his embrace of war, as he "declares everyone and everything outside himself to be a prima facie opponent and he asserts the rule of man at the expense of the rule of law" (Wood 176). The effect is genocide: "since nothing lay outside God, not even chaos, God could have no witness, that is, no other or nothing by which he could define himself and have his identity" (Mugerauer 6). While one could hardly argue that the judge is construed as a god, it is easy to argue that he may be the opposite, a devil. It is unclear whether the judge is the cause or a product of the gory universe we face in the novel.

Because violence is so pervasive in McCarthy's portrayal of the West, the characters, and particularly the Glanton gang, seem to constitute a cult that treats war as a deity. The novel does leave some space for ambiguity between its discourse and the judge's discourse, a space that often goes unnoticed by many readers, as the gory detail in which the Glanton gang's actions are described becomes the dominant trait of the narrative, along with the twisted charm of the judge's arguments. This space of ambiguity is one of the elements that allows the novel to resonate so powerfully as it crosses cultural environments. By de-emphasizing the subjectivity within the western approach to otherness, and by discursively reducing everything, including westerners, to equal status as objects of such an optical democracy, the novel offers a possibility to reconfigure subjectivities in a different manner. Put differently, a Mexican reader might find more to like in this radically egalitarian vision than in the more typically America-centric *Lonesome Dove*.

Blood Meridian offers a different relation to history—though it follows historical documents closely, the novel refuses to admit relations of causality that come from outside the narration, blocking the possibility of directly embracing historical events as a preferred frame of reference. The kid, for whom "[a]ll history [is] present in that visage, the child the father of the man" (3), is the space from which the history of any nation is invited to enter the mythology of the frontier. The cruelty inflicted in the novel is both harder and easier to stomach than that kind of mythology, for what nation's history has not been generated out of the need for a debased war machine like the Glanton gang? What nation has not originated in a group of lawless, bloodthirsty men like the gang? And what nation, deep inside, is not ashamed of its origins? In this way, the horror not only resonates with the backdrop of the Native American genocide in the United States. It also resonates with other horrors in the past of other cultures. In my courses, it resonates against the backdrop of the strongman novel (e.g., Juan Rulfo's *Pedro Páramo* or Carlos Fuentes's *La muerte de Artemio Cruz* [*The Death of Artemio Cruz*]), though it could certainly be read against the conquest novel or the dictator novel as well. The thing that is notably different about *Blood Meridian*'s effect, as opposed to the resonance produced with the genre of the western and its glorification of genocide, is that the novel's horror is not as naturalized.

My approach to teaching *Blood Meridian* is centered on multiculturalism not because people of different ethnicities participate in the novel, but because by depicting imperialist violence, McCarthy allows us to critique the way in which modernity has developed in parallel with supremacy. I teach *Blood Meridian* in a graduate course centered on outlaws in the Americas, and the course's central hypothesis is that banditry is a reaction to society's tendency to transform too much consumption into capital, which leads to the domination of the many by a few. By the time we study McCarthy's novel, we have covered biopolitics, Marxism, and cultural capital. The unit in which we read *Blood Meridian* aims to help students think through freedom with a discussion of the way in which capital accumulation shapes itself in the image of Georg Wilhelm Friedrich Hegel's master-slave struggle. We discuss Hegel with regard to *Pedro Páramo* and F. Scott Fitzgerald's *The Great Gatsby* as we attempt to understand what Hegelian life and death are struggling for. In this vein, some of the texts against which *Blood Meridian* resonates are different from those one would likely find in an English class. As I note, they do not naturalize the violence of genocide in the Americas in the same way that the western does, but notably, in novels related to Latin American strongmen, dictators, and the conquest, the leading figure that produces the violence that swallowed up the continent is not the hero but the villain of these novels. Contrasting two novels with very similar structures, such as *Pedro Páramo* and *The Great Gatsby*, tends to lead to the same conclusion. The character who turns to violence and oppression to fill an existential void—a void imagined to have been produced in the wake of unrequited love—is not romanticized. The consequences of the phantasm of freedom chased by both Jay Gatsby and Pedro Páramo are obvious to every reader.

In resonating against these two traditions, the optical democracy of violence in *Blood Meridian* produces different meanings. In particular, the violent development of the Glanton gang then signifies in different ways: it is the violence that exterminated Native Americans, but it is also the drive for freedom and power that produces in businessmen like Gatsby a seemingly unquenchable thirst for money, since money stands as a palliative for a void that is impossible to fill. It is also the drive to power that fuels the narcissistic, dreamlike state that Pedro Páramo builds in the eponymous novel. In *Blood Meridian*, the drive for dominion is stripped of the romantic love with which the despots in these other novels dress their thirst for power, and it is represented by the judge, a man for whom whatever exists without his consent exists against him.

The scene in chapter 2 of *Blood Meridian* where the kid runs into a hermit can be interpreted differently when different resonances are considered. Because the hermit had been a slave dealer, it stands to reason that he would concoct a world vision that ends up justifying the status quo:

> The way of the transgressor is hard. God made this world, but he didnt make it to suit everybody, did he?
> I dont believe he much had me in mind.
> Aye, said the old man. But where does a man come by his notions. What world's he seen that he liked better?
> I can think of better places and better ways.
> Can ye make it be?
> No. (19)

But the logical pathway that leads to acceptance of the status quo is predicated on circumstance, as the inability of one individual to change the world does not imply that it is impossible for it to change. One of the first projects depicted in the novel, "to try whether the stuff of creation may be shaped to man's will or whether his own heart is not another kind of clay" (5), aims precisely at knowing whether people can change the world or whether they will be changed when they confront it.

The judge creates an ontology based on principles articulated by Hegel, who in the "Lordship and Bondage" section of *Phenomenology of Mind* talks about life and death judgments, which configure individuals as lords or servants in the following way: "it is solely by risking life that freedom is obtained; only thus is it tried and proved that the essential nature of self-consciousness is not bare existence" (Hegel, par. 187). Hegel then proceeds to establish that "[i]in the same way each must aim at the death of the other, as it risks its own life thereby; for that other is to it of no more worth than itself; the other's reality is presented to the former as an external other, as outside itself; it must cancel that externality" (Hegel, par. 187). *Blood Meridian* reveals a pervasive human need to cancel what Hegel calls externalities in order to build a universality that encompasses everything. Survival first and later fulfillment are predicated on dominating others in order to prevent them from dominating and, most important, because the culture requires the recognition of submission as a precondition of self-consciousness. In such a construction, war is ultimately the guarantor of everything, since the way one verifies the existence of one's own mind is by the domination of others. Yet the novel does leave philosophical wiggle room by not fully endorsing this worldview. The hermit offers us another consideration when he states that "[a] man's at odds to know his mind cause his mind is aught he has to know it with. He can know his heart, but he dont want to. Rightly so. Best not to look in there. It aint the heart of a creature that is bound in the way that God has set for it" (19). When people look at their own hearts, they may find out how easy it is to believe that a boot's natural place is on another person's throat—when it's one's own boot and not one's throat.

If we contrast *Blood Meridian* with McCarthy's novel *The Road*, we can see a different presentation of the idea of the violent apocalypse. Despite the generalized violence that has taken over the world of *The Road*, the father and the son find themselves with the boot on their throats and somehow come to the conclusion that there is something to be done in the world amid the horror.

In her story "The Ones Who Walk Away from Omelas," Ursula K. Le Guin describes a utopian city called Omelas, whose happy society is predicated on the torture of a small child in a basement (329–36). The happiness of most is then dependent on the misery of one, in a reverse image of the dystopia proposed in *Blood Meridian*, where the possible happiness of anyone is based on prevalent misery. Taking *Blood Meridian* out of the context in which it is most commonly understood shows that it is possible to be more aware and to walk, as some of the citizens in Le Guin's story do, away from Omelas and into a different mode of understanding.

NOTES

[1] More on this subject can be found in Daugherty; Wallach, "Judge"; and Mundik.

[2] Wood and Cant are good examples of scholars who study McCarthy's work in these terms, relating it to the tradition of the western.

[3] Braune and Baker are the most relevant scholars who study the novel from an object-oriented ontology perspective.

[4] For scholarship that shares this position, see Baker; Braune; and Eaton.

[5] For examples of such ecocriticism, see McGilchrist; Guillemin, *Pastoral Vision*; and Sanborn.

[6] I point here to a confluence between tool-being and Gilles Deleuze's notion of anorganic life: "the organism is that which life sets against itself in order to limit itself, and there is a life all the more intense, all the more powerful for being anorganic" (Deleuze and Guattari 554). The terms *tool-being* and *anorganic life* are full of virtualities and resist actualization, though Harman does point out some differences between them.

Ecocritical Approaches to McCarthy

Kevin Trumpeter

Ecocriticism emerged as a distinct field in literary studies in the 1990s, and its popularity has grown over the past two decades, largely in response to widespread anxiety about global climate change. Ecocritics have been engaged in drawing people's attention to poetry, prose, and other works of art that assist readers in recognizing the deleterious impacts human civilization has had on the nonhuman world, and Cormac McCarthy's works, with their nuanced attention to humanity's frequently antagonistic relation to the environment, offer a productive point of departure for exploring these issues. This essay will touch on some fundamental concepts in ecocritical discourse (including wilderness, ecocentrism, the pastoral, the Anthropocene, and collapse) and identify representative passages drawn from McCarthy's expansive body of work that suggest how these ecocritical concepts can enrich students' understanding of these texts.

While ecocriticism has greatly expanded its scope in recent years to analyze a much wider variety of landscapes, cultural perspectives, literary genres, and artistic media, the field began to coalesce around a group of scholars interested in promoting the study of nature writing and pastoral literature. An explanation of these two closely related genres therefore provides a logical entry point for teaching students about the development of ecocriticism as an interpretive approach, and these modes of literary discourse are also instrumental for understanding the environmental issues addressed in McCarthy's fiction.

Nature Writing, Wilderness, and Ecocentrism

Though McCarthy's works, as fictional narratives, differ from more conventional examples of nature writing, which tend to be essayistic, autobiographical accounts of their authors' experiences living in or traveling through a specific wilderness, the thematic significance of the wild and the wealth of lyrical descriptions of natural phenomena in McCarthy's works suggest some important affinities with the nature writing tradition. McCarthy's works display the same formidable erudition about animal behavior, plant taxonomy, and geologic systems that is found in works by celebrated nature writers like Henry David Thoreau, Aldo Leopold, Rachel Carson, Edward Abbey, Barry Lopez, Annie Dillard, and many others. Encouraging students to attend to richly described wilderness settings provides a useful approach to reading a text like *Blood Meridian*, a novel whose episodic plot and cipher-like protagonist eschews the standard devices for unifying a narrative. The book is packed with vivid natural imagery that does little to advance the plot but rather invites readers to linger over the majesty of the western landscape. Take, for example, a passage like this one: "The crumpled butcherpaper mountains lay in sharp shadowfold under the long blue dusk and in the middle distance the glazed bed of a dry lake lay shimmering like the mare imbrium and herds of deer were moving north in the last of the twilight, harried over the plain by wolves who were themselves the color of the desert floor" (105). Setting is something that other interpretive approaches tend to gloss over while focusing instead on the interaction of human characters, but an ecocritical approach might begin by attending to seemingly uneventful passages like this one, whose offbeat metaphor ("crumpled butcherpaper mountains") defamiliarizes the landscape and invites contemplation. Such passages can have an even more profound effect if students have a stock of mental images that they can associate with what McCarthy is describing. Instructors can project photographs by artists such as Ansel Adams ("Mount McKinley and Wonder Lake" or "Mount Williamson") while they or students read the passages aloud in class in order to illustrate how McCarthy's panoramic descriptions aim to capture the sublimity of the mountainous western landscape.

It can also be instructive to pair McCarthy's novels with more conventional examples of nature writing from a contemporary writer like Edward Abbey, whose essays more explicitly address why wilderness landscapes inspire him (and, perhaps by extension, McCarthy) to focus on them so intently. For example, in the opening essay to his collection *Desert Solitaire*, Abbey finds himself at a loss to describe what he finds so enchanting about a particular rock formation. After an abortive attempt to find a satisfactory metaphor for conveying his awestruck impression, he explains that

> [t]he personification of the natural is exactly the tendency I wish to suppress in myself, to eliminate for good. I am here not only to evade for a while the clamor and filth and confusion of the cultural apparatus but also to confront, immediately and directly if it's possible, the bare bones of existence, the elemental and fundamental, the bedrock that sustains us. I want to be able to look at and into a juniper tree, a piece of quartz, a vulture, a spider, and see it as it is in itself, devoid of all humanly ascribed qualities, anti-Kantian, even the categories of scientific description. . . . I dream of a hard and brutal mysticism in which the naked self merges with the nonhuman world and yet somehow survives still intact, individual, separate. Paradox and bedrock. ([Touchstone] 6)

Abbey's passage can be used to illustrate for students the ideal of ecocentrism (or biocentrism), one of the key concepts in early ecocritical discourse, which serves as the desirable alternative to humanity's default anthropocentrism, the deep-seated belief that the beings of the natural world are nothing more than resources that can and should be exploited to fulfill the needs and desires of humans. Environmental problems have often been interpreted as the inevitable outcome of an anthropocentric worldview, and many ecocritics have looked to nature writing as a genre uniquely capable of fostering the kind of ecocentric worldview expressed in Abbey's desire to see the things of the world "devoid of all humanly ascribed qualities."[1]

The explicit articulation by Abbey of his ecocentric aspirations can help students make sense of some of the more elliptical passages in McCarthy's novels. *The Crossing*, for example, opens with the adolescent hero Billy Parham riding into the "rich and wild" country of New Mexico where his family plans to homestead (3). He sneaks out of the house one night soon after arriving to watch a wolf pack hunting in the moonlit desert and observes that "they seemed of another world entire" (4). Wolves, which in the twentieth century were hunted nearly to extinction in the United States, serve as a synecdoche for the wild, nonhuman world that Billy reveres and, like Abbey, desires to merge with. Later in the story, the teenage Billy traps a wolf, the last of its kind in the region, which has strayed up from Mexico and is killing cows from the Parham family's herd. Rather than shoot the animal, Billy embarks upon a precarious journey across the border to return the wolf to the mountains of Mexico, thereby acknowledging a value in the wolf that exists beyond humankind's reckoning.[2] Students can read McCarthy's novel as accepting the challenge that Lopez poses in *Of Wolves and Men* for authors to write about "a whole wolf" in a way that represents these animals as more than "two-dimensional symbols," a literary accomplishment that would signify that "man" had "finally quit his preoccupation with himself and begun to contemplate a universe in which he was not central" (270). Periodic attempts by Billy to delve into the consciousness of the wolf demonstrate his interest in cultivating a more primal, ecocentric worldview, even if descriptions of that consciousness ultimately founder in the face of the wild animal's insurmountable otherness. As one passage explains, the flames of a campfire reflected in the wolf's eyes "burned out there like gatelamps to another world. A world burning on the shore of an unknowable void" (McCarthy, *Crossing* 73). When the wolf dies, the novel again resorts to tropes of unknowability to describe Billy's quest for a transcendent understanding of the wolf's wildness: "He took up her stiff head out of the leaves and held it or he reached to hold what cannot be held . . . which cannot be held never be held and is no flower but is swift and a huntress and the wind itself is in terror of it and the world cannot lose it" (127). Billy's desire to cross the "unknowable void" separating the human world from that of wild nature defines Billy's pursuit of an ecocentrism that, as the unpunctuated flow of ambiguous imagery in the passage suggests, is difficult and perhaps even impossible to fully articulate. Addressing the ambiguity in such passages can prompt students to articulate their own ideas about what an ecocentric mode of thinking might look like and why it might be desirable.

To further illustrate how the concept of ecocentrism is useful for understanding McCarthy's environmental thinking, students can also be directed to attend to the description of "optical democracy" in *Blood Meridian*, which refers to a lack of discernible hierarchy in McCarthy's descriptions of the natural world (247). This absence disrupts the default anthropocentrism with which most readers are accustomed to read a textual landscape and, by extension, the natural world we all live in (Phillips 443–44; Guillemin, *Pastoral Vision* 73–101). McCarthy's insight about the lack of metaphysical hierarchy in an ecocentric view of the world helps account for *Blood Meridian*'s intense focus on natural phenomena and also for the absence of symbolism in the novel that in other literary discourse typically justifies extensive descriptions of nonhuman things. To highlight the ecocentric character of McCarthy's descriptive prose, the description of optical democracy can be paired with Ernest Hemingway's "Hills Like White Elephants," in which the author contrasts the dry, brown countryside on one side of a river valley with the fertile farmland on the other in order to reflect the metaphorically barren and fertile futures the young woman in the story contemplates as her lover tries to coax her into having an abortion. Hemingway's anthropocentric use of natural description contrasts instructively with the wilderness spaces McCarthy describes, which aren't clearly identifiable as symbols and whose value is better understood in the light of ecocentric standards that nature writing has traditionally encouraged readers to acknowledge and respect.

Pastoral, Environmentalism, and the Anthropocene

While McCarthy shares the nature writer's keen appreciation for wilderness, his work can also be read as an example of the closely related genre of pastoral, a mode of writing that addresses the encroachments of urban civilization not only on wilderness areas but also on sparsely settled rural landscapes that coexist harmoniously with the natural world (Guillemin, *Pastoral Vision*). Traditional pastoral imagery, which was codified in the art and literature of the burgeoning Roman Empire, depicts shepherds enjoying lives of ease amid bucolic landscapes that had a nostalgic appeal for readers who had recently migrated to the empire's urban centers. These pastoral landscapes were defined as an idealized middle ground where the advantages of a growing urban civilization (e.g., safety, security, and the beauty of human culture) were balanced with those of the wilderness (e.g., excitement, freedom, and the beauty of wild nature). The middle ground in pastoral tends to be more agrarian than wild, so McCarthy's focus on subsistence farmers in the writer's Appalachian fiction and on ranchers in the western stories makes the pastoral dialectic between city and country an effective conceptual frame for understanding McCarthy's work.

McCarthy, however, offers readers a distinctly grim version of the pastoral genre in which the industrial order inevitably outpaces his pastoral heroes' efforts to escape it. His novels are almost always set in the past, so the reader's interest in the lives of these pastoral heroes is overshadowed by the melancholy realization that their way of living is doomed to extinction. The hopelessness that characterizes McCarthy's pastoral imagination nevertheless aptly reflects the apocalyptic sensibility of the late twentieth century, and providing students with a brief overview of some of the influential texts and key concepts through which the environmental movement has been popularized in the past few decades can help them better understand the pessimism that pervades McCarthy's revision of the pastoral tradition.

McCarthy's first novel was published in 1965, three years after Rachel Carson's *Silent Spring*, whose success in mobilizing opposition to the indiscriminate use of chemical herbicides and pesticides is roundly cited as a watershed event in the development of the environmental movement in the United States. The environmental movement grew throughout the 1960s and 1970s, fueled by concerns over littering, overpopulation, air pollution, oil spills, species extinction, and deforestation, among many other issues. Doomsday scenarios such as Carson's ("silent spring" refers to the prediction of a world depopulated of birds) and the one Paul R. Ehrlich depicts in his bestselling Malthusian polemic, *The Population Bomb*, have been a prominent feature in the development of environmental discourse in the United States. Such apocalyptic rhetoric fosters a widespread sense that the natural world, and humanity's ability to survive in it, is increasingly and perhaps irremediably imperiled. Bill McKibben's *The End of Nature*, a popular environmentalist polemic of the late 1980s that laments the impossibility of locating any place on earth where industrialization has not had a measurable impact, sums up a widely felt sense of hopelessness among Reagan-era environmentalists. The default tone of alarmism within environmental discourse was validated even more powerfully throughout the 1990s and early 2000s by increasing public attention to the seriousness of global climate change, as reflected in the commercial success of Al Gore's documentary film, *An Inconvenient Truth*, which warned a broad international audience about the potentially dire consequences of a warming planet.

Discussions concerning climate change within ecocriticism have focused in recent years on the concept of the Anthropocene. The term, popularized in the early twenty-first century by the climate scientist Paul J. Crutzen, proposes that the fossil-fueled impact of the industrial revolution upon the earth's ecological systems has become profound enough to constitute a new geological epoch (Crutzen and Stoermer). The distinctly pessimistic treatment of pastoral themes in almost all of McCarthy's work indicates how difficult it has become in the Anthropocene to convincingly imagine the kind of idealized middle ground that pastoral narratives traditionally celebrate.

The failure of the pastoral is a thematic formula that McCarthy uses to structure many of his works, beginning with his first novel, *The Orchard Keeper*. The story is set in the 1930s and offers readers a nostalgic representation of the approximate era and rural environs in which the author spent his own childhood. The would-be pastoral hero is "Uncle" Arthur Ownby, one of the last living representatives of the pioneering mountain people who first settled the Tennessee valley and whose names "[o]n the lips of the strange race that now dwells there . . . are myth, legend, dust" (246). Ownby is the eponymous orchard keeper, watching over a grove of peach trees that "went to ruin twenty years before when the fruit had come so thick and no one to pick it that at night the overborne branches cracking sounded in the valley like distant storms raging" (51). The defunct orchard evokes a tragically neglected paradise and suggests a fall that can be understood along pastoral lines. McCarthy doesn't indicate why no one was there to pick the fruit, but students can be encouraged to draw their own inferences by examining the changing nature of employment opportunities for other major characters in the book. Sylder, for example, works for a local fertilizer plant and, later, as a moonshine runner, whose reliance on an automobile is another indication of how modern technology is becoming an integral part of life for this "strange race" of modern southerners who are growing increasingly alienated from the pastoral lives and ideals of their forebears (246).[3]

The water tank looming over the orchard—which Ownby "had been pondering for some time" (51)—is another essential symbol to help students understand the story's pastoral dialectic. McCarthy describes the fenced area around the tank as "[a] barren spot" "where the trees had been plucked from the ground and not even a weed grew" and where the tank "stood surveying the work, clean and coldly gleaming and capable of infinite contempt" (93). The silent hostility exuded by the personified tank toward the surrounding orchard, along with the tank's contagious sterility, indicates that the tank is meant to function as an antipastoral symbol. Ownby clearly interprets it as such when he shoots holes in it, an act of symbolic resistance to the encroaching industrial culture that leads to a shootout with the local authorities and forces Ownby to flee to a more remote part of the mountains. Though he tries to escape the advances of the modern world, he is soon arrested and placed in a mental hospital where he will live out his remaining years. Unable to adjust to the new industrial order, Ownby is also unable to find a viable path of resistance or escape. The novel's other pastoral figure, John Wesley Rattner, a boy whose interest in trapping indicates his desire to preserve the disappearing folkways that are necessary to sustain the pastoral existence of the previous generation, also ends up leaving Red Branch at the end of the novel. The book closes with the young Rattner hitchhiking westward, perhaps in search of some pastoral middle ground that is no longer possible to find in the Appalachians in the era of the Tennessee Valley Authority.

A lesser-known work by McCarthy that pairs well with *The Orchard Keeper* is his screenplay *The Gardener's Son*, about a murder in a South Carolina mill village that was based on historical events and made into a 1977 film that aired on PBS. The film highlights how the agrarian economy and culture in the rural South were gradually eclipsed by the rise of industrialism in the years following the Civil War. The pastoral figure is Patrick McEvoy, who is employed as the eponymous gardener until James Gregg inherits his father's estate and eliminates the position. While the elder Gregg is a formidable, paternalistic figure in the town, the son is described as "a different cut" (2). James, who embodies the decadent values of the wellborn, is eager to enrich himself and the company shareholders at the expense of his employees' welfare and has a reputation for seducing the uneducated mill girls. Passing details in the story reveal that the McEvoy family was lured away from its small farm to the mill in Graniteville by the prospect of earning wages, making the McEvoys representative figures of the shifting economic culture of the postbellum South. The greenhouse and orchard that Patrick McEvoy is paid to care for initially suggest some hope that an interest in the natural world will be preserved under the new industrial regime (albeit under artificial conditions); however, when McEvoy's son Robert returns to Graniteville to attend his mother's funeral, he discovers that the greenhouse and orchard have fallen into neglect because his father is now employed as a common factory hand. Nothing is left in the greenhouse but "withered pottings" (40), and the orchard's trees have "barren limbs" (43). The laconic explanation Robert receives from the company guard—"Not big on gardens anymore. Gardens is always the first thing to go" (42)—indicates how traditional pastoral values have been abandoned as the factory comes to dominate all aspects of human life. Watching the film in class can help emphasize this conflict for students, particularly if they are asked to attend to how the filmmakers use sound to establish mood in the film. Quick cuts between the cacophonous noise accompanying shots of the mill machinery and the relative quiet of the scenes in the greenhouse or countryside create a stark contrast that signals to viewers that the factory is a "machine in the garden" (Marx)—a violently intrusive force of industrial modernity imposing itself on an otherwise pastoral setting. Robert, the troubled antihero who murders the younger Gregg in a violent act of resistance against the corrupt industrial system the factory owner represents, is arrested and hanged. While *The Orchard Keeper* offers westward migration as a potential escape from the new industrial order, the tragic ending of *The Gardener's Son* indicates the deadly consequences for those who rebel against it.

Among McCarthy's western novels, the first volume of the Border Trilogy most explicitly transplants the anti-pastoral themes developed in the Appalachian fiction. *All the Pretty Horses* begins in the late 1940s with the death of John Grady Cole's grandfather, a Texas rancher who instills in John Grady a love for the wild western landscape and for the horses that allow ranching culture to thrive there. Following the grandfather's funeral, John Grady's mother, an aspiring actress who prefers city life, immediately sells the ranch, depriving John Grady of the pastoral sanctuary he intended to inherit. John Grady (much like the similarly named John Wesley Rattner in *The Orchard Keeper*) longs to continue living the pastoral existence of bygone generations, so he rides his horse into Mexico to find the bucolic middle ground that was rapidly disappearing in the postwar United States. He finds what he is looking for, but due to his various transgressions against Mexican authority figures (e.g., the hacendado, Alejandra's great aunt, and the captain), he is soon cast out of Eden to return to the United States. The book concludes by describing the desultory horseback journey around the Texas plains that occupies John Grady's next few years. Descriptions of "pumpjacks . . . ranged against the skyline . . . [like] great primitive birds welded up out of iron by hearsay in a land perhaps where such birds once had been" (301) emphasize the conflict between the technological world of oil derricks and fossil fuel consumption and the worlds, both primal and agrarian, that this new order is supplanting. The book opens with John Grady's hallucinatory vision of Native Americans riding across the plains "like a dream of the past" and closes with a group of actual Native Americans "watching him vanish upon that landscape solely because he was passing. Solely because he would vanish" (5, 301). Using classroom discussion to juxtapose these passages, which describe the sequential passing of Native and pastoral cultures, prepares students to think about the next logical step in this progression: the postpastoral and postcollapse worlds of the Anthropocene that McCarthy depicts in two of his other novels.

Ecological Collapse and the Return of the Wild

Unlike much of McCarthy's other work, *Suttree* takes place mainly in an urban setting and a rather Dickensian one at that: the river is little more than a sewer, trash is scattered everywhere, and an atmosphere of dank squalor pervades much of the novel. *Suttree* depicts a world in which the wild or rural spaces imperiled in McCarthy's other novels are already spoiled beyond much hope of recuperation, and while Cornelius Suttree, like other McCarthy heroes, seems intent on establishing a pastoral retreat from the modern industrial world, the scarcity of spaces untainted by human industry radically limits his options for pursuing that goal. Polluted as the river might be, Suttree is attempting to live off of it by running trotlines, but this ostensibly pastoral occupation seems farcical given the surrounding urban blight. Students can be encouraged to explore how *Suttree* pursues McCarthy's pessimistic vision of pastoralism to its logical extremes. Other novels focus on tracing how the fossil-fueled industrial order supplants the pastoral world of McCarthy's increasingly anachronistic homesteaders, but *Suttree* offers a vision of the world consonant with the idea of the Anthropocene in which nature, as humankind once defined it, is radically undermined. While the thematic conflicts in most of McCarthy's novels operate within the parameters of the traditional nature-culture binary that undergirds pastoral aesthetics, *Suttree* presents a pastoral story influenced by the same deconstructive ways of thinking about nature (such as those found in the work of Bruno Latour, Donna Haraway, or Timothy Morton) that have inspired a great deal of twenty-first-century ecocritical scholarship and debate. The novel focuses on a menagerie of down-and-out characters (such as the ragpicker, Gene Harrogate, the goatman, the junkman, Reese, and Michael) who cobble together shelters from urban detritus and, like Suttree, earn a living on the littered fringes of the modern industrial economy. These characters find ways to adapt to an emerging postnatural wilderness in the junk-strewn margins of an increasingly ubiquitous metropolis.

The world of *Suttree* is a world pervaded by a sense of imminent environmental collapse, a theme that McCarthy explores most explicitly in his latest novel to date, *The Road*. *The Road* has attracted a great deal of ecocritical interest as a contribution to the burgeoning genre of "cli-fi" (Thiess; Christensen; Bragard; and Wright)—which consists of speculative fictions dedicated to exploring worst-case scenarios for a world radically modified by the effects of climate change.[4] The world in McCarthy's novel is virtually depopulated in the wake of an unspecified disaster that leaves a father and his young son to wander an ashen landscape and hide from small clans of cannibalistic survivors while desperately hoping to locate a safe haven that they both understand is unlikely to materialize.

The Road marks the ne plus ultra of McCarthy's pastoral pessimism, making it an excellent text to conclude a course or unit on the influence of pastoral aesthetics on McCarthy's ecocritical imagination. McCarthy's pastoral heroes, from Ownby and McElvoy in the South to John Grady Cole and Billy Parham in the West, inevitably fail in their quest to find a satisfactory compromise between their pastoral past and the industrial future. Suttree survives for a while in the urban world that displaced the agrarian one but ultimately flees the city in the unlikely hope of finding something different. For the father and the boy in *The Road*, the triumph of the modern industrial system that McCarthy's pastoral heroes lament turns out to be rather short-lived. Despite its supposed advantages, the modern industrial world not only wipes out the pastoral middle ground that McCarthy's characters love but also self-destructs, leaving a new postcollapse wilderness governed by the primal directives of violence, hunger, and fear. This is a new wilderness, as wild and brutal as that of the wolves McCarthy describes in *The Crossing*, but lacking the redemptive counterpoint of a sublime natural beauty that might awaken and invite ecocentric identification. *The Road* emphasizes "the fire" that the father and son carry (83)—a metonym for the ethical, caring behavior they preserve for each other and for the few other characters they encounter—and the boy's unexpected adoption by another small band of apparent fire carriers at the end of the story, and this emphasis suggests, however vaguely, that some new utopian order might rise from the ashes of the burnt world. But given McCarthy's unwaveringly bleak chronicle of humanity's rapid downhill slide in the twentieth century from pastoral idealism to Anthropocenic reality, the hopeful note feels anomalous, if not disingenuous. In the novel's elliptical closing passage, readers may rightly infer that a deceptively stable ecological system that has sustained human life for millennia is the referent for the "thing which could not be put back. Could not be made right again" (287). Most of McCarthy's novels are nostalgic, inviting readers to look back with regret at losses past. The grim vision of things to come in *The Road*, on the other hand, relies, like much ecocritical discourse, on an appeal to an apocalyptic fear that can easily provoke despondency but might also inspire some readers to seek interventions capable of averting the prophesied disaster.

Students who delve into what McCarthy has to say about foregone pastoral conflicts are not likely to come away feeling reassured. His is clearly a pessimistic vision that speaks to the very serious environmental concerns that confront humanity as it becomes ever more entangled with an industrial modernity that has supplanted more bucolic modes of existence that McCarthy is old enough to remember and elegize. Though the answers are not guaranteed to be comforting, engagement with McCarthy's texts along ecocritical lines should demonstrate to students that the questions his novels raise about humanity's once and future relation to the nonhuman world in all its wild, pastoral, industrial, and postcollapse manifestations are timely and well worth contemplating.

NOTES

[1] For more examples of this prevalent feature of first-wave ecocriticism, see Glotfelty and Fromm; and in particular, essays such as Love.

[2] Indeed, McCarthy and Abbey not only wrote about these ecocentric values but also "reportedly tried to reintroduce wolves, illegally, in New Mexico" (Greenwood 65).

[3] The novel's reference to the fertilizer industry marks not only a shift from farming to manufacturing in the New South but also the development of the commercial farming that supplanted the small-scale subsistence farmers of Ownby's generation.

[4] Other recent narratives in this vein that could be read in conjunction with *The Road* include Atwood, *Oryx*, *Year*, and *MaddAddam*; Bacigalupi, *Windup Girl* and *Water Knife*; H. Simpson; Rich; and Hunter.

The City and the Landfill: Teaching Waste, Toxicity, and Southern Environmental History in *Suttree*

Benjamin Mangrum

The Tennessee River flows southwest from Knoxville to Chattanooga and then turns in a long loop to join up with the Ohio River in western Kentucky. The river features prominently as both a setting and a mythic force in *Suttree*, Cormac McCarthy's last Tennessee novel. The protagonist, Cornelius Suttree, often simply called Sut, lives on a houseboat on the river and finds companionship mostly among the residents of a nearby Knoxville slum named McAnally Flats.[1] In addition to providing a livelihood for many characters, the river also functions as a conduit for distributing urban waste throughout the Tennessee River valley and the South more generally. In the novel's italicized prologue, the river "*flows in a sluggard ooze toward southern seas, running down out of the rainflattened corn and petty crops and riverloam gardens of upcountry landkeepers, grating along like bonedust, afreight with the past, dreams dispersed in the water someway, nothing ever lost*" (4). The novel presents the Tennessee River as a multiple and ambiguous natural signifier: the river is a source of plenty that makes the soil fertile for those who own or work the land, even as it distributes detritus and pollution.

Readers of McCarthy will not be surprised to find the river's mythic resonances bound up with an insistent attention to the "ugly facts" of southern history, as Dana Phillips describes the representational matrix of *Blood Meridian*. The presence of the Tennessee River in *Suttree* alludes to the novel's many precedents in southern and modernist fiction.[2] Much like the river, the novel is "*afreight with the past*" (4), preserving rather than washing away whatever has gone into it. Suttree, for instance, fails to escape the legacy of his affluent southern family. And although many characters hope that the waters will relieve them of moral and commercial pollution, the river instead bears testament to the permanence of whatever has been left behind.

A later moment in the novel returns to these regional and metaphysical themes. In a characteristic use of free indirect discourse, the narration recounts Suttree's observations of the "swollen river" after the water level begins to rise from heavy rains:

> Bearing along garbage and rafted trash, bottles of suncured glass wherein corollas of mauve and gold lie exploded, orangepeels ambered with age. A dead sow pink and bloated and jars and crates and shapes of wood washed into rigid homologues of viscera and empty oilcans locked in eyes of dishing slime where the spectra wink guiltily.
>
> One day a dead baby. Bloated, pulpy rotted eyes in a bulbous skull and little rags of flesh trailing in the water like tissuepaper. (306)

Suttree, who has also lost a child, finds that human life has become like dross in the wasteland he inhabits. After seeing the dead infant in the current, Suttree immediately oars "his way lightly through the rain among these curiosa" and "fe[els] little more than yet another artifact leached out of the earth and washed along, draining down out of the city" (306). In the literal waste of the river, he finds bleak tokens of the human condition. And in a potent description of the role of waterways during the expansion of southern urban centers, this passage also suggests how the Tennessee River becomes the city's fluid landfill. Given the markers of class that are present in this and other scenes, the river becomes a receptacle for the city's lower classes as well as for toxic waste. Refuse becomes a category that flows freely between class and ecology, socioeconomic inequality and commercial production (see McCoy 85–99).

Yet even as the novel's industrial waste, class divisions, and existential nausea are dressed in the garb of a contaminated nature, the novel also presents the semblance of a remedy by looking to the natural world. Whenever Suttree is fishing, for example, he is often "in concert" with nature, as Louis H. Palmer III writes, and thus seemingly reinvigorates "the Romantic belief in the essential innocence and purity of nature, contrasted with the depravity of humans" (173–74). On the other hand, when Suttree wanders in the mountains, he imagines that if he were "to come to himself in this obscure wood he'd be neither mended nor made whole but rather set mindless to dodder drooling" with the doppelgänger that haunts him throughout the novel (McCarthy, *Suttree* 287). Suttree often confronts the image or phantom of his dead twin while alone in seemingly pastoral landscapes. If nature functions as a remedy for the ills of the modern world, it also serves as a theater of terrible specters.[3]

The next section of this essay addresses specific environmental issues that teachers might raise during course meetings and includes potential supplemental readings. The final section discusses assignments that aid students' reflections on the novel, including student-generated lesson plans for prompting discussion of *Suttree* in relation to McCarthy's more commonly assigned apocalyptic novel *The Road*, and that give students the opportunity to write for nonacademic audiences.

Southern Environmental History in Suttree

The desolate scenes of waste, polluted waterways, scatological imagery, and dying mussel beds in *Suttree* offer opportunities for teachers to discuss the environmental degradation of the American South in the twentieth century. The following discusses a few of the novel's environmental concerns that teachers might consider.

History of the Tennessee Valley Authority

Created in 1933, the Tennessee Valley Authority (TVA) fundamentally reshaped the environmental terrain throughout much of the American South by constructing massive irrigation and hydroelectric power systems. The TVA was part of President Roosevelt's assemblage of New Deal programs, but it also became a touchstone for organized labor and political conflict beginning in the late 1930s, a role that culminated during the 1950s with the trials of fifteen white-collar TVA employees for their alleged communist activities (Purcell). McCarthy's father was a senior lawyer for the TVA, and his obligations to the federal agency brought the family to Knoxville around 1934 (Luce, *Reading* 19, 21–22). Given these historical events and the importance of the Tennessee River to the TVA, to McCarthy's life, and to *Suttree*, instructors should at least mention this federal agency when teaching the novel.

William Prather's work on *Suttree* offers a model for criticism that explores the historical and environmental background of a literary text. Drawing out the importance of Knoxville to southern environmental history, Prather connects Suttree's observations about displacement with "the history of the Tennessee Valley Authority (TVA) and its influence on the lives of people living along the Tennessee River" (40). As Prather's essay shows, the lives of characters who inhabit the river and its environs reflect the destructive imprint of the TVA's damming projects and environmental engineering. Prather's analysis also draws from one of the seminal environmental histories of the Tennessee Valley, Donald Davidson's two-volume study *The Tennessee: Rivers of America*, which shaped how many in the valley understood themselves in the postwar era.

In addition to Prather's essay and Davidson's study, teachers might also consult Christopher J. Manganiello's *Southern Water, Southern Power* for a sense of the competing political and environmental interests at work in TVA projects. This additional reading would provide more political context for class discussions of the TVA and the river that runs through Knoxville. Chapter 3 of Manganiello's monograph (69–91) is an accessible and engaging account of the emergence of a "New Deal big dam consensus" throughout the South (69). Knoxville does not feature prominently in this study, but Manganiello does briefly mention the many sources of the Tennessee River valley's water pollution that were discovered in the late 1930s (153). While Prather's essay models a scholarly argument about *Suttree*, Manganiello's account would allow an instructor to situate *Suttree* within the region's environmental history.

Mussel Beds and Ecosystem Decline

Commercial mussel fishing in North America began in the mid-1800s. Those who fished for mussels used the shells for buttons and also hoped to find freshwater pearls. The mussel population in North America has been in slow decline as a result of market demand for these items (Anthony and Downing). The exploitation of mussel beds was first documented through research conducted by the United States Fish and Wildlife Service in 1956–57 in a lower part of the Tennessee River near Pickwick Dam. Later published in a 1960 report by George D. Scruggs, the research traces the effects of the brail fishing method on mussel populations in the mainstream reservoirs of the Tennessee River. This fishing method exacerbated challenges created by the century-long exploitation of mussel fauna. Brailing appears to have first been used on a broader scale (i.e., to service markets rather than individuals and families) around 1942. (I have displayed a short *YouTube* video depicting mussel brailing to help students visualize this practice ["Brailing"].) Scruggs's report gives some context to this method of fishing, which is used in McCarthy's novel, and its effects on mussel beds. The report also illustrates how federal authority perceived mussel fauna at mid-century.

Commercial fishing for mussel species in the Tennessee River (most commonly, *Pleurobema cordatum* and *Fusconaia ebenus*) had effects on the species' population and on the wider river ecosystem. However, brailing for commercial markets wasn't the only challenge to the ecosystem. There is also a demonstrable relation between the status of mussel populations and the impoundment of the Tennessee River through reservoirs and damming projects, first during the 1920s, then later, and to a greater extent, by the TVA. Most impoundments on the Tennessee River are below Knoxville, but the TVA built Fort Loudoun Dam on the river above the city in the early 1940s. Wendell R. Haag's 2009 essay is an excellent source to assign to students to facilitate class discussion of the issue of impoundment alongside Suttree's experience in a mussel camp (see also Bates). While many species continued to exist under the altered conditions of the multiple impoundments of the Tennessee River and its tributaries, Haag cites the extinction of at least one species of mussel, *Epioblasma personata*, during the 1920s and 1930s as a result of impoundment (119).

Suttree's experience with mussel brailing occupies a relatively short section of the novel (McCarthy, *Suttree* 306–63). However, the episode provides an occasion for instructors to introduce important ideas in environmental studies, including resource commercialization, the environmental costs of federal technocratic planning, and the Anthropocene. Also, the decimation of mussel beds in *Suttree* seems to anticipate the enigmatic and potentially Romantic vision of trout beds that concludes *The Road*: "Once there were brook trout in the streams in the mountains. You could see them standing in the amber current where the white edges of their fins wimpled softly" (McCarthy, *Road* 286). If an instructor were to pair these novels, such a comparison would convey the recurring sense in McCarthy's novels of environmental loss—that is, the mourning of what "once" was, or of what one "could see," before the effects of human activity despoiled American waterways.

Industrialization, Landfills, and Urban Effluence

Suttree's prose form very often mimics its urban and natural settings, as well as the existential condition of its characters. Knoxville, for example, is "*constructed on no known paradigm, a mongrel architecture reading back through the works of man in a brief delineation of the aberrant and disordered and mad*" (3). The almost picaresque style of *Suttree* follows closely this architectural madness, as no known narrative center comes into view across the novel. Yet this mimicry between the city's architecture, the novel's prose form, and Suttree's existential displacement has decisive links to the effects of industrialization and concentrated toxic waste. In terms of Knoxville's history, instructors can consider the case study of David Witherspoon Inc., which managed contaminated scrap metal on behalf of the Atomic Energy Commission beginning in 1948. The corporation disposed of the contaminated metals (some containing radioisotopes) in an economically depressed neighborhood of South Knoxville. The disposal occurred on three landfills, and during the late 1990s the Office of Environmental Restoration and Waste Management (part of the Department of Energy) began to assess remedial action for the "past, present, and potential future releases of hazardous substances" (*Remedial Investigation*).

The public health consequences of having industrial production and toxic landfills near residential areas are well-known and are often amplified by class and racial disparities. As a way to link up McCarthy's novel with recent work in ecocriticism, teachers might introduce Heather Houser's idea of "ecosickness," or the affective and somatic damage caused by chemical exposure and toxic ecosystems. *Suttree*, like much of the other contemporary fiction that Houser analyzes, "shows the conceptual and material dissolutions of the body-environment boundary through sickness and thus alters environmental perception and politics" (3). Sickness in *Suttree* is widely distributed, but students may rightly query whether illness stands in for the human condition or is differentiated among characters. Robert Bullard's now-classic 1990 study *Dumping in Dixie* was one of the first scholarly studies to identify the racial dimensions of the siting of landfills and the importing of garbage into the American South. In a more recent essay, Bullard explains related racial disparities in environmental and public health: "Urban air quality is a major concern to people of color since they are disproportionately concentrated in the nation's polluted environments. According to National Argonne Laboratory researchers, 57 percent of whites, 65 percent of African Americans, and 80 percent of Hispanics live in 437 counties with substandard air quality" ("Confronting Environmental Racism" 92).

Moments in *Suttree* attend to the racial dimensions of environmental hazards. For example, one of the novel's Black characters, Ab Jones, lives not far from Suttree's houseboat. When Suttree visits Ab, he finds "boards in the reeking gloom splotched with a greenish phosphorescence, a sinister mold that glowed faintly" (112). The toxic, perhaps even radioactive, material lining the home of Ab Jones may stand in contrast to the more subtle forms of pollution that surround the lives of the novel's White characters. Introducing this aspect of the novel in the first or second course meeting on the book would give students an opportunity to evaluate *Suttree*'s attention to the well-documented history of environmental racism in the South, including whether the novel grapples adequately with that history.

In addition to the environmental and human costs of landfills, the novel also explores the links between urban expansion and industrialization. The development of urban metropolises in the American South generally lagged behind the rate of growth in most northern cities. However, cities began to expand in the region after the Civil War, and by 1920, there were several larger metropolitan cities in the South. The expansion of urban centers changed the South's economic character. As Donald E. Davis explains, "The growth of southern cities ensured that industrialization and heavy manufacturing would prevail across the southern landscape, including large areas of the Lower South that had historically resisted such development" (159). In short, urban development was closely tied to the rise of industrial capitalism in the region.

Suttree often explores this link between industrial capitalism and urban development. For example, the novel's opening sets as a prominent feature of its backdrop a looming image of industrial production: "*Factory walls of old dark brick, tracks of a spur line grown with weeds, a course of foul blue drainage where dark filaments of nameless dross sway in the current*" (4). Later, as the novel follows the wanderings of Harrogate, it presents the following scene: "A row of black fisherman sat along the ties where the tracks crossed the creek, their legs dangling above the oozing sewage" (99). Harrogate calls out to the fishermen, who do not answer him. After walking further, Harrogate then "studied the landscape beyond. A patch of gray corn by the riverside, rigid and brittle. A vision of bleak pastoral that at length turned him back toward the city again" (99). As this passage suggests, the waste inside the city and the wasteland of formerly pastoral landscape beyond it reflect the totalizing costs of development. In fact, one of the complexities of *Suttree* is that the loss of the pastoral leads almost everyone except for Suttree to turn "back toward the city again." The urban wasteland appears to be the only recourse for so many characters because the landscape "beyond" has been decimated. In such moments, there appears to be no divide between country and city or garden and machine. Vistas of blighted nature recur in *Suttree*, as if such landscapes were the last bleak remainder of urban industrialism.

In one course on contemporary literature and southern environmental history in which students read *The Road*, not *Suttree*, I assigned the entirety of Paul S. Sutter and Christopher J. Manganiello's *Environmental History and the American South: A Reader*. This volume's essays model an impressive range of environmental histories and in my course supported readings of contemporary fiction by writers like Janisse Ray, Ernest Gaines, Ron Rash, and Jesmyn Ward in addition to McCarthy's *The Road*. The volume only indirectly addresses issues pertinent to the Knoxville of *Suttree*. Still, the contributions by Mart Stewart and Craig E. Colton raise ideas that are helpful for thinking about the concept of nature and its presence in the built environment of Knoxville. Although *Suttree* depicts 1950s Knoxville as having abundant refuse and polluted waterways, the current advertising for tourism in Knoxville draws heavily on the city's outdoor appeal. Colton's essay is especially helpful on this front. Referring to a different urban context, Colton writes that the ostensibly natural spaces that have been recreated in southern cities "are shaped to resemble pre-urbanized environments, that function in an urban setting as part of an evolving concept of parks and open spaces, and that stand as concrete evidence of public attitudes and environmental policies" (433).

Assignments and In-Class Activities

The assignments and in-class activities discussed below can enrich students' reflections on *Suttree* and give students the opportunity to think creatively and to write for nonacademic audiences.

Student-Generated Lesson Plans

Students can be asked to generate lesson plans either in every class session or retrospectively, after completing *Suttree*. Both versions of this in-class assignment invite students to imagine themselves in critical and scholarly roles. In the retrospective version, students imagine thematic problems, creative assignments, and even alternative course syllabi that would offer different modes for analyzing the novel. My prompt for this assignment typically resembles the following: "How might you teach *Suttree*? What is essential for analyzing the book as a text that engages with the southern literary tradition and the region's environmental history?" Students might answer this question by creating a one-page syllabus, designing an assignment, or sketching an arc of lesson plans for teaching the novel. The retrospective iteration of this activity offers the instructor a chance to reflect on students' ongoing questions and interests and to consider what was left out of course sessions and what questions were inadequately addressed. The assignment also prompts students to internalize the course discussions. They imagine themselves as instructors who name the key terms and issues to be discussed in the class.

During my time as a visiting professor at Davidson College, I asked students in several courses to do both versions of this activity in response to *Suttree* and *The Road*. Rather than teaching *Suttree* as a product of southern literary history, one senior English major proposed that the novel be taught as a culminating text in a course on American masculinities. This student suggests that the course examine the character Ishmael in Herman Melville's *Moby-Dick* and Ben Franklin and then move to the artist Jackson Pollock and the character Holden Caulfield in J. D. Salinger's *The Catcher in the Rye*. *Suttree*, this student proposes, stands in a long line of books about the American cult of masculinity. Another student proposed to situate the book in a course on narrative omissions. This sophomore explains that she might teach what is *not* in the novel. For example, she notes that Suttree's son isn't mentioned after the funeral scene. Why? These patterns of narrative omission might lead a class to think about McCarthy's lacunae at the level of both form and plot. How do these lacunae function narratively? What do they signify formally and philosophically?

Two junior English majors proposed daily discussion activities that would center on the philosophical debates staged by McCarthy's writing. For instance, these students envisioned in-class debates in which participants would take on the role of Suttree's father or the man's wife in *The Road*. The man and woman in *The Road* discuss the value of life in a dying world and whether it is ethical to keep their son alive when he can only expect suffering. The two students imagined that such debates would take approximately fifteen minutes of class time and would serve as opportunities for exploring the characters' ways of viewing the world.

Students also made practical suggestions in their lesson plans to help future students navigate *Suttree*. For instance, one student suggests creating a character list that students could access through *Google Docs* or a similar shared platform and that they would update at the start of each class or between classes. Finally, students' retrospective lesson plans regularly affirmed that close reading specific passages prepared them for the next night's readings. Close reading in class increased their engagement with the novel out of class.

Creative Assignments

After a semester of thinking critically about environmental writing, students often embrace opportunities to contribute to this body of work through their own creative projects. For example, in one sophomore-level course I offered on American environmental writing, students encountered fiction by McCarthy alongside ecopoetry, nonfiction essays, philosophical treatises by naturalists, and an eco–horror film. Several students chose to write narratives that draw on McCarthy's use of gothic and apocalyptic tropes. These narratives grew out of in-class discussion of the two genres.[4] I've found that this assignment works best when students present synopses or selections of their creative work to the class before completing and submitting the work to the professor for evaluation.

Digital Platforms and Writing for Nonclassroom Audiences

In one version of the course on southern environmental literature, I used the popular digital platform *Medium* to offer students an opportunity to write for nonacademic audiences. *Medium* is a free publishing community that allows users to collect articles under what the site calls a Publication, which functions much like a blog. As the administrator of a class Publication, an instructor can easily track the readership of posts in the Publication and can view the anonymized analytics data for each essay. Conveying this information to students can help them see how their writing finds readers outside the classroom. Here's a portion of the description for this assignment:

> Using essays published in *The Atlantic* and *Conservation Magazine* as a model, each student will research a topic of cultural, political, or environmental importance to the American South and write an article about it. The article may focus on an issue from the region's past or a present-day problem. Your article should present an argument or focused appraisal of

> the chosen problem. While you are not expected to write your article in academic prose, your writing should still be formal and persuasive. You must conduct research using legitimate sources and submit a bibliography (with a minimum of six sources) to the professor in addition to posting your work to our publication on *Medium*. Your bibliography may include assigned readings from the course that are relevant to your topic.

To help students with this assignment, I provided a list of suggested topics. Students wrote their articles on such topics as environmental challenges to Native communities in North Carolina, a history of the Wild and Scenic Rivers Act, the racial inequalities of mass transit in Charlotte, and, more closely related to *Suttree*, the environmental challenges pertaining to brownfields.

These creative, nonacademic, and digital assignments ask students to inhabit the texts they read and the academic work they produce. Much like the image of Suttree sitting in a forest and finding himself unable to "tell where his being ended or the world began" (286), McCarthy's fiction asks us to reflect on the boundaries of our habitations. Creative and nonacademic assignments are a fitting answer to that request.

NOTES

[1] As Inge notes, Suttree's nickname alludes to one of "the most popular humorous characters in nineteenth century Southern fiction," that is, "George Washington Harris's Sut Lovingood, a Tennessee prankster and hell-raiser who enlivened the hills of Knoxville with his high-spirited antics and often catastrophic happenings" (17).

[2] See Vescio; O'Gorman; and Cant 104–06.

[3] Instructors may assign the potent criticisms of the Romantic view of nature by Cronon and by Morton.

[4] Instructors might point students who are interested in apocalyptic fiction to Buell.

"Freeze This Frame": McCarthy on Page and Screen

Mark Steven

"The ugly fact," Cormac McCarthy once confessed, "is books are made out of books" ("Cormac McCarthy's Venomous Fiction"). But McCarthy's books derive their aesthetic resources from cinema as well as from other books. The truth of this claim can be seen in the fact that several of his novels began their life as screenplays as well as in McCarthy's prose, which, as John Cant phrases it, "reflects the visual style that classical narrative cinema employs to disguise its own mythic forms" (218). Between these observations, and notwithstanding the realization that the novels are rife with citations and allusions to films, another "ugly fact" insists on itself: McCarthy's books have always been engaged in a mutually transformative dialogue with cinema, to such an extent that any serious consideration of McCarthy's literary oeuvre necessitates an engagement with cinema, or what McCarthy once described as "the fourcornered reality of making a film" (qtd. in Crews 304). Dedicated McCarthy scholarship has only recently attuned itself to this necessity. As Stacey Peebles has demonstrated, McCarthy's "novels are really only half the story," and rather than living out a cliché as the reclusive luddite behind an old typewriter, McCarthy "has routinely welcomed others into his creative projects and, just as routinely, has demonstrated a keen interest in writing directly for film and theatre as well as a desire to see how filmmakers would bring his writing to the screen" (*Cormac* 2). If all of this is true, and McCarthy is an author whose work must be understood on both page and screen, then instructors will have to modify their teaching practices accordingly. To that end, I want to situate McCarthy in a tradition of cinematically engaged writing in order to introduce the kind of thinking required for this revised approach to his work, and then to offer three practicable suggestions for teaching McCarthy's literary output in relation to cinema.

Before McCarthy: An Introduction to Cinematic Modernism

After a trip to a picture house in the early 1920s, Virginia Woolf speculates in one of her essays that "[a]ll the famous novels of the world, with their well-known characters and their famous scenes, only asked, it seemed, to be put on the films." "What could be easier," she asks, "and simpler? The cinema fell upon its prey with immense rapacity, and to the moment largely subsists upon the body of its unfortunate victim" (173). If, for the working novelist, cinema arrived as a threat of lycanthropic proportions, then to the philosopher-critic it presented new possibilities for humankind by fundamentally transforming lived experience. For Walter Benjamin in the mid-1930s, the advent of cinema meant the widespread development of an "optical unconscious," a new mode of sensory perception shaped by the industrial production and mass distribution of photographic technology:

> Then came the film and burst this prison-world asunder by the dynamite of the tenth of a second, so that now, in the midst of its far-flung ruins and debris, we calmly and adventurously go traveling. With the close-up, space expands; with slow motion, movement is extended. The enlargement of a snapshot does not simply render more precise what in any case was visible, though unclear: it reveals entirely new structural formations of the subject. (250)

While modern imaging technologies were the principal catalyst for this new mode of perception, literature adapted to this mode through medial self-awareness, by developing strategies that were unique to language-based media and that were used to assert sovereignty from a new aesthetic regime ushered in by the movie camera. In other words, literature endeavored to retain its autonomy if not its heretofore unrivalled purchase on human consciousness. The concrete means by which it did so gave shape to what we now call literary modernism.

Modernist literature opportunistically borrowed forms and themes from the cinema but also strove to set itself apart from that new medium by granting the reader access to regions of being from which cinema is denied entry. That is what readers encounter, perhaps most famously in the work of McCarthy's direct antecedents, as the venerable stream of consciousness. Media theorist Marshall McLuhan describes stream of consciousness as an inscape whose modernist reformulation should be thought of as a reaction to "the reel world" of cinema and its redistribution of perception into a kinaesthetic torrent of surfaces experienced at the rate of twenty-four frames per second (310). In contrast to this new dispensation, literature proposed an alternative, unfilmable experience, which James Joyce famously called "the ineluctable modality of the visible," the epiphenomenal and affective impress of optical perception in the age of its mechanization (45). "Joyce," claims McLuhan, "knew more about the effects of the photograph on our senses, our language, and our thought process than anybody else" (262).

The writers who are most invested in cinema at an economic level—who have been driven to work in the film industry by pecuniary need—have traditionally been the most responsive to it in their literary aesthetic. William Faulkner is exemplary of this group of writers in his use of cinema to, as John T. Matthews argues, "symbolize key shifts associated with modernity" (*William* 60). At one point, for example, Faulkner figures an industrial vista cinematically as "a scene like something out of an Eisenstein Dante" (*If I* 157), a hellscape made for celluloid. To give this figure a theoretical gloss, Fredric Jameson formulates an inflexible law of artistic remediation: "whenever other media appear within film, their deeper function is to set off and demonstrate the latter's ontological primacy" (*Geopolitical Aesthetic* 84). The unique achievement of Faulkner's prose is how it mobilizes that law on behalf of literature, undertaking formal maneuvers precisely to assimilate into its fictional substance cinematic technologies that do not belong on the page. If, as Benjamin claims, cinema "reveals entirely new structural formations of the subject" (250), literature aims to surpass that revelation by presenting it in a language that cannot be translated back into visual media.

What was true for the modernist authors, who acclimatized to cinema in ways that inspired new acts of literary creation, is also true of McCarthy. Like Faulkner, McCarthy has looked to cinema for what he has called "movie money," a potentially easy way to subsist as a writer when grant funding dries up (Peebles, *Cormac* 21–22). More generally, McCarthy's novels are highly aware of their relation to cinema; they even seem to be engaged in an apotropaic process of what psychoanalysts might call secondary revision, in which they anticipate the cannibalization of their literary forms by other media. "We're not survivors," stipulates one character in McCarthy's *The Road*. "We're the walking dead in a horror film" (55). Elsewhere in the same book, this identification with another medium is registered as the force of doom itself. "Freeze this frame," we read. "Now call down your dark and your cold and be damned" (19). Yet McCarthy does not simply represent cinema as an object for narration, nor is his prose style cinematic in the sense that it might bear some resemblance to scenic description or even to a screenplay. Rather, and again like Faulkner, McCarthy subsumes the cinema formally into his prose, where it serves as an aesthetic stimulant, an impetus for stylistic and technical innovation. In good modernist fashion, McCarthy's books perform their own refusal to become cinema at the level of stubborn stylistic singularity. While *The Road* seems to have been written with the film rights uppermost in mind, since its uncomplicated plot and syntax make it amenable to adaptation, it also features moments of formal efflorescence that serve to distinguish it as an irreducibly literary artwork.

The medial lesson taken from literary modernism is not that literature seeks to emulate cinema, or that its syntax somehow becomes cinematic, but that, when written and cinematic media gravitate together, each finds ways to absorb the other while asserting its own irreducibility. The challenge for teaching the works of McCarthy in relation to cinema, then, is to simultaneously affirm the singular achievement of his literary fiction and to consider that achievement in relation to the determining presence of another, rival medium: to avoid belittling his novels as the bombastic repackaging of more popular forms, which are increasingly pitched toward the bestseller list and blockbuster adaptation, but to nevertheless show what the novels do with popular and cinematic forms and how they remake mass culture in their own image. Or, as McCarthy tells the Coen brothers, "a novel's a novel and a film's a film, and they're very different" (McCarthy, "Hollywood's Favorite Cowboy"). Teaching McCarthy in relation to cinema means preparing students to discover how literature coexists, competitively and productively, with cinema. In what follows, I propose three relatively concrete lessons that can be adapted to teach these ideas and to consolidate an understanding of McCarthy as an author whose works manifestly embody the effects of the film medium on the existing cultural technologies of literature.

First Lesson: Blind Intransigence

If we want students to realize that McCarthy's prose both reacts to and adapts elements from cinema, and also that it asserts its own status as literature when doing so, then the first challenge is for students to break with the cliché that literature can somehow be like cinema. To achieve this break, I propose that teachers ask their students to try adapting for cinema those passages that most obstinately refuse adaptation. Here it is worth pausing to observe the herculean ambition of James Franco. Given that Franco has directed and starred in an adaptation of McCarthy's novel *Child of God* and has flirted with the idea of directing the novel *Blood Meridian*, it is instructive that the other three novels that Franco aspires to adapt or has adapted are all defiantly anticinematic: *Ham on Rye*, by Charles Bukowski; *The Sound and the Fury*, by Faulkner; and *House of Leaves*, by Mark Z. Danielewski. From Bukowski's inebriate first-person interior, through Faulkner's associative temporal leaps and clashing familial psyches, to Danielewski's glyphic architecture, these are books that can only ever be books, and Franco appears to be profoundly aware of this. "In some ways," he reflects, "*Blood* seems un-filmable. It is almost Biblical in its prose. [McCarthy's] terse prose utilizes vocabulary only found in the crannies of annals of the Old West and the specialized spheres of working men. [McCarthy] captures the slang of forgotten peoples so deftly, it's as if they were his barroom friends" (Franco). This is consonant with McCarthy's own take on that novel as an object of adaptation. When asked if *Blood Meridian* is unfilmable because of its sheer darkness and abject violence, McCarthy is quick to respond: "That's all crap. The fact that it's a bleak and bloody story has nothing to do with whether or not you can put it on the screen. That's not the issue. The issue is it would be very difficult to do and would require someone with a bountiful imagination and a lot of balls. But the payoff could be extraordinary" (McCarthy, "Hollywood's Favorite Cowboy"). Perhaps something in Franco's and McCarthy's views suggests why the completed adaptations of novels by McCarthy rarely enjoy critical favor—his writing, more at the level of form and style than in its narrative content, challenges cinema. To adapt *Blood Meridian* would require an admixture of creativity and courage absent from the more outwardly faithful because objectively literal adaptations that have already been made.

While cinema is primarily a visual medium, in this first lesson we proceed by seeking out those moments in McCarthy's fiction that reroute narrative perception away from vision and by asking students to plan adaptations of precisely these moments: to describe how they would translate exemplary literary fiction into cinematic scenes or visualize the invisible. This lesson should provide an opportunity to think about the kinds of literary matter that remain irreducible to what André Bazin calls the "imaged reality" of film (31). That blindness is a recurring trope throughout McCarthy's oeuvre helps us with this lesson, since the author's work provides scenarios perceived through a sensory manifold devoid of sight.

One of the most harrowing examples of this trope is the old man in *The Crossing* whose eyes were sucked out of their sockets in a Mexican prison camp:

> He said that the light of the world was in men's eyes only for the world itself moved in eternal darkness and darkness was its true nature and true condition and that in this darkness it turned with perfect cohesion in all its parts but that there was naught there to see. He said that the world was sentient to its core and secret and black beyond men's imagining and that its nature did not reside in what could be seen or not seen. He said that he could stare down the sun and what use was that? (283)

The task of this lesson is for students to imagine a film from the perspective of such a subjectivity. What would it mean to envisage "eternal darkness," a Weltanschauung that is "black beyond men's imagining," in cinema? This question is undeniably perverse—and, for that reason, can be conducive to lively conversation in class—but it also suggests an understanding of literature as defensively nonvisual. It establishes that McCarthy's novels are unlikely to be cinematic in the sense of having a formal resemblance to film or being adaptable. In order for students to think about McCarthy between page and screen, they will need to develop a better understanding of the mediations between those two distinct forms.

Second Lesson: Convergent Swarm

After students find passages that seem distinctly uncinematic, they should locate moments in McCarthy's fiction that seem closest to cinema, and for which a direct comparison with some cinematic precedent can be compellingly made. In other words, for the second lesson they should choose texts that are narratively and tonally similar, typically emerging from a shared tradition or genre. If McCarthy's literary fiction is meaningfully indebted to cinema, then this is especially true of film genres such as the western, which enjoys immense global popularity. As McCarthy claims, "There isn't a place in the world you can go where they don't know about cowboys and Indians and the myth of the West" ("Cormac McCarthy's Venomous Fiction"). Although McCarthy conceptualized *Blood Meridian* as his contribution to the western genre, instructors should remind students that this novel was written and published in the aftermath of the Vietnam War, when the genre's romantic ideal of frontier exploration undertaken by a hero was revised as the experience of inchoate terror and primitive accumulation. Instructors can represent this transformation in cultural myth as the force that opened up a chasm between the star-driven classicism of the films of Howard Hawkes and the much grislier films of Sam Peckinpah. Students might therefore compare moments in *Blood Meridian* with revisionist westerns, such as those of Peckinpah, or with war films.

Steven Frye correctly compares McCarthy with Peckinpah, a director for whom "the camera image might be employed to capture a sense of actuality that moves beyond mimetic representation to the psychological sphere" ("*Blood Meridian*" 111). In making this comparison, Frye recounts two battle scenes, one from *Blood Meridian* and one from Peckinpah's film *The Wild Bunch*, to show the extent to which McCarthy might be drawing on Peckinpah's ultraviolent and affectively charged aesthetic. Frye describes the final shootout in Peckinpah's film, in which slow motion is used to simulate subjective horror, and the Yuma massacre in *Blood Meridian*, in which narration appears to emulate cinematic technique in its vivid, kinetic imagery. "As the battle ensues," he reflects, "quick close-up shots blend with wide-angle images of the soldiers and the townspeople fighting the bunch. Normal motion combines with slow motion, the latter usually when someone is being shot or falling. There is virtually no sound but gunfire" (112). This aesthetic, designed to amplify the brutal actuality of violence, may find its equivalent in McCarthy's prose style: in the pacing and rhythm of the writer's syntax; in a diction that focalizes intersubjective chaos; and in a show of optical details, which together produce a "visual montage" that "blends group movement and individual movement as the language pace is slowed by modifiers in the same manner as the film, in which slow motion is employed particularly when people are killed" (113). There is no need to inhibit class discussion with a reading of McCarthy's prose for its similarity to film; instead, here Frye's clarification that film and prose are mutually irreducible is essential.

"Of course," Frye writes, "it is impossible to translate the medium of film to prose directly, but an indirect use of a cinematic aesthetic can be seen. Departing from his frequent use of ornate language, anachronism, metaphor, and stylistic complexity, McCarthy describes the Yuma massacre almost entirely in visual terms, using parallel construction to mimic the shifts from shot to cinematic shot" (113). Here I want to suggest inverting Frye's reading: although this scene in *Blood Meridian* seems cinematic at the levels of narrative, character, and setting, it also departs from what Frye calls "parallel construction" by way of style and technique. Here is the first sentence of McCarthy's description, from which Frye draws his reading: "They swarmed up the hill toward the fortifications where the Americans lay sleeping and some were mounted and some afoot and all of them armed with bows and clubs and their faces blackened or pale with fard and their hair bound up in clay" (*Blood Meridian* 274). This sentence does not reproduce unmediated content or conventions from cinema; instead, it aspires to have the energy of a cinematic scene but to express that energy in distinctly literary ways. We can hear as much in its galloping polysyndeton that combines with monosyllabic diction to echo Anglo-Saxon poetry and through which it emphatically recasts those "visual terms" within the domain of literature (Frye, "*Blood Meridian*" 113). Indeed, other critics have noted that the oldest surviving poem written in this style, *Beowulf*, is the literary grandfather to *Blood Meridian* (Crews 58–60). Even in what could potentially look like a game of mimicry, literature obviates absolute identification with cinema by capitalizing on its historical strengths.

For this lesson students may also compare moments in McCarthy's fiction with films from other genres. Episodes of horror and macabre, from *Child of God* or *The Road*, have narrative and visual equivalents in grind-house splatter films, and especially in those directed by George A. Romero, Sam Raimi, and Tobe Hooper. Moonlit vistas and horsemen in silhouette from any number of novels by McCarthy are evocative of Charles Laughton's *Night of the Hunter*.

With two texts in hand, one literary and one cinematic, the lesson proceeds by way of a three-stage comparison. First, students describe the cinematic text in as much technical and affective detail as possible. Second, they describe the literary text as an indirect response to the genre inhabited by the film. The purpose here is to stress the similarities between the two texts and to begin thinking about McCarthy's prose as a potential adaptation from cinema. Third, students describe how the literary text, McCarthy's prose, seems to embellish upon its potentially cinematic content: are there specifically linguistic and literary qualities, from allusions and archaisms through sound and syntax, that augment or supplement what appears to be a cinematic sensibility? What does the prose supply that cinema cannot? While answering these questions might lead students to McCarthy's literary antecedents—from John Milton to Herman Melville, the Bible to Samuel Beckett—the objective of this lesson is to show that literature responds to cinema by drawing upon its own resources, which can make us think and feel in ways that cinema cannot. If successful, this task will productively undermine the evaluative clichés about the comparison of film and literature, such as the idea that a book is always better than the film or that a film can somehow bring the text to life.

Third Lesson: Catfish and Melons

Whereas the first two lessons demonstrate that McCarthy's fiction lives in competition with cinema—that it utilizes forms that cannot be remade as visual media and that it adapts reactively from film—the final lesson begins by insisting that we not underestimate the value of cinema: cinema can achieve things literature cannot. According to Christian Metz, cinema "tells us continuous stories; it 'says' things that could be conveyed also in the language of words; yet it says them differently. There is a reason for the possibility as well as for the necessity of adaptations" (44). For this lesson, I want students to think about what the reasons for adaptation are, how the commercial imperatives for cinema translate into aesthetic form, and what happens when we move from the relatively insular medium of literature—the production and reception of which frequently takes place in solitude—to an industrial, collective art form, over which the individual has much less control. Simultaneously, however, I want students to think about McCarthy's fiction as unique: what makes the adaptation of a McCarthy novel different from, say, that of a novel by Toni Morrison or by Thomas Pynchon? Here students compare McCarthy's novels to their cinematic adaptions and describe what a film might add that was absent or impossible in the literary source material.

Since the production of McCarthy's screenplay *The Gardener's Son* in 1977, there have been a number of adaptations of the novels: Billy Bob Thornton's *All the Pretty Horses*, Ethan Coen and Joel Coen's *No Country for Old Men*, John Hillcoat's *The Road*, and Franco's *Child of God*. To understand how cinema can augment literary narrative requires thinking about the totality of this very different form: how a description becomes mise-en-scène, how perspective is represented by a type of camera shot, how characters meld with their actors, and how temporality now unfurls by a logic of discontinuous edits. To illustrate the force with which all of this can transform narrative, an instructor can direct students away from discrepancies in content so that they can instead think critically about questions of affect. In short, they should consider how it feels to encounter an episode on screen as opposed to on the page.

The best film with which to answer this question is undoubtedly the Coen brothers' *No Country for Old Men*. While the directors describe their creative process as one of slavish fidelity to the literary source—"One of us types in the computer," they claim, "while the other holds the spine of the book open flat"—this film is unique among adaptations because of its specifically cinematic achievement (Coen and Coen). That is to say, this film capitalizes on cinema's inimitable strength as a medium, just as the novel does with literature. "The significance of the cinema," claims Mary Anne Doane, "lies in its apparent capacity to perfectly *represent* the contingent, to provide the pure record of time" (22). No mood or affect responds to an aesthetics of contingency quite so powerfully as suspense: the wilfully delayed reckoning with one of many probable outcomes. Whereas in a literary text suspense is an effect of the characters and the plot, in film it emanates from the formalization of scenes and is obtained in the relation between the camera's negotiation of space and the pacing of action. Joel Coen describes cinematic narration as "the physical work that somebody does that helps reveal who they are and is part of the fiber of the story," and as "the fact that you were thrown back on that, as opposed to any dialogue" (McCarthy et al., "Conversation").

Take, for example, the episode in which Llewelyn Moss prepares to ambush Anton Chigurh in a hotel room. In the book, their first encounter takes the shape of an epiphany. "At that moment," we read, "Moss realized that he was not going to open the bathroom door. He was going to turn around. And when he did it would be too late. Too late to make any more mistakes or to do anything at all and that he was going to die" (McCarthy, *No Country* 111). If students compare the two iterations of this episode, it becomes clear not only that has the plot changed—in the film, tension breaks explosively when Chigurh punches out the cylinder lock and Moss replies with a shotgun blast—but that the change seems responsive to the medium: reading simply doesn't allow for the same kind of shock tactics that we experience with cinema and that make us jump (00:56:30–1:00:55). On the page, McCarthy gives us a moment of reflection, the grammar and mood of which dilate so as to look to both the past and the future, whereas on the screen we only have the pure, instantaneous present of an action image. That's what makes this scene in the film so manifestly thrilling.

Finally, it is worth asking students about the ways that literature persists or fails to persist into cinematic remediation. Rather than serving as a conventional adaptation from page to screen, the film *The Counselor*, for example, is an ensemble production for which McCarthy received credit as screenwriter and as executive producer and on which Ridley Scott was director. This film recapitulates more of the tropes that we associate with McCarthy than with Scott and amounts to a tale of warring cartels around the Texas-Mexican border. Despite its obvious commercial and aesthetic potential—it banks not only on McCarthy and Scott but also on an ensemble cast of stars—this film was almost unanimously deemed a failure. As Peebles states, it "was certainly criticized—wrongly for its lengthy dialogue sequences and complicated plot and rightly for its treatment of women" (*Cormac* 189). My sense, however, is that what rendered this film so critically abject on both of these levels is its failure to transliterate from literature to cinema. The film was unable to decode an ultimately literary narrative into the visual syntax of cinema, which exacerbated its worst ideological tendencies.

This charge registers against the film's most infamous scene, in which manifestly senile dialogue combines with visual exploitation, when Cameron Diaz's femme-fatale character, Malkina, "fucks" Reiner's car (00:48:21–53:59). The scene begins as an exchange between Reiner (played by Javier Bardem) and Michael Fassbender's eponymous Counselor. "You remember that yellow California I had?" asks Reiner, and a flashback sequence begins, opening with a long shot of a sports car driving across a golf course at night and under sprinklers. He is in the passenger seat, and Malkina has been driving. They park on a rise. "For no particular reason that I could see she slides off her knickers and hands them to me and gets out of the car and I ask her what she is doing and she says I am going to fuck your car." The sequence cuts between Reiner, who narrates the flashback to the Counselor, and the narrated memory, in which the shots inside the car largely match Reiner's perspective, watching Malkina closely as she removes her underwear, exits the car, and mounts the windshield. Then, as Reiner stutters briefly in the voice-over, the camera takes position directly overhead, looking down on Malkina as Reiner gazes slack-jawed up through the windshield. The film then continues to cut between this overhead shot and his point of view, both of which are scored by thumping techno and the squeaking of flesh on glass.

Some psychoanalytic film theory will help students make sense of what they see in this scene. "Traditionally," writes Laura Mulvey, "the woman displayed has functioned on two levels: as erotic object for the characters within the screen story, and as erotic object for the spectator within the auditorium, with a shifting tension between the looks on either side of the screen" (11–12). The scene in *The Counselor* has evidently literalized this tendency, taking the male gaze to its dopiest limit, but what has drawn critical ire is less the visuals than the rhetorical flourish with which Reiner rounds out his description. "It was like one of those catfish things, you know, one of those bottom feeders you see going up the side of the aquarium sucking its way up the side of the glass." There will be value in asking students what is wrong with this scene at the level of aesthetic realization, speculating on whether or not it appears to be utilizing the best medium for its narrative content, and how that potential misalignment of form and content might contribute to its obvious misogyny.

The scene is better suited to page than to screen. For readers of McCarthy it will be reminiscent of an episode in *Suttree* in which one character copulates with inanimate objects:

> When the light of the sealedbeam cut over the field he was lying prone upon a watermelon with his overalls about his knees. The beam swept past, stopped, returned to fix upon his alabaster nates looming moonlike out of the dark. He rose vertically, pale, weightless, like some grim tellurian wraith, up over the violated fruit with arms horrible and off across the fields hauling wildly at the folds of old rank denim that hobbled him. (32)

The humor of this passage is not in the image of a man copulating with melons, which is hardly visualized; it is, rather, in the dissonance between that image and the language with which it is described: "alabaster nates," "grim tellurian wraith." These are not phrases uttered by a character. They are, instead, the stylized form given to the omniscient narrator. "Somebody has been fuckin my watermelons," is one description offered from within the novel's diegetic space, as is, more quizzically, "He's damn near screwed the whole patch. I dont see why he couldnt of stuck to just one. Or a few" (33). There is good reason to speculate that the infamous catfish scene from *The Counselor* is trying to recreate this brand of humor. To transpose this material off of the page and onto a screen means that narration is no longer omniscient but instead issues from the mouth of a character and so belongs to an individual personality, while the objective visualization literalizes the simile and negates its potential incongruity. This is literary as opposed to cinematic humor, and its transposition from a written to a visual medium means the decomposition of its forms.

These lessons have been designed to promote a theoretically sophisticated approach with which students can appreciate the aesthetically productive relations between writing and cinema and to counter the clichés that occupy too much thinking about these media. These lessons facilitate an understanding of how a literary work might articulate its narrative in ways that are fundamentally incompatible with cinema, by insisting upon its own aesthetic and medial autonomy; how literature reacts to cinema in moments of multimedial affiliation, when literature sublates the other medium by using its own forms and techniques; and how cinematic adaptation might add, formally and affectively, to literary narrative while nevertheless retaining the traces of that older medium within itself. Understanding the relation between writing and cinema allows students to grasp the unique capabilities and tremendous possibility of each medium as well as the aesthetic singularity of McCarthy's literature.

LITERARY PAIRINGS AND CONTEXT

Maps and Legends: Teaching McCarthy as a Postsouthern Novelist

Nell Sullivan

Identifying Cormac McCarthy as a southern writer can be somewhat vexed in a southern literature course. Students readily identify as southern most novels from his Tennessee period because of their explicit geographical references, but students also perceive a thematic disjunction between these Tennessee novels and the other southern novels in the course because McCarthy does not foreground questions of race, southernness, or Lost Cause mythology. Moreover, McCarthy left the South for the Southwest both imaginatively and physically in the 1970s to write *Blood Meridian*. His characters also often seem to head west: John Wesley Rattner at the end of *The Orchard Keeper*, Suttree in his eponymous novel, John Grady Cole in *All the Pretty Horses*, and even the "grim triune" on the first page of *Outer Dark* (129). For Robert Brinkmeyer, McCarthy's mid-career turn to the western genre was a postsouthern gesture common among contemporary southern writers that signaled "anxieties about origins and construction of postmodern society, particularly the embedded ideologies that define 'progress' and civility" (*Remapping* 30).[1] In that sense, the divide between McCarthy's Tennessee novels and westerns is not schismatic. The postsouthern critical construct is useful for analyzing the relation between these novels in a McCarthy course, but more important, the novels themselves can exemplify what *postsouthern* means in the context of southern literature. This essay describes an effective approach for using McCarthy's *Outer Dark* and *The Road* as representative postsouthern texts.

My undergraduate southern literature course focuses primarily on postbellum fiction. I begin with an overview of southern history, southern exceptionalism, and critical formations of southern literature, making explicit my general goal for the semester: to explore tensions in the texts related to the South's dual history of slavery and military defeat. The syllabus ranges chronologically from the New South to the postsouth, covering post-Reconstruction plantation and negrophobic narratives (by Thomas Nelson Page and Thomas Dixon), tragic mulatto narratives (by Charles Chesnutt), works by the Southern Agrarians (such as Allen Tate), works from the southern renaissance (by William Faulkner), works representing the mid-century southern grotesque and gothic (by Flannery O'Connor and Carson McCullers), grit lit (by Dorothy Allison or Larry Brown), and postsouthern narratives (by Randall Kenan, Edward Jones, and McCarthy).[2] The course is designed to put these texts in dialogue, especially texts by Faulkner, O'Connor, and McCarthy. As Michael Kreyling notes, all southern writers after Faulkner, including McCarthy and O'Connor, "have known that post- began with 'Faulkner'" (*Inventing* 157).

Teaching southern literature requires more than putting individual authors into the southern framework, especially for undergraduate students who have not previously studied regional literature qua regional literature. The course must help students define what southern literature is in the first place. The mid-century critics who championed the southern renaissance and Faulkner's place in it also sought to define (or, after Kreyling, "invent") southern literature as a whole (Kreyling, *Inventing*). For these critics, southern literature must have the oft-cited sense of place (which encompasses culture, community, and geography); reveal the author's and preferably the characters' awareness of the burden of the region's history (see Rubin; Woodward; L. Simpson), especially in relation to race; and be to some degree "Christ-haunted," in O'Connor's famous phrase ("Grotesque" 44). Lewis Simpson notes that twentieth-century southern literature ensconced a "vision of social order at once strongly sacramental and sternly moralistic" (255). The representative texts that I teach from the plantation tradition, the tragic mulatto tradition, the southern renaissance, and the mid-century southern grotesque and gothic demonstrate these various aspects of the larger southern literary tradition. By century's end, however, novelists and critics alike recognized that the South is as much a "metadiscursive space" as a geographical place (Romine 35) and that it is often "an ideological construct rather than a place" (Greeson 10). Modernity's homogenizing effects inevitably transformed the New South into what James Cobb, after George Washington Cable, calls "the No South," a South virtually indistinguishable from everywhere else in the United States (Cobb 213; Cable 47)—but the idea of the South persisted.

To lay the groundwork for the postsouthern segment of a southern literature course, I establish the elements of postmodernism, the postsouthern, and their intersections. Simpson coined the term *postsouthern* to describe the state of southern letters in the late twentieth century, when the myth of southern exceptionalism and the narrative of one South, united by shared agrarian values and a glorious past, had been vanquished. Postsouthernism, in short, is what happens when southern writers confront the postmodern condition, which Jean-François Lyotard defines as "incredulity toward metanarratives" (xxiv), or grand narratives, the big, abstract stories that humans use to explain history and control their place in it. Matthew Guinn uses the term "mythoclasm" to describe the postsouthern incredulity toward the southern metanarrative (xii). In a slightly different vein, Frederic Jameson defines postmodernism as the terminus of the modernization process, where "nature is gone for good" in the ultimate triumph of capitalism and commodification; for him, postmodernism also attempts to "think the present historically in an age that has forgotten how to think historically in the first place" (*Postmodernism* ix). In class I stress the ways in which Lyotard's and Jameson's versions of postmodernism inform the constructions of postsouthernism developed by Simpson's heirs, critics such as Guinn, Martyn Bone, Scott Romine, and Kreyling.

Postsouthern writers like McCarthy retain continuities with the South's historical and literary past even as they diverge from the tradition. Thomas Haddox argues that postsouthern writing recycles "the content of the past, by redeploying all its familiar tropes" (567). As Brinkmeyer suggests in *The Fourth Ghost*, contemporary southern writers cannot quite be "free from the past" (325–26). I find it useful to introduce students to the terminology that scholars use to discuss the postsouthern engagement with the past. In *Inventing Southern Literature*, Kreyling uses the term "parody" to describe the motivated (but not necessarily mocking) imitations of the works of other southern authors, while elsewhere he uses "intertextuality" to describe the way writers inscribe the memory of earlier texts in their own works and suggests that the distinctive South remains only in such intertextual traces (*South* 16, 194). John Matthews revives the poststructuralist concept of text as palimpsest to describe *The Road*'s engagement with the history of slavery and the dehumanizing events that followed it, including lynchings ("Moveable South," 67); the palimpsest signifies writing over past erasures whose traces haunt the new text, just as "the pale palimpsest of advertisements for goods which no longer existed" bleeds through the whitewashed billboards in McCarthy's novel (*Road* 127–28). Jameson uses "pastiche," a more neutral term than parody, to describe the postmodern scavenging of different texts or genres; pastiche involves "the cannibalization of all the styles of the past" and "the increasing primacy of the 'neo'" (*Postmodernism* 18).

A brief survey of critics' descriptions of McCarthy's works can illustrate this generic cannibalization for students. *Outer Dark* is "postmodern local color" (Guinn 98), the rest of McCarthy's Appalachian fiction is "neo-Southern Gothic" (Hobson 9), *Blood Meridian* is routinely labeled a neowestern, and *The Road* is alternately "the New Southern Gothic" in the form of a zombie narrative (Ellis, "*Road*" 71), a road narrative (Woodson), and sentimental fiction (N. Sullivan, "Good Guys"). Instructors could choose many McCarthy novels to exemplify postsouthern writing;[3] however, I focus on *Outer Dark* and *The Road*—both of which have unspecified southern settings—to demonstrate the postsouthern play on the southern literary and historical past.

Outer Dark: *The Class of '68*

Outer Dark was published in the annus horribilis 1968, the year when French students and workers joined forces for massive demonstrations that had the collateral effect of accelerating the development of postmodernism.[4] The Tet Offensive that year augured defeat for American forces in Vietnam. Martin Luther King, Jr., and Robert Kennedy were assassinated that year, and the Republican Party's so-called southern strategy successfully co-opted White Dixiecrats, who helped elect Nixon. Such political realities confirmed that the modernization and homogenization of the South could not heal racial and class ills. Unlike McCarthy's other Tennessee fiction, *Outer Dark* is not set in contemporary East Tennessee but in a preindustrial nineteenth-century South with unmappable geography. As Dianne Luce notes, "[I]ts deliberately underdetermined and ambiguous locale contributes to the novel's parabolic qualities" (*Reading the World* 62), while its "topographical dislocations are ecological as well as cultural, with swamps abutting uplands, pasturelands adjacent to deep forests," and the setting represents "many ecological systems of the American South" (117). Although its antique and slightly dreamlike setting might suggest a reactionary turning away from contemporary issues, *Outer Dark* reflects the zeitgeist and marks McCarthy's postsouthern debut. Providing the historical context helps students understand the ways McCarthy confronts prevailing critical and ideological constructs.

Like the dreamlike setting in *Outer Dark*, the novel's literary terrain is familiar but transformed to reflect postsouthern impulses. Luce notes its metanarrational aspects, positing Culla Holme as the novel's "dreamer" and implicit narrator (62). McCarthy also employs pastiche, notably of O'Connor and Faulkner. His prose is Faulknerian, and the italicized chapters, like Faulkner's italicized passages, suggest a different level of consciousness. Further, Rinthy Holme recalls Lena Grove in Faulkner's *Light in August*, as both characters undertake a purposeful journey, live in relative innocence, and are fecund. The brother-sister incest in *Outer Dark* provides a gothic element that recalls Faulkner's *The Sound and the Fury* and *Absalom, Absalom!* While Faulkner's gothic remains contained in some dark house—"Dark House" being the working title Faulkner used for both *Light in August* and *Absalom* (Polk 24)—*Outer Dark*'s sexual guilt and horror become unhoused and peripatetic, as do most aspects of McCarthy's novels, according to Jay Ellis (*No Place for Home*) and Terri Witek. Neither sibling in *Outer Dark* remains domiciled, and by the novel's end, Culla roams aimlessly while "little sister" falls asleep—forever—by a "dead fire" that contains her chap's bones (238, 237).

In class discussions and brief essay quizzes, I invite students to consider how McCarthy also cannibalizes O'Connor's short story "A Good Man Is Hard to Find" to produce his "grim triune" (*Outer Dark* 129), whose bearded leader is, like the Misfit in the O'Connor story, a homespun nihilist with no shirt and ill-fitting clothes. The only named member of the triune, Harmon, resembles

O'Connor's jocular Bobby Lee, whose name memorializes General Robert E. Lee in an example of what Romine calls "conspicuous southernness" (38).

The abrupt, unsentimental violence in *Outer Dark* also shows the influence of O'Connor, but as Guinn says of *Child of God*, "McCarthy has adopted O'Connor's fundamentally pessimistic vision of humanity but declined her theology" (100). For example, when the bull pierces Mrs. May's heart in the O'Connor story "Greenleaf," the character "continued to stare straight ahead but the entire scene in front of her had changed . . . and she had the look of a person whose sight has been suddenly restored but who finds the light unbearable" (*Complete Stories* 333). This restored vision betokens spiritual knowledge, as the dying woman seems "to be bent over whispering some last discovery into the animal's ear" (334). In contrast, McCarthy's snakehunter dies not with theological understanding but a question, "Minister?" as the bearded one's "fist rose in an eruption of severed viscera until the blade seized in the junction of his breastbone and he stood disemboweled" (*Outer Dark* 129). McCarthy retains O'Connor's violence and the formal trinity but substitutes blindness for the epiphanies that O'Connor awards her protagonists. When Culla remarks on the chap's missing eye, the bearded one says pointedly, "Some folks has two and cain't see" (232). More so than O'Connor, McCarthy gives the lie to the Southern Agrarians' belief in southern society as a sacred community. Students particularly recognize this postsouthern waning of the sacramental in the triune's cannibalism. The mute one parodies a communicant at the altar as he "knelt forward with hands outstretched and his nostrils rimpled delicately. The man handed him the child and he seized it up, looked once at Holme with witless eyes, and buried his moaning face in its throat" (236). The scene is Christ-lorn, not Christ-haunted. The novel ends with a blind man walking unwarned into a swamp, a scene that underscores the absence of Christian or pastoral redemption in this work.

The novel's most postsouthern aspect, however, is the way the setting echoes the plantation economy of the preindustrial South, an aspect that must usually be teased out in class discussion. Instructors can remind students of Luce's observation that the novel's setting is an amalgam of locations in the South, and thus not specifically Appalachia, whose topography did not lend itself to large plantations. Because Rinthy and Culla lack the historical consciousness of Faulkner's characters, students may initially perceive them as free of the southern past. But *Outer Dark* retains trace memories of the Old South in the episode involving Culla's brief employment with Squire Salter and Salter's subsequent murder. Here we also see *Outer Dark*'s intertextual relation to Faulkner's *Absalom, Absalom!*, which recounts Thomas Sutpen's attempts to build both a dynasty and a large plantation, Sutpen's Hundred. Salter's place resembles a small-scale version of Sutpen's Hundred, "a large two-storey house fronted with wooden columns" (McCarthy, *Outer Dark* 41), where Culla instinctively uses the back door. Like Sutpen in *Absalom, Absalom!*, Salter is ruthless and looks Culla over "as he would anything for sale"

(42). At his house, we meet two of the novel's three African American characters, his unnamed housekeeper and the mute servant John. Like Sutpen, Salter claims to be a self-made man: "What I got I earned. . . . Daybreak to backbreak for a Godgiven dollar" (47). His claims are undermined by the presence of his Black servants, his hiring Culla at a deep discount, and his status as squire: that is, as a landowner and local grandee. When the triune dispatches him with the brush hook stolen from his own barn, they act as poor White avengers and projections of Culla's own resentment: *"when the next one came up behind him sideways in a sort of dance and swung the brush-hook it missed his neck and took him in the small of the back severing his spine and when he fell he fell unhinged sideways and without a cry"* (51). Salter's death by farm implement in *Outer Dark* mirrors Sutpen's murder in *Absalom, Absalom!*, which Wash Jones commits using a rusty scythe belonging to the victim, a murder that the character Quentin imagines as likewise silent, *"since always that which merely consummates punishment evokes a cry while that which evokes the last silence occurs in silence"* (Faulkner, *Absalom* 151). Jones is similarly motivated by class resentment: he kills Sutpen, whom he reverently calls "Kernel" (229), because Sutpen refuses to acknowledge the baby he fathered with Jones's granddaughter and compares her unfavorably to his horse.

Outer Dark also contains a nod to miscegenation, the gothic heart of *Absalom, Absalom!* To outdo Faulkner's combination of miscegenation, incest, and homoeroticism in the Judith-Henry-Bon triangle, McCarthy shows the recently disinterred corpse of a White man posed in a coffin with the murdered Black sexton, suggesting miscegenation, homosexuality, and necrosexuality: "the old man shared his resting place with a negro sexton whose head had been cut half off and who clasped him in an embrace of lazarous depravity" (*Outer Dark* 88). I ask students to compare this scene in *Outer Dark* with the one in *Absalom, Absalom!* and with the negrophobic narratives that they studied earlier in the semester. The fear of miscegenation in *Absalom, Absalom!* drives Sutpen from Haiti to Yoknapatawpha County and drives his son Henry to kill Bon. In *Outer Dark*, the horror of miscegenation erupts in and is immediately deflated by McCarthy's macabre spectacle of the sexton's "lazarous depravity." Anxiety about racial mixing becomes absurd in the light of the novel's real horrors.

The Road: *Don't Tell about the South*

The Road provides students perhaps the clearest example in McCarthy's oeuvre of postsouthern writing and of what Walsh, after Bone, calls McCarthy's postsouthern sense of place (Bone, *Postsouthern Sense*). This novel marks McCarthy's conscious return to an altered version of the region that students may not immediately recognize as the South. Wesley Morgan painstakingly uses textual clues to chart the route taken by the novel's protagonists, the man (also

Figure 1. Map showing part of the route taken in *The Road*, based on Morgan, "Route." This partial route runs roughly southeast from Middlesboro, Kentucky, passes through East Tennessee and North Carolina, and ends near Pendleton, South Carolina. TypeStyle Graphics Studio.

known as Papa) and the boy, south through the Great Smoky Mountains and into the coastal lowlands ("Route"; see fig. 1). McCarthy subtly signals locale by using the word "south" twenty-one times; John Sepich and Christopher Forbis's online resource "A Concordance to *The Road*" is an excellent tool students can use to find each instance of the word. Walter Sullivan famously accused McCarthy of being "bereft of community and myth" (72). *The Road* literalizes this critique of McCarthy's Appalachian fiction and depicts a world without neighborhoods—the very word "neighborhood" is unfamiliar to the boy (McCarthy, *Road* 95)—and without communities, unless one counts the blood cults and gangs of cannibals, self-consuming communities with implicit expiration dates.

The novel's elliptical and fragmented cartography recalls the geographic vagueness of *Outer Dark* and provides students a vivid counterpoint to the specificity of Faulkner's South. Faulkner's *Absalom, Absalom!* includes a helpful map of Yoknapatawpha County that shows the locations of Sutpen's Hundred, the Sartoris Plantation, Varner's store, and the roads to Memphis and Mottstown. Faulkner implicitly understood what Franco Moretti describes as the power of maps to make "the connection between geography and literature explicit . . . because a map is precisely a connection made visible" and allows readers "to see some significant relationships" they may have otherwise missed (Moretti 3). *The Road* does not include an actual map but contains the figure of a map: "The tattered oilcompany roadmap had once been taped together but now was just sorted into leaves and numbered with crayon in the corners for their assembly" (McCarthy, *Road* 42). Using Morgan's research, the class can use a mapping app to trace the protagonists' movements in *The Road* through the real South, though the journey becomes elliptical to the point of disorientation, and Morgan loses the protagonists' trail near Pendleton, South Carolina. Place references must be pieced together just like the leaves of the tattered road map, which becomes a metaphor for the increasing disjunction between the mythic South and the real one. The map in *The Road* recalls John Grady's useless map in *All the Pretty Horses* and the fanciful maps drawn for Billy in *The Crossing*. In *The Road*, the man points on the map to the route that he and the boy take, a route that is marked by "black lines" signifying "state roads" (42), a term that confuses the boy, because "there's not any more states" (43). The man later "sat studying the twisted matrix of routes in red and black with his finger at the junction where he thought that they might be. As if he'd see their small selves crouching there" (86), and eventually, like the students reconstructing his route, he stares at the map realizing that "he'd little notion of where they were" (121). Yet the man still imagines the South as having "a redemptive agency" (Walsh 52), and not merely because he believes it will be warmer there.[5] Nostalgic yearning also drives him, as when he returns to his childhood home (McCarthy, *Road* 25–27). Indeed, Morgan argues that the deliberately indirect route to the coast acquaints the boy "with his roots" and provides McCarthy with a fictional return to his own ("Route" 46).

But the South the protagonists find is not that of the man's memory or of popular imagination. At one point, the man identifies the words "See Rock City" painted on a barn (McCarthy, *Road* 21). Such advertisements, still common along I-75 and I-24 in the Southeast, suggest the South's commodification of place in the postwar tourist boom, which was fueled in part by the interstate highway system that features so prominently in *Suttree* and in the epilogue of *Cities of the Plain*. In *The Road*, any pastoral dreams that the man and boy still harbor are nullified by the death of the flora and fauna that once undergirded the South's idyllic image. They pass through woods of "huge dead trees" that once held "mayapple and pipsissewa. Ginseng" (39). The man realizes at various points that trout, crows, cows, seabirds, and probably dogs are extinct.

Industrial artifacts, on the other hand, will remain "for hundreds of years. Thousands, even," like the TVA dam built to power the modernized South (19–20). In the poem "The Cotton Boll," the Confederate-era poet Henry Timrod extolls southern agriculture as "Weav[ing] Edens of the sod." *The Road* suggests the passage from Timrod's antebellum Eden, to the New South, and finally to the "No South" (Cobb 213), a post-apocalyptic wasteland that offers little hope of redemption. Every page in the novel witnesses the death of nature that for Jameson signifies the end point of modernism, the place of postmodernism. The Southern Agrarians' dream, already "ossifying and disappearing" in McCarthy's Tennessee novels (Walsh 51), is mummified in *The Road*.

Given the novel's focus on starvation and cannibalism, its elegiac evocations of southern foodways provide a visceral way to help students recognize its southern dimensions. The man discovers a country ham "gambreled up in a high corner" of a smokehouse: "Deep red and salty meat inside. Rich and good. They fried it that night over their fire, thick slices of it" (McCarthy, *Road* 17). He later awakens with the "uncanny taste of a peach from some phantom orchard fading in his mouth" (18). The narrator recites a litany of recovered agrarian plenty in jars filled with home-canned "[g]reen beans. Slices of red pepper standing among the ordered rows. Tomatoes. Corn. New potatoes. Okra" (206). The man and the boy also find one of the last cans of Coca-Cola in the postcommodity South. Brian Donnelly sees the Coke as a "critique of [the] excessive consumption" that attends the triumph of global capitalism (73), but the drink's New South provenance also imbues it with southern nostalgia. The "bubbly" Coke is thus "a treat" that bonds father and son to each other and to their dead southern past (McCarthy, *Road* 23).

Such nostalgic moments are countered by lingering traces of historical traumas. McCarthy cannibalizes the plantation narrative, and reading scenes where elements of this narrative appear reminds students that *The Road* indeed runs through the South. The post-apocalyptic blood gangs resurrect the institution of slavery for labor and sex, as the man and the boy witness a blood gang passing with their "wagons drawn by slaves in harness" and with a "consort of catamites" (92). Having students explore the *Oxford English Dictionary* entry for "catamite" fosters a crucial aha moment for them. McCarthy also ponders antebellum slavery directly, offering two antebellum mansions in the novel—"the unheimlich home," where people are cannibalized (N. Sullivan, "Good Guys" 92), and the hospitable home with "double stairs that swept up to the columned portico" and a pantry stocked with delicious canned vegetables and "english china" (McCarthy, *Road* 204, 207). While the second mansion offers remnants of Timrod's Edenic South, its graciousness is already rendered suspect by the memory of the first house. Much like Sutpen's Hundred in *Absalom, Absalom!*, that first, "once grand house"—"tall and stately with white doric columns across the front" and "a port cochere at the side" (McCarthy, *Road* 105)—is where "[c]hattel slaves had once trod those boards bearing food and drink on silver trays" (106). Sutpen built his grand design on the backs of slaves, who "carried plank by plank and brick by brick out of the swamp" (Faulkner, *Absalom* 28), slaves likewise built the first mansion in McCarthy's *The Road* with the "handmade brick of the house kilned out of the dirt it stood on" (106).

Reusing the trope of the haunted plantation house, McCarthy reveals that this house is haunted by more than antebellum slaves when the man and boy discover captives being consumed piecemeal in the cellar: "Huddled against the back wall were naked people, male and female, all trying to hide, shielding their faces with their hands. On the mattress lay a man with his legs gone to the hips and the stumps blackened and burnt" (110). Both Matthews and Ellis connect this gothic scene to American slavery. For Ellis, the cannibalism relates both to "our historical memory of slavery" and to the New South's valorization of mass production and consumption ("*Road*" 61). For Matthews, "the mansion signifies the open secret that terror *made* America" ("Moveable South" 67), and the novel's unspecified apocalyptic event stems from America's "origins in colonial violence" as something "permanently, catastrophically ruinous" (68).

The issues of race and American slavery have usually been intertwined historically and imaginatively. In *The Road*'s evocations of slavery, however, race curiously recedes because McCarthy eschews racial markers, even for the "chattel slaves" (106). If there are "not anymore states," as the boy says (43), then rhetoric about states' rights can no longer be used to enflame racism or obscure racist actions. Interestingly, the Australian-born and Canadian-raised director John Hillcoat, a regional outsider like Shreve McCannon in *Absalom, Absalom!*, injects the issue of race in his 2009 film adaptation of *The Road*.[6] Invariably, students who view the film question Hillcoat's casting of the African American actor Michael Kenneth Williams as the thief in a cast that is otherwise thoroughly White. McCarthy notes that the thief is an "outcast from one of the communes" who is missing fingers on his right hand (255), has eyes that dart "wildly" in response to Papa's threats (256), and ends up standing before Papa and the boy as "the nude and slatlike creature" (258), but nowhere in the four pages devoted to this episode does McCarthy mention racial attributes. Some students wonder whether Hillcoat's casting choice for the thief is a recursion to the stereotype of the brutish Black criminal found in the negrophobic narratives such as Dixon's *The Clansman*, which students studied earlier in the course. Did the director read this "creature," who threatened the good guys' survival, as necessarily a Black man? If none of the characters is assigned a race in the novel, why did Hillcoat choose the thief to be the lone Black character of import? Is the novel, as opposed to the film, postracial in the sense of having moved beyond race, or does McCarthy expect his audience to read his racially unidentified characters as White, in what might be considered yet another form of racism? The man does consider the boy a "Golden chalice," which may refer either to the boy's possible blondness or to his divine nature (75). McCarthy uses racial descriptors elsewhere (e.g., *Outer Dark*'s "negro sexton" [88] and "Black and white Jackson" in *Blood Meridian* [81]), so their absence in *The Road* is instructive and provides fodder for class discussion. I have argued that using apocalypse as a plot device in his work enables McCarthy to overturn gender norms (N. Sullivan, "Good Guys" 84); perhaps it also relegates race to the "old and troubling issues resolved into nothingness and night" (McCarthy, *Road* 28).

The postsouthern begins with the end of the southern metanarrative, a point I stress to students as we examine the man's attempts to uphold the southern storytelling tradition and preserve "old stories of courage and justice as he remembered them" (41). McCarthy, like Faulkner, is concerned with the nature of narrative: how it is constructed and by what authority. In *Absalom, Absalom!*, Faulkner depicts the importance of storytelling and the metadiscursive nature of the South through the dialogue and joint narration of Quentin and the Canadian Shreve, who demands, "*Tell about the South. What's it like there. What do they do there. Why do they live there. Why do they live at all*" (142). The South, for Shreve, is born in the telling. The boy in *The Road*, a post-apocalyptic child, is likewise an outsider to the southern experience and the American experience more generally. His traumatic experiences in the unheimlich plantation house and elsewhere demolish the South's grand narratives, which were already tottering in *Absalom, Absalom!* While Shreve enters imaginatively into Quentin's reconstruction of Sutpen's story—Faulkner calls their collaborative storytelling "some happy marriage of speaking and hearing" (*Absalom* 253)—the boy ultimately declines to hear the man's stories or to tell his own: "Those stories are not true," he says (McCarthy, *Road* 268). His refusal underscores the extinction of the southern metanarrative.

On the last day that we discuss *The Road*, I have students perform a close reading of its final paragraph, which serves a narrative function analogous to that of the epilogues of *Blood Meridian* and *Cities of the Plain*. Together, we wonder why *The Road* "should come to such a place," to quote McCarthy's *Outer Dark* (242). Students who have viewed the film often note how its final, hopeful tone is at odds with the novel's ending. It seems that Hillcoat has harkened to the advice of the band Drive-By Truckers in its song "A World of Hurt": "to roll the credits" before anything else can go wrong. By ending the film with the boy's loving embrace by a family with a dog and adding the comforting dialogue, "We don't have to worry about a thing," Hillcoat restores the narrative of a (relatively) idyllic, redemptive South, a world where, in Stacey Peebles's words, "loss . . . can be ameliorated" (*Cormac* 129). But in the novel, McCarthy does something very different. When we turn to the language of the final paragraph, students inevitably note that the passage begins elegiacally with "Once" and that the boy is absent, undercutting the hope inspired by his adoption by the veteran's family (*Road* 286). Students also seize upon McCarthy's reintroduction of map imagery, though "maps of the world in its becoming" involves cosmic rather than regional cartography, and the grammatical coordination of "maps and mazes" suggests losing, not finding, one's way. The world evoked by these figurative maps is irredeemably lost, "could not be put back. Not be made right again." McCarthy's statement about the brook trout points our attention to prehistoric time: "In the deep glens where they lived all things were older than man." Finally, students notice, with a little prompting, that the last word is "mystery," whose suggestion of divine revelation brings us back to the work of O'Connor, though here the revelation does not seem to be made to any human agent (287). Despite its setting and intertextual traces, McCarthy ends *The Road* by turning away from the burdens of southern history and toward something greater, the mystery of geologic time. McCarthy's gesture recalls Jameson's notion of postmodernism as thinking "historically in an age that has forgotten how" (*Postmodernism* ix). The earth's story, McCarthy suggests, began well before the English settlement at Jamestown in 1607, did not end with the Civil War in 1865, and will continue, even after the last Coke has been consumed, with or without humanity.

NOTES

[1] Throughout this essay, I follow Kreyling, *Inventing*, which does not capitalize *postsouthern*.

[2] In this undergraduate course, I limit readings and thus omit many worthwhile writers and styles. The readings may be too limited for some instructors, but the following combinations of assigned works are manageable for students and work well together to meet course goals. To cover the post-Reconstruction plantation narrative, I assign Page's story "Marse Chan: A Tale of Ole Virginia" (1–38), along with Timrod's poems "Ethnogenesis" (100–04), "Cotton Boll" (125–31), and "Ode, Sung at the Decoration of Graves of Confederate Dead" (209–10). Excerpts from Dixon (297–305, 318–26) illustrate the blatant negrophobia of the period. I assign Chesnutt as an example of the tragic mulatto narratives that were written to oppose the plantation and negrophobic narratives. As we move into the modern period, I assign a few poems by the Southern Agrarians, such as Tate's 1928 "Ode to the Confederate Dead" (479–82) and a novel by Faulkner, usually *Absalom, Absalom!* I assign O'Connor's "A Good Man Is Hard to Find" (*Complete Stories* 117–33) and "Revelation" (488–509) to exemplify the southern grotesque. I assign either Allison or Brown as an example of grit lit. Finally, I assign two texts from the postsouthern category, generally McCarthy's *Outer Dark* or *The Road* and a second full-length text such as Kenan or Jones.

[3] See, for example, Guinn's reading of *Suttree* (91–109), Jackson's analysis of *Blood Meridian* and the border fiction, and Walsh's pairing of *The Road* with Richard Ford's *The Lay of the Land* as postsouthern exemplars.

[4] Rivkin and Ryan provide a helpful discussion of 1968 as a seminal year in the development of poststructuralism and postmodernism.

[5] As we discuss early in the semester, climate is an oft-cited element of southern distinctiveness, beginning with Thomas Jefferson's letter to François-Jean de Chastellux, dated 2 September 1785.

[6] In *Absalom, Absalom!* Shreve, Quentin's Canadian roommate, forces Quentin to confront the issue of race in their joint retelling of Sutpen's story. Similarly, in his cinematic adaptation of McCarthy's novel, the director Hillcoat reveals (perhaps unwittingly) or invents the novel's latent racial content by introducing the racist trope of Black criminality through his decision to relegate the film's only Black actor to playing the thief.

Teaching McCarthy's Western Novels from the Perspective of the Western

Alex Harmon

For several years, I have taught courses that examine the western genre in the context of its role in, and reflection of, social change in the United States. Though the western has proved to be a remarkably hard-wearing genre—often pronounced dead and just as often considered to be in revival—what John Lenihan wrote in his 2002 article in *Organization of American Historians Magazine* about teaching the genre remains true today:

> For today's college student . . . the Western is itself something of a historical artifact, preserved on the shelves of video stores and recirculated like other old movies on television, but rarely experienced as a current feature at the local multiplex. Consequently, the first order of business in teaching the Western is to define a subject with which most students have but a passing acquaintance. (27)

Lenihan is writing in particular about film westerns, of which I teach many, but the statement is perhaps doubly true for literary examples of the genre. In many cases my students will have watched relatively recent western films—such as Ang Lee's *Brokeback Mountain*, Quentin Tarantino's *The Hateful Eight*, or the 2010 Coen brothers' remake of *True Grit*—and can infer backward from the concerns of those works to consider the interests of the genre more generally. But in no case have my students read any of the foundational western novels (e.g., Walter Van Tilburg Clark's *The Ox-Bow Incident*, Owen Wister's *The Virginian*, or Charles Portis's *True Grit*) or more contemporary interventions into the literary genre. This is all to say that when we, as scholars and critics, approach Cormac McCarthy's so-called western novels, we think we know something of what we are getting into. But for students, reading these novels is another matter.

Truth be told, even the scholars and critics are divided. McCarthy's engagement with the American West now spans five novels—*Blood Meridian*, the Border Trilogy, and *No Country for Old Men*. Though the first and fifth novels are markedly different from those in between, these works are often understood to be McCarthy's western novels because they expose and revise the mythologies that underwrite narratives of the American West in literary and popular culture and in the ideologies of settler colonialism that continue to implicitly structure those narratives. *Blood Meridian* is the first, the most highly regarded and critically examined, and by far the most violent of the novels. For that final reason Barcley Owens, in a book whose title (*Cormac McCarthy's Western Novels*) marks the continuity of this group of texts, nevertheless maintains a sharp divide between *Blood Meridian* and the Border Trilogy. He writes that *Blood Meridian* "is a product of its post-Vietnam era. In stark contrast, the Border Trilogy is grounded in the nostalgic, mythic remembrance of the Old West and American cowboys" (xi). Owens has little patience for critics who understand *Blood Meridian* as a revisionist western with a moral engine that propels a critique of the mythologizing of the history of the United States, and he characterizes the scholarship that has located a moral center in the book as a "defense" of McCarthy built on "elaborate [interpretive] paradigms" (10, 11).

Those critics who, unlike Owens, read *Blood Meridian* as a critique—whether of the western's romanticization of violence (e.g., David Holloway, Kate Montague, and many others), the coherence of national mythologies after Vietnam (e.g., Vince Brewton and Megan Riley McGilchrist), or the imperial and hegemonic impulses of global neoliberalism (e.g., Dan Sinykin)—have the interpretive advantage of being able to trace a genealogy among McCarthy's western novels that unites them rather than divides them. While the pitiless violence of *Blood Meridian* and *No Country for Old Men* brooks no wistfulness for a romantic West that never was, the more nostalgic Border Trilogy ultimately evacuates its own commitment to that sentimentality.

What these critics agree on is the shared sense that McCarthy's novels have played an essential role in the redefinition of the American West in literature and popular imagination. Conversely, the western, as an autochthonous American genre, has left an indelible mark on McCarthy's fiction. This reciprocal relation to the western is central in McCarthy's construction of meaning. In other words, thinking about McCarthy's western novels through the western genre proves useful for understanding them as part of a larger project that examines the contours of the genre, without suggesting that the novels all conduct that work in the same way. This perspective allows readers to see the extreme violence in *Blood Meridian* as of a piece with the nostalgic romance in *All the Pretty Horses*. Teaching the novels in the context of a course on the western makes this link obvious, as students build on what they have learned from earlier examples of the genre to construct critical paradigms about the novels that engage the range of myths that the western has been built on and that the genre has since been used to criticize or even dismantle. Likewise, subgenre distinctions aside, teaching these novels as westerns provides a way to think through the scholarly problem of the mythic versus the sociological-political readings of these novels: the western has always accommodated both.

Working through the complicated depictions of the West offered by these novels, students gain insight not only into the western genre, and not only to the ways history and mythology have been inextricably bound in the American West. These novels also introduce for students the broader question of intertextuality. As McCarthy famously said in an early interview about his work, "The ugly fact is that books are made out of books. . . . The novel depends for its life on the novels that have been written" ("Cormac McCarthy's Venomous Fiction"). Critics have drawn authorization from this admission of McCarthy's to trace his artistic lineage to William Faulkner and Herman Melville. In the classroom, the statement is equally useful for encouraging students to think of the novels as the literary descendants of other narratives of the American West—that is, not to simply posit an atavistic hellscape that arises completely from the mind of the author but to reach back intertextually to earlier topoi, language, and analyses of texts and myths that have built those narratives. Ultimately, reading McCarthy's novels as a part of the western genre vividly demonstrates for students the idea of literary tradition—both its power and its mutability.

For students to read westerns productively, they must first achieve fluency in a wide range of historical, legal, and cultural norms that have arranged the way the American West organizes American culture. It is difficult or impossible to read below the surface of these texts without knowing something of the history of western settlement and the ways in which that settlement entered into the American imagination through the western. Immensely helpful in this regard are Richard Drinnon's *Facing West: The Metaphysics of Indian Hating and Empire Building* and Richard Slotkin's *Gunfighter Nation: The Myth of the Frontier in Twentieth-Century America*. In particular, Drinnon's "The Problem of the West" (*Facing West* 443–68) introduces students to the idea that from the time of earliest colonization imperial impulses structured the American imagination and political will, and it introduces the ways in which those imperial aspirations required and found a constitutive other in Native societies. These relatively straightforward disclosures fracture standard histories that students bring to the class, including the surprisingly resilient narrative of the disappearing Indian and the settler making his way through the wilderness to claim free land in the Oklahoma land rushes and free gold in the California gold rush.

Likewise, *Gunfighter Nation* is indispensable for helping students come to terms with how Indian hating and its attendant mythologies continue to structure American life and culture.[1] This realization is crucial for any class on the western, because examples of the genre both reflect and advance their contemporary political zeitgeists.

The rest of this essay examines mythologies about savagery and civilization, wilderness, and manifest destiny and suggests classroom strategies for both framing and disrupting them using McCarthy's western novels. It must be stated at the outset that these thematic units bleed into one another substantially; I see this as a strength rather than a weakness, one that allows students to envision the many associations that configure American cultural experience and its interpretation.

Savagery and Civilization

The dichotomy between savagery and civilization is arguably the western's most central concern. In 1893, the historian Frederick Jackson Turner characterized the American frontier as "the outer edge of the wave—the meeting point between savagery and civilization," and that characterization made its way relatively unaltered into the early examples of the western. Examples appropriate to the classroom abound: students might watch D. W. Griffith's 1913 short film *The Battle at Elderbush Gulch*, in which an unnamed and intensely hostile group of Indians attack a frontier town; their provocation is that a Native man was killed by settlers after attempting to steal a puppy, which belonged to two young White sisters, and eat it. The film neatly encapsulates a great many of the elements attendant to the discourse of savagery and civilization as it plays out on the fictionalized frontier. The settlers are depicted not as land-grabbers but as the defenders of innocence and vulnerability, which are embodied by the girls and the puppy (as well as by a mother-infant dyad trapped in one of the cabins besieged by the tribe). The Native people themselves are aggressive, arguably drunk, and, as the film makes clear, "fueled by an ever-ready spark of hatred" (00:13:10). The tiny settlement is finally saved by the cavalry, whose arrival signals the triumph of the United States over Indian tribes and characterizes the frontier town as the vanguard of national settlement and nationalist sentiment.

Students readily notice these elements, as well as the fact that the violence by the White characters in the film is largely threatened rather than actuated. The frontier is a place of danger, but ultimately the idealized national project prevails over the demonized Indians. Other texts could also work well. John Ford's *The Searchers* features a captivity narrative that similarly pits White innocence against trumped-up Native barbarism. What is important in these examples is the way that the violence of the nation—legal and geopolitical—is occluded by personal stories of innocence and valor "at the meeting point of savagery and civilization" (Turner).

Becoming familiar with these standard generic topoi and narratives prepares students for the ways in which McCarthy both explores and shatters such elements in his work. *Blood Meridian* is perhaps the best example, because of its setting at the Texas-Mexico border during the height of the Indian Wars, and because of its startling violence, which is neither confined to non-White characters nor valorized as a necessary evil for the advancement of a noble national project. Some of McCarthy's most densely occlusive passages render new meaning for students when read in this way. Asking students to close read one or more of McCarthy's descriptions of Native characters is particularly useful in this regard. Many critics have described these descriptions as deeply racist. Jay Ellis, for example, argues that "McCarthy's description of Indians . . . amounts to xenophobia, a caricature of the racial other as having no identity beyond that of animals dressed in the garb of colonial violence" (*No Place* 174). Yet reading these seemingly overdetermined Native characters through the critical lens of the western yields alternatives to Ellis's perhaps oversimplified reading.

Exercise

The below exercise encourages students to work closely with the language of *Blood Meridian*—language that my students often find difficult to penetrate. The exercise also helps students see what such opaque and allusive language accomplishes in terms of the novel's broader themes and intertextual engagements.

> First, read the description of the Comanche attack in McCarthy's *Blood Meridian* (52–53). Next, recall the images of Native people in Griffith's *The Battle of Elderbush Gulch*. With a partner, discuss what Griffith's depictions have in common with McCarthy's, and how they are different. Then write down any words that you don't know or don't understand in context.

Considerations of what the depictions have in common range widely but tend to gravitate toward questions of savagery: the film's Native characters are drawn primarily from stereotype and have become utterly predictable mainstays of the western generic imagination. However, McCarthy's "Indian drovers," though described outright as a "legion of horribles" (*Blood Meridian* 55), diverge from the stereotype of the savage Native American at seemingly every turn. Students note that although the passage describes them as half naked, it immediately goes on to describe their dress as "attic" and "biblical" (56), working against a simple binary between the savage and the civilized. Likewise, much of what is "horrible" in this passage derives from the accumulation and modification of the detritus of Western history. This point gets driven home as students endeavor to make meaning from what seem to at first be nonsensical details. As we discuss the passage, in which the Indian drovers are bedecked in the effluvia of Western civilization, students are also encouraged to think about what it means, in particular, for a novel in the western genre to mark rather than obscure the violence of the consolidation of power in the New World. In turn, we contemplate the power of the novel's critique lodged inside a genre that has traditionally celebrated empire building by the United States.

Wilderness

Unlike *Blood Meridian*, the novels of the Border Trilogy do not wholly eschew romanticism in favor of brutality. These novels, in fact, hew closely to certain generic conventions: for instance, by including rhapsodic passages about western landscapes and by romanticizing horses and wild animals. Reading these novels as westerns demonstrates the ways in which they both draw on and complicate the genre's fixation on wilderness. Since students have read Turner's frontier thesis as a point of entry into the discourse of wilderness as a counterpoint to civilization in the American West, we consider how this discourse authorizes the generic topoi of the western, and the ways in which the western extends discourses of taming the wilderness and the progress of Western civilization that are embedded in Turner's work. Especially useful in this regard are some of the classics of the genre, such as Zane Grey's *Riders of the Purple Sage*, in which the protagonists escape from a repressive Mormon community (and philosophical regime) by disappearing into Utah's canyon country and allowing the wilderness to remake them even as they make a home in it. Students are quick to point out that the plot of the novel echoes Turner's work uncannily, especially passages like this one in Turner's essay:

> The wilderness masters the colonist. It finds him a European in dress, industries, tools, modes of travel, and thought. It takes him from the railroad car and puts him in the birch canoe. It strips off the garments of civilization and arrays him in the hunting shirt and the moccasin. It puts him in the log cabin of the Cherokee and Iroquois and runs an Indian palisade around him. Before long he has gone to planting Indian corn and plowing with a sharp stick, he shouts the war cry and takes the scalp in orthodox Indian fashion. In short, at the frontier the environment is at first too strong for the man. He must accept the conditions which it furnishes, or perish, and so he fits himself into the Indian clearings and follows the Indian trails.

Grey's protagonists fit themselves "into the Indian clearings" in order to escape the confines of an overly strictured religious life, and in that action they come to embody the figure of the pioneer, both as a part of the wilderness and as agents who work to "master" it. And it should be noted that, in both Turner's essay and Grey's novel, the Indian—who is also part of the wilderness—comes temporally before the settler and then seems to vanish, neatly vacating spaces that are then occupied by the settler.

Later examples of the western genre include the George Stevens classic film *Shane*, which is read rarely for its considerations of landscape and wilderness, but rather for its portrayal of the single-minded settler carving out a place in the hostile landscape of the West by using his gun as his tool. Students also watch Alejandro Iñárritu's *The Revenant* in this unit and contemplate how the myth of (White) man versus nature continues to have traction as a thematic explanation of what constitutes Americanness.

In the context of these conventional narratives about the danger of wilderness and the concomitant need to pacify that danger—in which the wilderness is depicted as a proving ground and as a potential site of national incorporation—even McCarthy's most orthodox descriptions of the western landscape stand out in contrast. Far from being a forge for American identity, especially masculine identity, McCarthy's landscapes are composed of the slippery terrain of loss. Take, for example, the first half of the novel *The Crossing*, a meditation on the power and vulnerability of the American western wilderness; the story is about a wolf that is trapped, saved, and ultimately slaughtered. Students struggle with the section of the novel that deals with the wolf's death, both because of its seeming fatalism and because it personally devastates them: as the protagonist Billy Parham comes to care for the wolf and even risks his life to save her, students likewise build affinity with the wolf. At times, my students claim that they cannot or do not want to continue with the novel after the wolf is killed, so distressed are they that an animal in which they have invested emotionally dies brutally midway through the narrative.

To clear a path for students out of such a disheartened perspective, I have them read the episode as a reexamination of the western topos of wilderness as the crucible in which the American man is formed. When I ask them to contrast the episode of Billy's passage across the western landscape with, for example, *Riders of the Purple Sage*, students point to the way the landscape in the latter work, though described as "a network of deceiving canyons" (Grey 21), in fact functions as a benign shelter for the righteous protagonists fleeing from the unjust strictures of Mormon society. If Billy Parham's wolf is an avatar for the idea of American wilderness, her ambivalent relationship with Billy can be read as an allegory for westward expansion that resists the typical binary of man and nature. Students note that Billy hopes to preserve the wolf by taking her to her home range but relies on his own misguided (and romantic) notions to determine that range. They observe that any possibility of mutuality is dashed from the beginning because of Billy's presumptive and flawed mission to preserve the wolf's wildness while aggressively controlling her. In this way, the students come to see the episode as a critique of western settlement that is achieved through the very generic topoi that typically celebrate it.

Manifest Destiny

Any discussion of wilderness in McCarthy's novels is necessarily tied to the third theme on which this essay dwells: manifest destiny, the nineteenth-century quasi-religious belief that the United States was destined to overspread the continent. For its early proponents, manifest destiny also meant the spread of democracy and the ideals of the agrarian republic to benighted regions in Mexico and what is now the western United States. Yet the idea has its political origins in the annexation of Texas and the question of whether that state would be a slave state or a free state. As in other thematic units, first I ground students in the political and legal regimes that structure the myth of manifest destiny, then I examine the ways in which the western genre both props up that myth (in the case of classic westerns) and challenges it (in the case of revisionist westerns and later revivals of the genre). So students begin by reading the 1845 article by John Louis O'Sullivan in which the term *manifest destiny* first appears:

> Why, were other reasoning wanting, in favor of now elevating this question of the reception of Texas into the Union, out of the lower region of our past party dissensions, up to its proper level of a high and broad nationality, it surely is to be found, found abundantly, in the manner in which other nations have undertaken to intrude themselves into it, between us and the proper parties to the case, in a spirit of hostile interference against us, for the avowed object of thwarting our policy and hampering our power, lim-

> iting our greatness and checking the fulfillment of our manifest destiny to overspread the continent allotted by Providence for the free development of our yearly multiplying millions. (5)

Students quickly identify the defensive posture and mythologizing tone of this passage and easily connect it to similar mythmaking projects in the western. Perhaps the quintessential western for understanding the cultural implications of the myth of manifest destiny is John Ford's 1962 epic *How the West Was Won*. The film presents the history of a single family over four generations as its members settle the American West. The film begins near the Erie Canal in 1839 and ends at the Pacific Ocean fifty years later, and in between it imagines the roles of mountain men, Civil War soldiers, railroad men, and lawmen (without consideration of women) in incorporating the Wild West into the nation both physically and narratively. The final images of the film are of two of the great public works of the early and middle twentieth century: the Hoover Dam and the Golden Gate Bridge. In this way the film posits a direct relation between the early pioneers and the modern industrialized West and suggests that the greatness of the nation was built on the backs of those first western settlers.

Although I would argue that all of McCarthy's western novels perform critiques of manifest destiny, students most readily identify the collapse of this particular myth in, unexpectedly, *No Country for Old Men*. The novel, set in 1980, tracks protagonist Llewellyn Moss as he finds and steals a stash of money from a drug deal gone wrong and is pursued relentlessly by serial murderer and fixer Anton Chigurh. Chigurh is a particularly chilling and ruthless villain because he has a distorted sense of justice that is tied up with the notion of fate. Several times in the novel he determines a potential victim's life or death with the toss of a coin; yet for Chigurh such an act is not arbitrary. Instead he claims that the coin represents a kind of predestined fate. Students understand this version of destiny as quite arbitrary indeed, and its quasi-religious substructure revises the discourse of manifest destiny, rewriting the inevitability it suggests in the darkest possible way.

Empire and Denial

McCarthy's novels are hardly the only westerns to criticize the United States' imperial ambitions. In fact, although critics like Owens insist that McCarthy's novels have little in common with revisionist westerns, on this count in particular it is useful to see them as part of the revisionist tradition. Slotkin's *Gunfighter Nation* can be used to introduce students to the revisionist western, loosely defined as a subgenre of the western that, beginning in the 1960s, challenged the aesthetic, imaginative, and ethical paradigms of the classics of the genre. These westerns took aim at some of the foundational myths of the genre with the goal of demythologizing and even parodying the American West of fiction and film. Sam Peckinpah's *The Wild Bunch* is a particularly vivid example of the revisionist tradition for students, because it emphasizes the revisionist western as a critique not only of generic conventions but also of the political realities that underpin those conventions.

Of McCarthy's western novels, *Blood Meridian* excavates questions of empire especially powerfully by contrasting its mythic, apocalyptic tenor with its setting at a particular historical juncture of American expansionism. As such, reading the novel provides students an opportunity to interpret the work both as a generic intervention that revises the western's standard mythologizing of the frontier as the site of American development and as an interpolation of the historical aggression endorsed by the discourse of American empire. Students experience these ideas most powerfully through the examination of primary source materials alongside readings from the novel. After a lesson outlining the United States' geopolitical aspirations toward expansion and consolidation of power in the early nineteenth century, students might compare, for instance, the text of the Monroe Doctrine to the mentions of the doctrine in *Blood Meridian*.

Exercise

For this exercise, students read the following passage from the Monroe Doctrine. They underline adjectives and verbs that refer to the United States and its actions and circle adjectives and verbs that refer to foreign powers and their actions. Then students pair up to compare their notations and to consider in what ways the descriptions of the United States and foreign powers differ.

> In the wars of the European powers in matters relating to themselves we have never taken any part, nor does it comport with our policy to do so. It is only when our rights are invaded or seriously menaced that we resent injuries or make preparation for our defense. With the movements in this hemisphere we are of necessity more immediately connected, and by causes which must be obvious to all enlightened and impartial observers. The political system of the allied powers is essentially different in this respect from that of America. This difference proceeds from that which exists in their respective Governments; and to the defense of our own, which has been achieved by the loss of so much blood and treasure, and matured by the wisdom of their most enlightened citizens, and under which we have enjoyed unexampled felicity, this whole nation is devoted. We owe it, therefore, to candor and to the amicable relations existing between the United States and those powers to declare that we should consider any attempt on their part to extend their system to any portion of this hemisphere as dangerous to our peace and safety. With the existing colonies or dependencies of any European power we have not interfered and shall not interfere. But with the Governments who have declared their independence and maintain it, and whose independence we have,

> on great consideration and on just principles, acknowledged, we could not view any interposition for the purpose of oppressing them, or controlling in any other manner their destiny, by any European power in any other light than as the manifestation of an unfriendly disposition toward the United States. ("Transcript")

After students analyze the passage from the doctrine, they read Captain White's explanation of the doctrine in *Blood Meridian* (34–35) and consider how White's understanding of the document, and its enforceability, compares with their own reading.

Students may realize after completing this exercise that the Monroe Doctrine is couched largely in defensive terms that cast the United States as potentially an ally or an unwelcome enemy of European powers. But when students read it alongside Captain White's interpretation, which evinces little faith in the ability of the United States to enforce the document but wholeheartedly embraces its most aggressive exhortations, they glimpse the violence masked by the beneficent and legalistic language of the text. They can then come to see the violence in the novel as a counternarrative to those elisions in the doctrine, and to the ways that violence is typically lent a veneer of grandeur by other works in the western genre.

The thematic approaches examined here represent only a sampling of the ways in which reading McCarthy's texts from within the western genre enriches students' understandings of both the novels and the genre more broadly. One might just as easily explore, for example, the hypermasculinity of McCarthy's western worlds or the issue of frontier justice as being both beyond the juridical bounds of the United States and constitutive of narratives of national belonging. In each of these instances and others, reading the novels as westerns provides insights into the stakes of McCarthy's dystopianism while also encouraging students to revise their analyses of American exceptionalist mythologies.

Teaching Cormac McCarthy in the context of the western has shaped my scholarly perspective on the western novels as well. Ultimately, I side with those defenders of McCarthy who detect in these novels both a moral universe and a critique of narratives about the United States that alter or ameliorate historical violence. I have come to this position partly out of my own readings of the novels, but largely from my students' readings, which again and again affirm the power of these novels to suggest to their readers alternative worlds to the mythological American West.

NOTE

[1] See Slotkin 1–28, 29–63, and 278–312. Slotkin's text proceeds chronologically, so the excerpts a teacher would choose depend on the dates of the primary texts with which the class is working.

McCarthy and the Nineteenth Century: Melville, Dostoevsky, and the Romance Tradition

Steven Frye

It is common practice among scholars of McCarthy to refer to his 1992 interview with Richard Woodward, in which McCarthy states that the "ugly fact is that books are made out of books. . . . The novel depends for its life on the novels that have been written" (McCarthy, "Cormac McCarthy's Venomous Fiction" 28). In this simple but pointed comment on his own practice as a novelist, he is quite honest and forthright. Throughout his career, McCarthy seems not to have been excessively concerned with the broad perspectives of mainstream critics, and he appears even less concerned here. In the limited context of his first interview, he seems more preoccupied with articulating an aesthetic practice that is not exclusive to him. His notion of literary creation is not new. It is articulated in more extended theoretical terms in T. S. Eliot's "Tradition and the Individual Talent," in which Eliot argues for a new kind of originality, one that McCarthy in more conversational terms implicitly endorses. The new and original work, the work that has a chance of transforming a living and organic tradition from within, must have a historical sense, the capacity to engage and rearticulate previous works and make them live in the consciousness of the reader in wholly new ways.

When Eliot alludes to Hamlet in "The Love Song of J. Alfred Prufrock," contrasting him with the poem's troubled persona, readers can never quite read the character of Hamlet as they did before. Hamlet, a clearly problematic hero in Shakespeare's conception, must then be read with the even more problematic modernist antihero Prufrock in mind. If Hamlet's heroic status requires any redemption at all, the character certainly achieves some measure of it through Eliot's use of him in a poem that has been credited with redefining and advancing the literary tradition significantly. Perhaps the works that McCarthy finds most admirable undergo this same process in his own fiction. McCarthy, guided by his aesthetic of influence, creatively reexamines, reenvisions, and rewrites such classic works as Herman Melville's *Moby-Dick* and Fyodor Dostoevsky's *The Brothers Karamazov*. Teaching McCarthy's work with an understanding of this process, and acknowledging the pervasive influence of the nineteenth century on works such as *Blood Meridian*, is central to allowing students to grasp the practice that informs McCarthy's novels.

When teaching *Blood Meridian*, I typically take an approach that involves minilectures, small group discussions, and discussions that involve the entire class over three seventy-five-minute class sessions. The minilectures are supplemented by a *PowerPoint* presentation. In the context of this process, I emphasize, among other things, McCarthy's relation to the American romance tradition: that is, the tradition of American fiction that emerges from the works of Edgar Allan Poe, Nathaniel Hawthorne, and Melville. These writers work in what might be called the dark romantic mode, as they emphasize themes of complexity, uncertainty, and mystery in a richly philosophical context. The key practice for all these writers is the use of polyvalence. Each of their works confronts often abstract metaphysical, psychological, and epistemological questions in the spirit of quest, but it does so ironically and with a simultaneous expectation of limited success or even failure. These three authors are Ishmael figures, fully engaging in the active search for meaning and truth, intellectually unwilling to leave off that search, but understanding the tragic plight of Ahab, who takes the search too far.

Poe orchestrates this polyvalence through his use of the ambiguous gothic mode in such works as "Ligeia," "The Fall of the House of Usher," and, in a different way, "The Cask of Amontillado." In these stories, conclusions as to the moral status of the protagonists, their sanity or insanity, and even the existence of ghostly spiritual realms are left ambiguous. In "Ligeia," one simply cannot say whether the narrator's beloved former wife has transmigrated into the dying body of the new wife. The narrator's perception that this transmigration has occurred may be the result of an opium fantasy. Or, to extend the uncertainty, the opium fantasy may have opened a perceptual capacity, as the narrator sees a transmigration that others cannot. The point is polyvalence and mystery.

In *Blood Meridian*, what is implied by the judge's dance at the novel's end? Judge Holden says he will never die. But can we trust that proclamation? Is he in fact the Gnostic demiurge or archon that many critics have claimed? Or is the judge referring not to his own physical death but to the perpetual and immortal principle of avarice and destruction that he represents? I begin teaching *Blood Meridian*, then, with a brief minilecture on the American romance tradition that emphasizes its dark romantic tendencies and, above all, its polyvalence. I contend that it is only by understanding McCarthy's participation in this tradition that the richness of this great novel can be fully understood and appreciated.

I continue with another introductory lecture that establishes the historical context for the novel. I note that the basic threads of the narrative are drawn from Samuel Chamberlain's memoir *My Confession: Recollections of a Rogue*. After recounting his experiences with the infamous Glanton gang of scalp hunters, which included the perhaps apocryphal Judge Holden, Chamberlain tells of becoming an American Civil War brevet general, and later a painter, writer, and public servant. The narrative is set during the Texas and Mexico border disputes in the early nineteenth century, and in my lecture I recount elements of the story and point to some of the ways in which Chamberlain's narrative and *Blood Meridian* are similar and different. At this most basic level, McCarthy is rewriting this semiautobiographical narrative, and in doing so he is transforming it according to his own dark vision and in alliance with the metaphysical, religious, and philosophical systems that he intends to bring to life in his novel—with his characteristic emphasis, shared by his predecessors Poe, Hawthorne, and Melville in the American romance tradition, on multiplicity of perspective.

In *PowerPoint* slides with photographs and paintings, I introduce the historical figure John Joel Glanton, who was an American soldier, mercenary, and scalp hunter, and who appears as a character in *Blood Meridian*. I emphasize that Judge Holden is as mysterious in history as he is the novel and that he may or may not have existed, because he appears only in Chamberlain's unreliable narrative and in *Blood Meridian* itself. I then discuss the critical reception of McCarthy's novel, pointing to the fact that initially *Blood Meridian* was greeted with mixed reviews and even vexed mainstream critics.

Once I have completed this lecture, which, despite the breadth of its content, takes only about twenty minutes, I divide the students into three or four groups and invite them to discuss a set of prompts projected on a *PowerPoint* slide that will begin our inquiry. The prompts are as follows:

> In as much detail as possible, outline the structure of McCarthy's *Blood Meridian*. What are its major events? What characters or conflicts dominate chapters or sections? How do the various sections differ?
>
> Consider the kid's background, character, and behavior in chapters 1–3. Explicate the kid's dialogues with the hermit and the Mennonite.
>
> Consider the early appearances of Judge Holden, with the preacher, in the paragraph in chapter 7 that begins, "The judge smiled," and in the dialogue in chapter 9 that begins, "They posted guards . . ." (85, 116).

Of course, these prompts lead to much varied discussion and some confusion, and I always take this opportunity to emphasize the dark romantic themes of ambiguity and uncertainty, as they become apparent in the novel's structure and dialogue, polyvalence and mystery. In synthesizing this discussion, I note that, like Melville, McCarthy aggressively and creatively engages in genre blending. Complete with the epigrammatic plot points that begin each chapter, the novel at its inception reads like the explorer narratives of the nineteenth century, particularly those of Washington Irving. The novel also involves characteristic features of the prototypical western, but with blended elements of the metaphysical romance, epistemological romance, gothic romance, picaresque, and the bildungsroman. In the context of the romance genre, the novel engages metaphysical questions in the narrative, including in the dialogues with the hermit and the Mennonite and certainly in the character and pronouncements of Judge Holden.

Foreshadowing the future, the Mennonite is a creative recasting of the prophet in *Moby-Dick*, whose words are a dark harbinger of a troubled future. The kid's interchanges with both the Mennonite and the hermit are vexing, evocative, and mysterious dialogues that do not offer any synthesis of the views presented in them, and in this they reflect the notion of dialogism as Mikhail Bakhtin defines it in *Problems of Dostoevsky's Poetics* and *The Dialogic Imagination*, where the term refers to the use of a variety of narrative voices. Introducing students to Bakhtin's notion of the dialogic is valuable, given the influence of Dostoevsky on

McCarthy that I later emphasize. Put simply, Bakhtin's concept is another way of emphasizing polyvalence. But Bakhtin associates dialogism with the novel as a genre—because narrative, exposition, and the various voices of characters express numerous and sometimes irreconcilable points of view. This dialogism is particularly prevalent in the tradition of the dark romance and is on full display in *Blood Meridian*. It is also prevalent in all of McCarthy's other works, including his novel in dramatic form, *The Sunset Limited*.

In groups, I invite students to explicate the following monologue that the judge speaks in chapter 7:

> The judge smiled. It is not necessary, he said, that the principals here be in possession of the facts concerning their case, for their acts will ultimately accommodate history with or without their understanding. But it is consistent with notions of right principle that these facts—to the extent that they can be readily made to do so—should find a repository in the witness of some third party. Sergeant Aguilar is just such a party and any slight to his office is but a secondary consideration when compared to divergences in that larger protocol exacted by the formal agenda of an absolute destiny. Words are things. The words he is in possession of he cannot be deprived of. Their authority transcends his ignorance of their meaning. (McCarthy, *Blood Meridian* 85)

At this point, given the obtuse nature of this passage and other passages spoken by the judge, I like to endorse any confusion that my students might be experiencing. I point to the idea that lack of clarity is part of the judge's point. He is a man of mystery, a "bloody old hoodwinker" (252), and much of what he says is designed to confuse and deceive. But I also argue that there is much philosophical portent in his statements. The central idea in this passage involves three principle and converging concepts: first, the notion of "absolute destiny," which suggests the metaphysical and cosmological determinism that McCarthy explores in *Blood Meridian* and many other works; second, the idea that the agenda and protocols of that destiny find meaning only through the person who witnesses and articulates them; and, finally, the notion that "[w]ords are things," which ironically echoes Ralph Waldo Emerson's *Nature*, in which Emerson argues that nature itself represents a kind of sacred text that the transcendentalist must learn to read. The judge seems to make the same claim; however, his reading of nature's text diverges from Emerson's in that it leads not to an apotheosis but to a worldview that celebrates the supreme holiness of war.

During the next class session, I begin with a short lecture introducing the major philosophical themes and concerns in *Blood Meridian*, issues that McCarthy shares particularly with Melville and Dostoevsky, and I include this quotation from chapter 1: "His origins are become as remote as his destiny and not again in all the world's turning will there be terrains so wild and barbarous to try whether the stuff of creation may be shaped to man's will or whether his own heart is not another kind of clay" (4–5). I point to the essential questions suggested by this passage. Does God exist? If so, what is his nature? To what extent does he care about his creation? To what extent does he control its nature? In a barbarous world and a seemingly indifferent universe, can we possibly make a claim for meaning, purpose, value, love, or any kind of moral machinery? What role does human agency (free will) play in a universe governed by elaborate systems of cause and effect? The more expansive questions suggested by this passage are introduced more fully as the novel progresses.

Before moving to the next set of group discussion prompts, I emphasize again the tradition of dark romantic ambiguity and uncertainty that comes to McCarthy directly from Herman Melville, and the dialogic aesthetic, drawn from Dostoevsky, that informs the formal features of *Blood Meridian*. Then, I briefly refer to some of the allusions and leitmotifs that find their way into the novel: of course, the novel alludes to *Moby-Dick* and *The Brothers Karamazov*, but it also alludes to the King James Bible, John Milton's *Paradise Lost*, and Joseph Conrad's *Heart of Darkness*, among others. Particularly as it relates to Melville and Dostoevsky, this is all by way of introduction, and I assure students that we will later explore the specific ways in which the works of these nineteenth-century authors inform *Blood Meridian*.

The next set of group discussion prompts are as follows:

> Select two or three passages in McCarthy's *Blood Meridian* that portray violence directly. Consider the issue of representation. How are the facts of experience transformed? Are the passages realistic (in antiromantic or journalistic terms), romantic (i.e., gothic, grotesque, or carnivalesque), or cinematic (when compared to violent films)?
>
> Explicate the dialogue in chapter 14 between Toadvine and the judge that begins, "Whatever exists . . . ," and ends, "That would be a hell of a zoo" (198–99).
>
> Explicate the dialogue in chapter 10 between the kid and the expriest Tobin that begins, "The expriest shook his head," and ends, "The kid turned the leather in his lap" (123–24).

Students come up with several passages that portray violence, some of which are surprising. But I am usually able to derive from their selections various elements that demonstrate the way McCarthy blends early- and late-nineteenth-century romantic and realist traditions. McCarthy clearly has an ear for regional dialect, the use of which was a common practice among late-nineteenth-century American realists such as Mark Twain and Bret Harte. But I emphasize that the stronger voice emerges from McCarthy's use of gothic, grotesque, and carnivalesque elements, and I often read aloud the Comanche attack scene at the end of chapter 4 to demonstrate how those realist and romantic traditions combine. As we tease out the dialogue between the judge and Toadvine, I emphasize the complexity and symbolic nature of the judge as a character, pointing to the fact that he is as emblematic as he is human. His will to power and domination reflects what McCarthy considers to be a fundamental human impulse but also, to echo the judge himself, a basic feature of the universe, whether that feature is considered from a physical or metaphysical perspective (307). I preview a later class discussion by emphasizing to students that these were, to adapt Melville's words, the mighty themes that informed *Moby-Dick* (349).

In this context, I suggest that to characterize the judge as evil is a massive oversimplification. Both McCarthy and Melville seek to illuminate the nature of evil, its origins and its contours, in their novels, and for McCarthy the judge serves that purpose. Yet in this context, even in the face of violence and brutality, from the expriest Tobin's perspective the world is animated by the ever-present voice of God, which people perhaps only recognize when it has stopped speaking. Of course, the dialogue between the kid and Tobin points to the grand metaphysical question that McCarthy explicitly shares with Melville. In *Moby-Dick*, Melville writes that "[t]o produce a mighty book, you must choose a mighty theme" (349), and McCarthy argues in the Woodward interview that good writers deal with issues of life and death (McCarthy, "Cormac McCarthy's Venomous Fiction"). McCarthy orchestrates a Melvillean polyvalence on the question of God when he allows Tobin's unorthodox theism to rest alongside a starkly naturalistic and materialist worldview: "In the optical democracy of such landscapes all preference is made whimsical and a man and a rock become endowed with unguessed kinships" (*Blood Meridian* 247).

This discussion concludes during the second class session. At the beginning of the next class session, I deliver another short minilecture that explicitly introduces the allusions to *Moby-Dick* in *Blood Meridian* and the similarities between the two novels. After the class has explored in discussion the various disparate and contending perspectives and has noted that McCarthy's aesthetic in many ways mirrors that of Melville and Dostoevsky, I point to specific passages in Melville's book. In chapter 41, Melville alludes to the ubiquitous nature of the white whale: "One of the wildest suggestings linked with the White Whale was the unearthly conceit that Moby-Dick was ubiquitous; that he had actually been encountered in opposite latitudes at the same instant of time" (154). With a blend of humor and seriousness, Melville suggests that the whale is more than what the first mate, Starbuck, thinks it is. It is not simply a beast; it is perhaps the ghostly manifestation of something transcendent, a "grand hooded phantom" and "snow hill in the air" (22). The whale is an apparition-like being that is simultaneously physical and metaphysical, immanent and richly symbolic.

McCarthy recasts this conception in chapter 10 of *Blood Meridian* in a dialogue between the kid and Tobin:

> I seen him before, said the kid. In Nacogdoches.
>
> Tobin smiled. Every man in that company claims to have seen that sootysoulded rascal in some other place. (124)

McCarthy is careful here to make the allusion his own. The judge's ubiquitous nature is tentative, and there is no reference made to characters having seen the judge in different places at the same time. But Tobin's comment is suggestive of Melville's passage and has the same effect, lifting the judge out of the normative realm and enlarging him in conception. Like that of the white whale, his metaphysical status is not clear. He seems at once immanently physical and evocative of other realms and mythic figures that transcend. But one thing is certain: he is more than a common man, and characters see certain meanings and principles in him that make him a metaphor for something absolute, whether that absolute can be expressed in terms of natural law or metaphysical principle.

Similarly, characters in *Moby-Dick* see certain meanings and principles in the great white whale, as Melville makes clear in Ahab's pronouncement to Starbuck in chapter 36: "Hark ye yet again,—the little lower layer. All visible objects, man, are but as pasteboard masks. But in each event—in the living act, the undoubted deed—there, some unknown but still reasoning thing puts forth the mouldings of its feature from behind the unreasoning mask. . . . To me, the white whale is that wall, shoved near to me" (140). For the second and third mates, Stubb and Flask, the white whale is simply an animal to be hunted. The first mate, Starbuck, who is thoughtful, reflective, and pious, understands the human capacity to transform things into symbols. He grasps Ahab's tendency to make the white whale the agent of a transcendent being, however undefined that being may be. But he also understands the danger in this tendency, and he argues that Ahab must leave off his obsession and recognize that the whale is, in fact, no more than a whale, as destructive, powerful, and portentous as it may seem. Like the kid in *Blood Meridian*, the narrator, Ishmael, is in a tenuous place, somewhere between Starbuck and Ahab, susceptible to the majesty of Ahab's intellect and obsession, but also able to see the practical reason of the first mate. It is this very tenuousness that drives the narrative forward in *Moby-Dick*, and the same is true in *Blood Meridian*, as the judge makes the kid his primary interlocutor. The allusion to *Moby-Dick* continues, even in the physical description of the judge. I invite the students to consider: Is Judge Holden, seven feet tall, bald, and cold white, the malevolence behind the pasteboard mask (McCarthy, *Blood Meridian* 6)? Has McCarthy taken *Moby-Dick* one step further, as his novel breaks through the mask and reveals the reality beyond? Or is the judge yet another mask "thrusting through the wall"? I emphasize the polyvalence in *Blood Meridian* again to students, and I argue that, like Melville, McCarthy's text is deliberately ambiguous here.

I continue this lecture by pointing to the influences of Dostoevsky, focusing specifically on *The Brothers Karamazov*. This novel involves several genre elements: It is a novel of sensibility in which three personalities stand in stark contrast. But the thematic heart of the novel involves a debate between the atheist, Ivan, and the devout Alyosha. Though Dostoevsky was himself quite religious, like McCarthy in *The Sunset Limited* he does not allow the religious voice to dominate the themes of the novel. Instead, he constructs a formal and polyvalent dialogue in which Ivan's voice and logic dominate initially, as Ivan argues for his position with the standard but compelling claim that a benevolent God cannot exist in the face of human suffering. In fact, he argues that he will not believe in God if even one child must suffer and die. Alyosha somewhat weakly responds, claiming that human beings must consider themselves responsible for each other and that under these conditions suffering might largely be abolished. His argument does not easily stand the intellectual test, which is precisely Dostoevsky's point. It is Alyosha's life of giving and sacrifice that works as his primary argument.

I then point students again to the theological questions that inform *Blood Meridian*, where Tobin posits God's existence through the pervasive and defining voice that animates the world and where the judge claims that war is God. The kid is largely silent, and his moral status is a matter of some debate. But many critics have argued for an ethical dimension to the novel, and the kid may function in a similar way to Alyosha insofar as his actions, his willingness to stay his bloody hand, may be a claim for the presence in the novel of a moral machinery if not of a divinity that shapes our ends. I point then to the similarity between the judge and the Grand Inquisitor in *The Brothers Karamazov*. As the Grand Inquisitor speaks to Christ and argues for the failure of his mission, he states: "There are three powers, only three powers on earth, capable of holding captive forever the conscience of these feeble rebels, for their own happiness—these powers are miracle, mystery, and authority. . . . But you did not know that as soon as man rejects miracles, he will at once reject God as well, for man seeks not so much God as miracles" (Dostoevsky 255). The judge emphasizes mystery and makes much the same point:

> The judge had been holding the femur upright. . . . There is no mystery to it, he said. . . . Your heart's desire is to be told some mystery. The mystery is that there is no mystery.
>
> Aye, said the expriest watching. . . . And no mystery. As if he were no mystery himself, the bloody old hoodwinker.
>
> (McCarthy, *Blood Meridian* 252)

McCarthy maintains the ambiguity regarding the mystery that the judge and the Grand Inquisitor reject, but the echo of Dostoevsky's novel is clear, and McCarthy seems to be creatively recasting the Grand Inquisitor's principal claim about the impoverished nature of belief.

After this lecture, I invite the students to gather in groups to consider another set of discussion prompts:

> Compare the Melville and Dostoevsky passages to the McCarthy passages. In what way does McCarthy's text reflect the work of the writers whom McCarthy admires? In what way does he revise or advance their

ideas? Put another way, to what extent does he fit T. S. Eliot's notion of a traditional author?

Explicate the judge's monologue in chapter 17 that begins, "The truth about the world . . . ," and ends, "a fact among others." Also explicate the paragraph a page later that begins, "On the rise at the western edge . . ." (McCarthy, *Blood Meridian* 245, 246).

Explicate the dialogue in chapter 17 that begins, "The good book says . . . ," and ends, "War is god" (249).

I suggest to the students that there is a pointed ambiguity in the concept of larger will, which is drawn from *Moby-Dick*. The judge is a clear allusion to and reconfiguration of the white whale itself. Like Moby-Dick, the judge may represent the larger will of a malevolent God. On the other hand, he may only be the "brute beast" of the first mate Starbuck's characterization (Melville 139), and in McCarthy's vision that larger will may be a deterministic natural law in a purely materialist context. In either case, both the judge and the white whale are representations of the Kantian sublime—ubiquitous, mysterious, and too large in magnitude and conception to be fully understood—and they evoke the idea of infinity.

Here I punctuate the class discussion with a series of slides that complicate the ethical implications of the judge and his pronouncements. The students, understandably, are at times quick to deem the judge evil, and sometimes they dismiss him on that basis. I point to the fact that in a note in the first draft manuscript of *Blood Meridian*, McCarthy clarifies that he has drawn the judge's words from Heraclitus and that similar reflections on the rejuvenating effects of war can be found in statements made by revered philosophers, writers, and politicians such as Friedrich Nietzsche, Émile Zola, Theodore Roosevelt, and Winston Churchill. I then suggest, in a synthesis of our discussion of the judge and his ethical status, that when we thrust through the pasteboard mask that is the judge, we find not an evil we can isolate, not a demon we can personify, but ourselves, the wars we've fought, the territories we've conquered, the science we've deified, justified in the words of people we eminently respect.

This complication must also be acknowledged as we ponder the moral status of the kid. He has participated in the horrific events of the narrative and makes no triumphant or dramatic rejection of the judge and his actions, only a partial but stubborn resistance toward the end. But the judge, perceptive as he is, sees something in the kid that stands apart and contradicts his edict of rapaciousness and war. The judge states, "There's a flawed place in the fabric of your heart. Do you think I could not know? You alone were mutinous. You alone reserved in your soul some corner of clemency for the heathen" (McCarthy, *Blood Meridian* 299). In this context, the kid achieves a peculiarly heroic status, not because he has in any way behaved heroically, but because he possesses a spirit of resistance not just to the judge but to a concept of war that has historically been widespread. Thus, to unequivocally pass judgment on the kid's behavior is to oversimplify the thematic implications of his character.

Finally, in the context of clarifying the polyvalent nature of *Blood Meridian*, I make sure to emphasize to students one of the more dominant perspectives on the judge's character, the Gnostic reading advanced by Leo Daugherty and by Dianne Luce (*Reading*). From their perspective the judge has a clear metaphysical status. I demonstrate the basic tenets of ancient Near Eastern Gnosticism, a first-century philosophy that asserts that the world is the creation of a destructive entity (a demiurge) who dominates the physical world. Trapped within the world are elements of a divine substance that can achieve freedom through gnosis, or knowledge of the good. Serving the demiurge are lesser gods called archons. I clarify that McCarthy is likely well aware of the discovery of the Nag Hammadi manuscripts, a collection of important Gnostic texts that were found in 1945 and fully translated by James M. Robinson in 1977. I point to the passage in McCarthy's *Blood Meridian* that is most significant to Daugherty and Luce's argument, where the judge stands over the coiner: "The judge enshadowed him where he crouched at his trade but he was a coldforger who worked with hammer and die, perhaps under some indictment and an exile from men's fires, hammering out his own conjectural destiny all through the night of his becoming some coinage for a dawn that would not be" (310). The judge in this passage presides over a coiner who, like characters in many of McCarthy's works, unknowingly hammers out destiny in a deterministic universe. The judge's metaphysical status in this dream-passage is clear. All that remains to conjecture is whether he represents a lesser archon or the demiurge itself.

This discussion typically concludes my treatment of *Blood Meridian*. The polyvalence and variety of perspective that emerge from the nineteenth-century romance can be also seen in many or most of McCarthy's other novels, especially in *The Crossing*, where these elements are explicitly thematized with multiplicity in the concept of storytelling. Polyvalence and variety of perspective are embodied clearly in the dialogic interaction in *The Sunset Limited*, which is a recasting of the conversation between Ivan and Alyosha in *The Brothers Karamazov*, and they appear as well in the ethical and religious tension between the man and the boy in *The Road*. Thus, the nineteenth-century romance tradition can be seen to influence in significant ways McCarthy's aesthetic and thematic interests.

Teaching *The Crossing* as the Making of a Mexican Corrido

Gene Young

Cormac McCarthy's novel *The Crossing* may be effectively taught from any variety of critical approaches, but it clearly carries an intimate and studied awareness of Mexican corridos, their history, how they are made, their place in the oral traditions of Mexico, and what they reveal about the country and its people. When Dueña Alfonsa says in McCarthy's *All the Pretty Horses*, "Between the wish and the thing, the world lies waiting" (238), she articulates the tragic course of the pendulum of Mexican history. If "the wish" represents, among other things, a romantic notion of Mexico, that wish is nowhere more evident than in the corrido, that paean to the outlaw, the impossible lover, the revolutionary, the folk hero. When these heroic stories become constructs of the popular imagination, mere fact gives way to romance, the "wish" of Dueña Alfonsa. *The Crossing* and *All the Pretty Horses* are part of McCarthy's Border Trilogy, and any reading of the trilogy that does not include some sense of how the novels are informed by the history and culture of Mexico is a limited reading. The Mexican corrido offers instructors a useful means of efficiently exposing students to those aspects of Mexican culture. In *All the Pretty Horses*, the corrido makes for enlightening and important background, but in *The Crossing*, it plays a central role in the story, and considering that role is one way to reach the fullest possible understanding of the novel. In fact, *The Crossing* can be taught as, essentially, the making of a corrido.

The corrido is an especially appropriate informing device for *The Crossing*. As Americo Paredes points out in *With His Pistol in His Hand: A Border Ballad and Its Hero*, strife-ridden borderlands, such as the Scottish-English borderlands and the border regions between Texas and Mexico, are particularly ripe for songs that emerge from folk traditions and that praise folk heroes who stand up bravely against repressive authority (2). The Mexican corridos are popular and widely sung in the rural areas of northern Mexico, as well as in Mexican communities in the United States, where both professional bands and ordinary folk continue to sing the old songs and create new ones. With the corrido, Cormac McCarthy chose the right vehicle for evoking the historical and ongoing tensions between individuals, between socially stratified groups in Mexico, and between entire nations. Commonly performed by small groups of musicians using folk instruments, the corrido would have been the protest form of choice by the Mexican country people who are represented in *The Crossing*.

This method of teaching *The Crossing* does not interfere with traditional literary-critical approaches. For instance, in a literature class, a framework on the making of the corrido embraces the teaching of conventional narrative theory and dovetails with anthropological theories about how hero myths (or animal legends) originate and play out in literature. In my folklore classes, this framework reveals the corrido's development as an object lesson in how folk ballads arise out of the oral tradition. In a southwestern literature course, the framework helps to establish the borderlands as areas of historical and continuing tension in the life and literature of the region. The framework does not replace the classroom need to examine, for instance, the legends of wolves, McCarthy's preoccupation with place and country, or the backdrop of World War II (and, as portrayed at the end of *The Crossing*, the emerging Cold War and nuclear age). On the contrary, reading *The Crossing* through the corrido reinforces and illuminates these other reading approaches. Finally, the corrido provides students insights into curiosities of the story and of storytellers in this novel (and indeed in most of McCarthy's fiction).

Introducing the Corrido to Students

I have taught *The Crossing* in a variety of classes at different levels: a traditional junior-level American literature survey, an upper-division folklore course, a course on southwestern literature (with an emphasis on Texan and Mexican border life and literature), a graduate seminar, and one senior honors seminar. Even in this variety of classrooms and student populations, this approach focusing on the making of the corrido works. However, I have also discovered (through bitter experience) that students need to know what a corrido is before they can consider the place and function of the corrido in *The Crossing*. To try to read the novel and learn about the corrido simultaneously only leads to confusion and frustration. Before they read the first sentence of *The Crossing*, students need to know that the corrido is a folk song, a ballad narrative sung largely by and for common people such as those in *The Crossing*: the campesinos from the *ejidos* (farming collectives), the workers who hoist Boyd Parham onto their flatbed truck and who later idolize him in song and story. These are the hospitable people whom we meet throughout the Border Trilogy (and whom McCarthy would likely have come to know in his travels in northern Mexico). The flowering period of the corrido was during the Mexican Revolution and in the decades that followed it. While corridos about romance, barroom encounters, and robberies—and these days, drug lords—are still a vital part of Mexican culture, the corridos of the revolution enlarged and romanticized the bravery of revolutionary soldiers fighting against the repressive federal government of Porfirio Díaz.[1]

The best-known corridos tell the stories of folk heroes who bravely defy authority—the government, a dictator, the law, or practically any other authority that oppresses the people. These corridos are often sprinkled with the miraculous or inexplicable, and they invariably exaggerate or alter the events on which they are based. Students should be shown the emergence and purpose of corridos. They should know how corridos are fluid: that they can emerge wholly out of the folk ballad tradition, but that they often are claimed by the people and enhanced through the oral tradition into variants. Importantly for our purposes, the corrido evokes and celebrates Mexico and the Mexican people by recalling and magnifying the deeds of folk heroes who have pursued justice for common people. This kind of corrido is similar to North American ballads about outlaws and bad men, but with an even larger dash of the miraculous, the impossible, and the mythic. Thus, we encounter in revolutionary corridos such as "La toma de Zacatecas" ("The Battle of Zacatecas"); "El Siete Leguas" ("The Six Leagues"), which stars the horse of Francisco "Pancho" Villa; and "Corrido de General Zapata" ("Corrido of General Zapata") heroes fighting against impossible odds who are shot from their horses and spirited away from the battlefield (and the mortal coil) by doves who transport their souls to heaven.[2] These revolutionary corridos, as we shall see, set a framework for the development in *The Crossing* of Boyd as an impossible hero, as well as for his brother's inability to come to grips with the myth created about this brash boy. Through this lens and with a measure of cultural background, students can understand *The Crossing* as the story of the making of a hero legend.

Engaging Students in a Corrido Story

Once students know what a corrido is, and before we begin our reading of *The Crossing*, I outfit them with a reading experience that vivifies the story behind one particular corrido. Students need to know what it is like to live as an ordinary Mexican in an oppressive and dangerous land—be that the borderlands of the United States or the Republic of Mexico itself. They need exposure to these essential elements: the historical struggles of common Mexican people against oppression and the tendency of those people to mythologize and glorify folk heroes who participate in the struggles. To capture these elements, we need a powerful story, powerfully told. In my classes that story is told by Paredes in the great *With His Pistol in His Hand*, which is about the corrido of Gregorio Cortez.

The historical tension over the border and the borderlands between Mexico and the United States is important to both the corrido about Cortez and McCarthy's Border Trilogy. It is not difficult to describe for students the long-lived animosity between the two countries and the long-abiding resentment many ordinary Mexicans feel toward the United States. Looming over all this is the border. When Billy Parham crosses into Mexico to return the she-wolf to her rightful place in *The Crossing*, he is not thinking about borders. When a young hacendado asks Billy what he is doing here below the border, governments loom—but only in the background. When the hacendado says, in English, "You think that this country is some country you can come here and do what you like," he is the voice of a government that sets borders, but the passion is personal. When Billy insists, "We was just passin through," the hacendado's reply is stinging: "Pasar or trespasar?" ("passing or trespassing?"; 119). To Billy, the border is an abstraction, a line in the sand made by laws. To the hacendado, it is something else again, and he is insulted by Billy's intrusion.

To help students understand these smoldering resentments at the personal level, I have found the best tool to be the book by Paredes. For certain classes I also use the 1982 film *The Ballad of Gregorio Cortez*, which hits dramatically hard in its depiction of the injustices done to Cortez and to the Mexican population in the lower border region of Texas during the early twentieth century. Depending on the class and the time available, I assign either the whole book by Paredes or excerpts, as discussed below. Likewise, I use the complete film or excerpts as needed.[3] (The film does not explore as deeply as the book, but it is intense in its dramatization of the story and the injustices done to Cortez and the Mexican populations of the lower border.) In essence, the Paredes study is about the making of a corrido, and it highlights elements of the corrido of Cortez that I want students to understand about the corrido of Boyd Parham and his revolutionary girl companion: the corrido's vivid portrayals of institutional injustice, including summary hangings, in the lower Rio Grande Valley (26–32); the protagonist who is cruelly victimized by authority (83–97) and who, in fighting back, becomes a ballad hero; the known elements of his story (which are amazing enough on their own; 34–49); and the magnification of the story's facts by ordinary people to produce a ballad legend (114–25). The second half of the book by Paredes includes a folkloric examination of ballad theory and a scholarly treatment of the many variants on the ballad composed and sung about Cortez. This section is useful for folklore classes but largely extraneous for literature classes.

"*The Ballad of Gregorio Cortez*"

The agents of authority in the Cortez corrido—as recounted in the film and Paredes's book—are a local sheriff and his deputy and later a posse of sheriffs, deputies, and deputized citizens; the Texas Rangers are also somewhat involved. Chapter 1 of Paredes's book vividly describes some of the injustices—such as summary hangings based on little (or nothing) more than the color of the victim's skin—perpetrated by Anglos acting either extralegally or nominally in the name of the law. Paredes then goes on, in chapters 2 and 3, to tell what is known about Cortez and about his story. To summarize, a misunderstanding occured between Cortez and law enforcement officers that was based on a stupidly inaccurate translation by a deputy sheriff who claimed to know Mexicans and their language, when in fact his knowledge of Spanish was rudimentary at best. When asked by the deputy if he had recently traded for *un caballo* (a horse), Cortez replied in the negative, saying that he had not traded for *un caballo* (referring to a male horse) but rather *una yegua* (referring to a mare). The deputy reported this to Sheriff Glover as a denial and a lie, whereupon the sheriff began to arrest Cortez. One thing led to another, and in self-defense Cortez shot Sheriff Glover, who later died. Thus ensued a days-long chase during which Cortez walked over one hundred miles and rode horseback for over three hundred, all the while pursued by an enormous posse that was advantaged by fresh horses and train transport and aided by the Texas Rangers. The chase is the stuff of legend. Cortez was ultimately captured and tried several times on varying charges, ranging from murder to horse theft. After a series of hung juries, overturned verdicts, and acquittals, Cortez was finally convicted of murdering the sheriff (but not the deputy). He was sentenced to life in prison at the Texas State Penitentiary in Huntsville in 1904 but was pardoned and released in 1913.[4]

In a chapter called "The Hero's Progress," Paredes then engages in a study of stories, folktales, ballads, and balladry, with the central focus being, of course, "The Ballad of Gregorio Cortez." Here Paredes takes up the question of story variants. In a salient passage, he describes the legend of Gregorio Cortez as being "made up of three kinds of ingredients: of straight fact, of fact exaggerated into fiction, and of pure folklore" (114), which is a perfect description of how Boyd's legend grows after he and the girl disappear at the end of book 3 of *The Crossing*. Paredes describes how it is known that Cortez was a good shot and superb rider and how the "broad outlines of the ideal border-conflict hero were actually present in Cortez." However, he goes on to say, "Other parts of the legend are mere exaggerations of the kind that one often finds in and out of folklore" (114). Cortez did perform deeds of tremendous skill and derring-do, but in legend, he is writ even larger: single-handedly fighting off a heavily armed posse of three hundred men and striking fear into the hearts of thirty armed men who are afraid to approach him. This parallels the outsized growth of the legend of Boyd Parham, the *güerito* (boy) hero. In reading of the injustices Cortez experienced, his resistance and flight, and how he became this legend, students will be better prepared to consider how Boyd's legend developed and why corridos give preference to the legend rather than to the known facts. Certainly, Anglo America has its own outsize legends, particularly of characters—such as Pretty Boy Floyd in the ballad composed and sung by Woody Guthrie—who are mythologized in the popular imagination to become Robin Hoods in modern dress. However, given the influence of popular history, religions (both native and Catholic), and shared imagination, Mexican narratives generally include the mythic in more pervasive and abundant ways. It is a pleasure sharing with students, by various means, how this mythic tendency creates fantastic songs and stories (and telenovelas) that are accepted by audiences as no different from (or superior to) hard fact.

At this juncture, students are ready for the next step: a presentation of how the events of the corrido inform the first novel in McCarthy's Border Trilogy, *All the Pretty Horses*. If the students have not already read that novel as a part of the course, they can learn enough by reading excerpts (132–37, 227–41, 247–55) and watching the video "La toma de Zacatecas," which includes an authentic musical performance of the corrido with a backdrop of historical film. Doing so will expose them to historical background that is also important for *The Crossing*, in particular the Mexican Revolution and its reverberations, as well as the role of women in that struggle. Students must understand the critical presence of Dueña Alfonsa in *All the Pretty Horses*. Her at-length explanation of the triumph and tragedy of the revolution (231–41) is a vital component of the novel and is singularly useful in preparing students for the appearance of the Mexican Revolution as background in *The Crossing*. Reviewing *All the Pretty Horses* is also useful for learning about the development of the corrido in the northern states of Mexico during and after the revolution. Appearing only indirectly (and not by name) but looming in the background of *All the Pretty Horses* is the Battle of Zacatecas, a critical turning point in the overthrow of Díaz and the defeat of his federalista forces. It is in this battle that Alejandra's grandfather died fighting on the side of the revolutionaries. While McCarthy makes no specific mention of the famous corrido "La toma de Zacatecas," which describes how streets were covered with the bodies of the dead, it clearly informs the novel.

Prepared by this review of the Mexican Revolution, students are ready to view Billy's girl companion in *The Crossing* as a kind of soldadera. Soldaderas were the women soldiers who fought alongside men—and were sometimes in command of them—on the revolutionary side in the Mexican Revolution. Again, *All the Pretty Horses* lays the foundation for us. When Dueña Alfonsa talks with John Grady Cole about the revolution and the sadness of national and personal loss, a particularly fraught and poignant moment comes when she says, "I could have been a soldadera" (230). Given her place in Mexican society, as a member of the intellectual class who helped spur the revolution, while most of the actual fighting was left to common folk, this is a telling statement. It also provides a way to talk about this phenomenon in class to help students arrive at a larger view of Boyd's companion, not so much as a girlfriend, but rather as a companion (possibly in arms).

Reading The Crossing *and Unlocking Its Mysteries*

Students are now equipped to read *The Crossing* and to absorb how Boyd is transformed into a ballad hero. Since they also have a sense of the Mexican embrace of the miraculous, they will have a far easier time grasping some of the more elusive magic realism of the stories of *The Crossing*—such as the fantastical map that the old gentleman draws in the dirt for the brothers, the puzzle of the gypsy stories of the airplane, or the curiosities in the story of the lapsed Mormon and his statement to Billy:

> Things separate from their stories have no meaning. They are only shapes. Of a certain size and color. A certain weight. When their meaning has become lost to us they no longer have even a name. The story on the other

> hand can never be lost from its place in the world for it is that place. And that is what was to be found here. The corrido. The tale. And like all corridos it ultimately told one story only, for there is only one to tell.
>
> (McCarthy, *Crossing* 142)

When Billy asks him, "What is the story?" he responds in a manner evoking the conventional opening of the corrido: "In the town of Caborca on the Altar River there was a man who lived there who was an old man" (143). The most typical elements of the corrido include an opening stanza that identifies the narrator and sets the events in time and place. In this case, the old man is the narrator. This manner of storytelling, and particularly the embrace of the mysterious and the miraculous, should not be an impediment to students' appreciation of *The Crossing*.

In this novel, more than in any of McCarthy's southwestern novels, the story takes center stage. The larger narrative navigates forward, building on stories about wolf-trapping anchorites, hermits who are lapsed Mormons, German Huertistas who suck out the eyeballs of revolutionaries, and airplane-bearing Romani. Of course, in the primary narrative of the novel, we observe compelling stories about the two New Mexican brothers Billy and Boyd—Billy's success in trapping the wolf and then its loss, the confrontation with the *manco* (one-armed man) over the ownership of the Parham horses, and the salvation of the mysterious girl, followed by Boyd's horrible wounding and remarkable recovery. Billy's claiming of the she-wolf from death in a dogfighting ring is a virtual film set piece, but no less remarkable is Billy's chilling barroom confrontation with an old revolutionary in the town of Janos, Chihuahua. In a novel so devoted to story, one of the most vital is the tale of the transformation of Boyd from wild cowboy adventurer to "hombre de la gente" ("man of the people"; 317) and revolutionary, a transformation that takes place far more in story than in fact. Viewed this way, the novel becomes the story of the making of a corrido. We learn firsthand the bare facts of Boyd's not inconsiderable exploits. But even these deeds fall short of what is needed to make a true ballad hero. Later, along with Billy, we uncover the miraculous tale that has blossomed from those facts. Even more in death than in life, then, Boyd becomes a folk hero, and nothing his plainspoken brother can do will contravene this folk story of the supposedly martyred boy revolutionary.

Boyd has passed beyond this world, and his story has passed beyond the limits of fact. As the old Mormon ascetic reminds Billy, in Mexico, substantial things have no being and no truth without their story (142). After he claims the wolf's body, Billy softly sings corridos his grandmother taught him, but he must have forgotten that the Mexican villagers have already created tales about how many children the wolf had devoured. Like John Grady in *All the Pretty Horses*, Billy knows the language of Mexico, but he has something to learn about its culture and practices. Still, he persists in bringing his pragmatic American version of truth into play. When he finds the outlaw girl whom he and Boyd rescued and with whom Boyd ran off, he gets another lesson. He asks her if she believes that Boyd would have killed a man. She says,

> All the world knew that the güerito had killed the gerente from Las Varas. The man who had betrayed Socorro Rivera and sold out his own people to the Guardia Blanca of La Babícora.
>
> Billy listened to all this and when she was done he said the manco had fallen from his horse and broken his back and that he himself had seen it happen. (McCarthy, *Crossing* 322)[5]

A moment later, Billy says, "No sabes nada de mi hermano" ("You know nothing of my brother"). "Quizás" ("Perhaps"), she replies. Then she goes on tenaciously defending the legend about Boyd that her people have created and claiming its transcendence beyond mere truth. "She said that in every family there is one who is different and the others believe that they know that person but they do not know that person" (323). Myth and legend have transformed Boyd into another robber-hero revolutionary after the mold of Cortez, Pancho Villa, or Juan Cortina, whose stories constitute the outlaw folklore of the lower Rio Grande borderlands.

Finally, during Billy's search for Boyd's final resting place, he hears an actual corrido of a *güerito*.

> In a bodega in the mountain town of Temosachic he first heard lines from that corrido in which the young güero comes down from the north. Pelo tan rubio ["hair so fair"]. Pistola en mano ["pistol in hand" (evoking Cortez)]. Qué buscas joven? Que te levantas tan temprano? ["What do you seek, young man? Why do you arise so early?"] He asked the corridero who was this joven ["youth"] of which he sang but he only said that it was a youth who sought justice as the song told and that he had been dead many years. The corridero held the fretted neck of his instrument with one hand and raised his glass from the table and toasted silently his inquisitor and toasted aloud the memory of all just men in the world for as it was sung in the corrido theirs was a bloodfilled road and the deeds of their lives were writ in that blood which was the world's heart's blood and he said that serious men sang their song and their song only. (375)

Soon after, Billy encounters a girl singing in a garden in Casas Grandes. She stops Billy dead in his path when she sings these two verses of a corrido:

> Pueblo de Bachiniva
> Abril era el mes
> Jinetes armados
> Llegaron los seis

Si tenía miedo
No se le veía en su cara
Cuantos vayan llegando
El güerito les espera (381)[6]

In the pueblo of Bachiniva,
April was the month,
came six armed horsemen.

If he was afraid,
it was not to be seen on his face.
When they arrived,
the güerito awaited them.

Could this be the corrido of Billy's brother, Boyd? Could it provide information about his whereabouts, or at least the whereabouts of his bones? Alas, no. Billy asks her if she knows any other verses, but she tells him she knows just the two:

> She said that it was an old corrido. She said that it was very sad and that at the end the güerito and his novia die in each other's arms for they have no more ammunition. She said that at the end the patrón's men ride away and the people come from the town and carry the güerito and his novia to a secret place and bury them there and the little birds flew away but that she did not remember all the words and anyway she was embarrassed that he had been listening to her singing. (381)

So, as the old Mormon tells Billy much earlier, "All tales are one. Rightly told, all are one" (143). And the real Boyd has been spirited away by the all-consuming myth of that one mysterious tale. These are puzzles for a student reader, but students who are already in tune with the corrido have a far better chance to unravel the mysteries.

Soon after, Billy meets Quijada, the Yaqui Indian and ranch foreman who had in a distant earlier time returned Billy and Boyd's stolen horses to them. The meeting is instructive. Quijada, a member of an ethnic group that is looked down on by the lowest classes of Mexicans, has achieved through his bootstrap efforts a measure of power and security as a *gerente* (foreman) of the Nahuerichic division of the Babícora, a great ranching estate. He is not deceived by myths and tales, and it is he who tells Billy the truth about his brother's demise and the fact that Boyd had killed two apparently random men in Galeana who did not work for the latifundio, or large ranch estate.[7] During their conversation, Quijada expresses an enduring, fundamental truth of Mexican history: "There is the latifundio of Babícora, he said. With all the wealth and power of Mr Hearst to call upon. And there are the campesinos in their rags. Which do you believe will prevail?" (384). He goes on to say, tellingly, "The soul of Mexico is very old. Whoever claims to know it is either a liar or a fool. Or both." About Boyd, Quijada says, "He didnt want to be taken care of. He wanted to shoot people" (385). Then the two engage the nature of the corrido.

> What does the corrido say? Billy asks.
>
> Quijada shook his head. The corrido tells all and it tells nothing. I heard the tale of the güerito years ago. Before your brother was even born.
>
> Don't you think it tells about him?
>
> Yes, it tells about him. It tells what it wishes to tell. It tells what makes the story run. The corrido is the poor man's history. Is does not owe its allegiance to the truths of history but to the truths of men. It tells the tale of that solitary man who is all men. It believes that where two men meet one of two things can occur and nothing else. In the one case a lie is born and in the other death. He looked at Billy. (386)

A moment later, he says to Billy, "Even if the güerito in the song is your brother he is no longer your brother. He cannot be reclaimed" (386). This dash of cold water onto the face of the romance is echoed by Alejandra's words in McCarthy's *All the Pretty Horses* when Alejandra leads John Grady to the Plazuela de Guadalajarita, where her grandfather died in the Battle of Zacatecas: "There was no mother to cry. As in the corridos. Nor little bird that flew. Just the blood on the stones. I wanted to show you. We can go" (253). In that same novel, Dueña Alfonsa intones that "[b]etween the wish and the thing, the world lies waiting" (238). Between the reality of Boyd's unheroic death and the romance of the corrido lies the elusive truth of the being whose bones Billy lugs to their burial place. By this point, most of the students reach a full appreciation not only of this compelling story but also of the enigmas therein. When they are asked which is true, the story told by the soldadera, the story told by the girl in the garden, or the one told by Quijada, I hope they will answer: What difference does it make? If they do, then the work of teaching *The Crossing* by way of the corrido is done.

NOTES

[1] See Tatum for more on the influence of this more modern version of the corrido.

[2] See *Mexican Revolution* for these corrido examples and others; "Corrido de General Zapata" is labeled "General Emiliano Zapata" on the album. For "El siete leguas," see Los Alegres. The corridos mentioned here merely represent possible assignments, depending on the class content, level, and focus. For instance, in my senior-level course on the novels of McCarthy, I would use only one instance of one corrido, "La toma de Zacatecas." In an upper-level folklore course, I would use several corridos, as well as variants, so as to emphasize their folk process of development. In my senior-level course on Texas culture and history, I would be more inclined to use an outlaw ballad such as "The Ballad of Gregorio Cortez," so as to highlight the history of tensions along the

Texas-Mexico border. In certain classes, I use various historical video presentations, such as those on José Alberto's *YouTube* channel (Alberto).

[3] My use of the film *The Ballad of Gregorio Cortez* varies according to the class. In my class on Texas history and culture, for instance, I usually show the entire film. For most classes, I use excerpts selected from the following: the opening credits, including the text and vocal performance (by Americo Paredes) of the actual corrido of Gregorio Cortez (00:00:20–04:05); the San Antonio newspaper reporter's interview of Deputy Boone Choate and the flashback dramatization of the shooting of the sheriff as told through Choate's deceitful account (00:14:20–25:10); the pursuit of Cortez and his storied evasion and escape (00:43:30–52:40); the betrayal and capture of Cortez (00:59:40–01:04:50); the unveiling of the truth of the shooting incident, followed by the flashback dramatization of the events as they actually happened (01:07:20–21:30); the trial and verdict (01:22:00–31:40); and the ending, including the prison train, a mythologizing folk drama, and the credits (01:37:50–45:52).

[4] It is a bitter disappointment to me and to my students to learn that after his release, Cortez took part in the Mexican Revolution, not on the side of the revolutionaries fighting injustice, but on the side of the dictator, Díaz. I suppose that in a corrido, this would have been reported otherwise.

[5] Here *güerito* means "pale youth"; *gerente*, "ranch manager"; and *Guardia Blanca*, "White Guard."

[6] Given McCarthy's tenacious devotion to authenticity in *All the Pretty Horses* and *The Crossing*, I expect that this fragment comes from an actual corrido, but I have not been able to find it in any archive or other source. One of the resources I share with students is a copy of a manuscript page of *The Crossing* from the Cormac McCarthy Papers on which McCarthy edits these verses in his own hand. These handwritten edits suggest to me that this corrido fragment may have been composed entirely or in part by McCarthy. However, because of my experience researching the authenticity of place in McCarthy's Border Trilogy, I continue the search for the original.

[7] Interestingly, the Babícora was a latifundio owned by William Randolph Hearst, a fact that testifies to the favors the Mexican government was paying to influential Americans—here long after the revolution. This presence of powerful American landowners was a point of resentment among Mexicans during the revolution, as it was during the time of this novel. It remains so today.

Cormac McCarthy Made Me Do It: Embodied Responses to Literary Studies

Nicholas Monk

I first read Cormac McCarthy's *Blood Meridian* on a road trip to the American Southwest. My companions and I approached the town of Presidio outside Big Bend National Park just as I came to this sentence in the book: "They traveled northeast as far as the town of Presidio on the Texas border and they crossed the horses and rode dripping through the streets." In that moment I was in two different Presidios. I felt elated, as if something mystical had taken place. The vividness of McCarthy's "barren peppercorn hills and the mountains and the flat brush country and running plain" was all around me (172). I felt that if I erased from my mind the trucks, cars, and telephone wires, I would at any moment see the kid, the judge, and the Glanton gang slouching in their saddles and holding their rifles crosswise, ready to slaughter anything that moved in the shimmering heat. This was a Southwest unique to me in this place and time, a combination of the political and physical geography of place, McCarthy's consciousness, and my own. It was then, and later when I looked out across the Rio Grande at the Sierra Madre in Mexico, that I felt I understood a truth that is central to McCarthy's writing: nothing, not even the material of the earth itself, is eternal. The insignificance of humanity and its works, captured in their nanosecond of geologic time, was vivid to me in those extended minutes. Thought and being became indistinguishable to me as my senses and intellect conveyed the same information. Their separation, or that of mind and body, had never seemed more erroneous.

McCarthy was therefore at least partly responsible, a short while later on the same trip, for my decision to swim across the Rio Grande and back. I was intoxicated by the romance of the landscape as McCarthy represents it in *Blood Meridian*, and as I saw it. I wanted to be closer to it, part of it. There was something too in the act of swimming that defied arbitrary borders, something in me that wanted to prove, physically, the permeability of imaginary lines delineating imagined nations. As McCarthy tells us, political borders cannot triumph over the geography of the Southwest—only geologic time can do that. There was both an ontological and an epistemological dimension to what I did as thoughts and actions flowed together. I also chose to swim because I felt a sense that I should respond to the grandeur of the surroundings with a dramatic gesture of my own. I did not ponder these matters in such language at the time, but I feel sure that a partly conscious awareness of them sanctioned my recklessness. As it happened, the river was not unkind, featuring little more than gentle currents, and pollution was noticeably absent. After I had swum back, looking perhaps like "some wholly wretched unholy baptismal candidate" (McCarthy, *Blood Meridian* 27), I looked back over the river. I felt like I had acted in the spirit of Edward Abbey, who demands that we physically and emotionally enter the landscape in order to "see" it: "get out of the goddamned [car] and walk, better yet crawl, on hands and knees, over the sandstone and through the thornbush and cactus. When traces of blood begin to mark your trail, you'll see something, maybe" ([Ballantine] xiv). I didn't bleed for the Southwest, but I took risks with both landscape and the authorities that patrol it. I wonder now what I might have said in defense or mitigation if I had been apprehended by those representing the law. Maybe only that Cormac McCarthy made me do it.

This is one example of how reading fiction has changed my life. My experience of the fiction of McCarthy forever altered my "being-in-the-world" (Wheeler).[1] I want others to find a route of their own to such an experience, and while it is vitally important that students engage with abstract ideas, I also believe they should experience the way literature can make us feel. I try to create learning spaces, therefore, where participants can engage with reading in ways that might develop in them a more embodied, visceral, or haptic response to the writing.[2] Informed by my commitment to the idea that learning at its best is a kinesthetic experience, and by the knowledge that reading literature has real effects on the reader's life, I have a developed teaching and learning workshop on texts by McCarthy and Paul Bowles. The workshops are designed to help participants move from a typical mode in higher education in which they are conditioned to absorb knowledge to a less typical one in which they are required to be ontologically engaged. In briefer terms, the move is from knowing to knowing through being and doing. The pedagogy that underpins this approach acknowledges that literature (fiction in this case) often produces subtle, complex, and layered commentary and represents a uniquely wide spectrum of experience, and that these features are more accessible to a body and a brain that are treated as part of the same whole.[3]

The workshop consists of an introductory activity, a principal activity titled theory building, an optional tableau or writing exercise, and a plenary or group reflection.[4] The workshop lasts for two hours, and in advance its participants are asked to read Bowles's "He of the Assembly" (*Stories* 311–25), "The Wind at Beni Midar" (340–51), "The Delicate Prey" (162–70), and "The Garden" (352–55) and McCarthy's *All the Pretty Horses* and *Blood Meridian*. Participants should also be aware that Bowles translated into English from Arabic the work of a number of important Morroccan authors such as Mohammed Mrabet and Driss ben Hamed Charhadi. The workshop's introductory exercise is called Clap, Snap, Stamp and is well-known in theatrical rehearsal rooms, where it is used to encourage performers to focus on and respond to other members of their ensemble. Participants are placed in pairs, then the facilitator asks for a volunteer to demonstrate the activity. The facilitator says "1," the volunteer responds with "2," the facilitator says "3," the volunteer responds with "1," the facilitator says "2," and the volunteer says "3." Essentially the two participants are counting up to 3 together. The demonstration ends, and the pairs in the group now take up the activity. After a minute the facilitator stops the activity and recalls the volunteer for another demonstration. This demonstration is identical to the last one except that "1" is replaced by a clap. The pairs then resume the activity. After a couple of minutes the facilitator stops the participants and recalls the volunteer for an additional demonstration. This demonstration is identical to the last one except that "2" is replaced by a snap of the fingers. Again, after a couple of minutes the facilitator stops the activity and recalls the volunteer. The demonstration is the same as the last one except that "3" is replaced by a stamp of the foot. The activity concludes with the pairs reverting to exchanging spoken numbers, as in the first round of the exercise. The facilitator then asks for feedback. Invariably participants talk about the need to collaborate, and the need to focus, in order to make the activity work. There is always a lot of laughter during the exercise as individuals and pairs fail. Already, however, participants are working with each other in an embodied fashion.

The warm-up activity is designed to prepare workshop participants for the principal activity, theory building. Theory building allows students to collaborate with each other in groups to discuss literary texts and develop ideas that they cocreate, represent visually, and sometimes embody. It allows them to create theories or narratives in which ideas are shared and outputs co-owned. This gives rise to a more complex, deeper, and varied experience than a student might expect to get from reading and analyzing a text alone. The activity demands that the facilitator prepare in advance a collection of images and fragments of text on laminated paper. The workshop is divided into smaller groups of up to eight. Each of the smaller groups receives the same handout of images and text. Twelve to fifteen laminated pages are sufficient. Each of the laminated pages should relate in some way to the subject matter of the workshop. It is crucial that the material not explain ideas, or be explicit about the intent or opinions of the facilitator, and that it be sufficiently open to permit a wide range of interpretation. Each group is invited to create a theory or narrative from the materials and to represent this as a pattern on the floor of the space. This part of the workshop should last around forty-five minutes. If possible, each group should be provided with a tablet or laptop and Internet access in order to discover and include an image or text fragment of their own. This stage allows students to better own the process and permits them to feel that they have greater control of its direction. The facilitator should intervene at various points to clarify with each group what images represent, to elucidate more opaque fragments of text, and to offer advice. When each group is satisfied with its narrative or theory and the pattern it has created, it invites the other groups, in turn, to enter its space and interpret its creation. I have used theory building in many pedagogic contexts, but what makes it such a good fit for studying the works by McCarthy and Bowles is the correlation between the very visual—often cinematic—style of both writers, the visual richness of the settings they use, and the connections that emerge between their works and an extraordinarily wide range of other texts. Such features allow participants to have thoughts and feelings that are both vivid and extensive.

The images for the session on Bowles and McCarthy include John Gast's *American Progress*; Anasazi structures at Canyon de Chelly ("Canyon"); a burning bush (McGill); interiors of abandoned houses half-full of sand at Kolmanskop, a ghost town in the Namib (P. Cooper); a still from a trailer for the film adaptation of *The Road* showing the man and the boy in a post-apocalyptic wasteland ("Road" 00:00:24); W. B. Yeat's poem "The Second Coming"; and a figure dressed as the professor after his transformation in Bowles's story "A Distant Episode" ("On Location"): "the men took him out, still in a state which permitted no thought, and over the dusty rags that remained of his clothing they fastened a series of curious belts made of the bottoms of tin cans strung together. One after another of these bright girdles was wired about his torso, his arms and legs, even across his face, until he was entirely within a suit of armor that covered him with its circular metal scales" (Bowles, *Stories* 410–11). I include in this session a laminated page that shows in twenty-four line charts the increases or decreases of various phenomena that affect the health of the planet: for example, urban population, frequency of great floods, number of motor vehicles, carbon dioxide concentration, and gross domestic product. I also provide the following quotations:

> "He was naked on a rock in the desert, in the stone age, a prey to homesickness for his own kind, his own epoch, for European man and his glorious history of desire and dreams. . . . Something Reptilian he felt here, something that had endured by immobility, a kind of life out of reach, like crustaceans in their armour" (Cather 102).
>
> "When I write 'paradise' I mean not only apple trees and golden women but also Scorpions, tarantulas and flies, rattlesnakes and Gila monsters, sandstorms, volcanoes and earthquakes, bacteria and bear, cactus, yucca, bladderweed, ocotillo, mesquite, flash floods and quicksand, and yes—disease and death and the rotting of flesh" (Abbey [Ballantine] 147).
>
> "[They] never paint for the callow purpose of declaring 'I am.' They paint as a means of maintaining the physics of the earth" (Kenneally 57).
>
> "That night he dreamt of horses in a field on a high plain . . . and they ran in that resonance which is the world itself and which cannot be spoken but only praised" (McCarthy, *All the Pretty Horses* 161–62).
>
> "The desert has inspired cultural fantasies and enabled real and imagined experiences of solitude, contemplative repose, divine revelation as well as anxieties of loss, disorientation and death" (Gersdorf 16).
>
> "In the neuter austerity of that terrain all phenomena were bequeathed a strange equality and no one thing nor spider nor stone nor blade of grass could put forth claim to precedence. The very clarity of these articles belied their familiarity, . . . and in the optical democracy of such landscapes . . . a man and a rock become endowed with unguessed kinships" (McCarthy, *Blood Meridian* 247).[5]

When each group has read the theory or narrative of every other group, the exercise is complete. This final element of theory building is crucial. The facilitator should always instruct the participants that the readers cannot be initially led but must reach their own conclusions. Those who have prepared the work will then comment on these conclusions, indicating whether the readers have interpreted the theory or narrative in the way intended. This part of the workshop allows participants to see that many interpretations are available and that these can be highly nuanced even if they are similar.

An optional next stage is to ask participants in each group to create a tableau of their theory or narrative by using their bodies. The rules are that each person in the group must be in physical contact with at least one other member and that they must be still and silent when the tableau is read by the other groups. Participants may use whatever props they find in the space. Movement can be added if there is time, so that a short performance is created. Another option would be to have a writing session in which participants produce a five-hundred-word commentary on their experience and understanding of the theory building activity.

I have seen a variety of narratives and theories represented in patterns on the floor of the space in response to the provided materials, as the work of groups tends to be distinctly different. Some groups will represent the desert as antithetical to human existence, while others will show the desert as a refuge. Nihilism recurs, as do a progression from lower to higher and varieties of ecological or spiritual experience. Some groups have produced theories concerning modernity and geologic time. Still others make connections to the Anthropocene and the posthuman. Although I claim that theory building allows participants to create their own knowledge, the materials provided can never be wholly uncontaminated by the interests and preconceptions of facilitators, indeed by their entire conscious and unconscious worlds. The addition of the participants' own images or fragments of text does mitigate this contamination, and if facilitators select the materials carefully, participants will find that they are able to feel ownership of the narratives they create.

The experience of working in this fashion can be profound for participants. It can also be challenging. The tableau activity can produce a range of responses—fear, embarrassment, or resistance—but the vast majority of participants overcome their concerns once they begin to collaborate with their colleagues and revisit their ideas. Under ideal circumstances, at this point in the workshop this groundwork will have produced a coherent move from individual reflection to collaborative reflection, to shifts in those reflections, and finally to the shared embodiment of an idea.[6] It is my hope that the workshop helps participants reintegrate embodiment and intellectual activity in the way that reading *Blood Meridian* and traveling through the Southwest did for me.

The theory building session on the works by McCarthy and Bowles offers distinct learning outcomes. Participants improve their ability to engage with the subject matter and thus develop their understanding. They are better able to work collaboratively, and at the same time they develop greater self-reliance as they take responsibility for their own learning. By embodying their understanding, participants can better remember difficult concepts and theories. Theory building provides a foundation from which participants can develop sophisticated and complex understandings of literary texts. Student feedback consistently shows that this is the case: students report greater confidence in developing and sharing knowledge and ideas in courses I run that involve theory building early on. Following my theory building workshop at the University of Nebraska, Omaha, a colleague at the university remarked that "[e]ven now, almost two years after our Embodied Learning Workshop, my faculty colleagues and graduate students continue to reflect on the inspiration they gained from Dr Monk's . . . visit to our campus." Other benefits can also emerge from theory building: a pattern from the session that posits an ecological theme might lead to a discussion of responses to the environment in the work of the authors, which in turn might lead to a discussion of ecocritical approaches to literature. Historical approaches might provide the basis for a discussion of modernity and the rational. Narratives and theories generated by participants in the theory building exercise very often lead to a focus on both nihilism and the posthuman, as they do in the workshop on texts by McCarthy and Bowles. Animals, in particular, feature prominently in images the students add.

The session on works by McCarthy and Bowles takes place in an undergraduate course, on either American literature or literature of the American Southwest, and immediately follows two seminars on Native American and Chicana/o literature, the second of which addresses landscape, cultural geography, and borders. The seminars feature work by Leslie Marmon Silko, Gloria Anzaldúa, Louise Erdrich, Vine Deloria Jr., Paula Gunn Allen, and others. Before the session on McCarthy and Bowles, students have already been exposed to ideas of fluidity—between nation states, between races and ethnic groups, between humans and animals, and between local and regional or global ecosystems. The session opens a space for the discussion of challenging ideas that are current in contemporary fiction, such as the posthuman and post-apocalyptic, and it suggests theoretical critiques such as new materialist analyses of anthropocentrism. The handout for the session is intended to help students reflect on how systems of being are organized in nonhuman ways and to analyze these systems in relation to assumptions that determine cultural practice. This comparative approach allows students to rethink the multifarious nature of subjectivity and to apply their hypotheses to familiar literary studies topics such as violence, feminism, regionalism, colonialism, and identity in its various forms.

When students participate in this session, they are already accustomed to the cultural importance of region in the United States, to the significance of landscape in American fiction, and to the notions of the immigrant writer.[7] The pairing of Bowles and McCarthy should not, therefore, seem unusual to students, despite the fact that Bowles predominantly wrote short stories and that McCarthy is most known for his novels. Nor should it be jarring that Bowles's work is set in North Africa and Sri Lanka for the most part and that McCarthy strays outside the United States only as far as Mexico. Nor should students be surprised that writers of two different eras are placed alongside each other or that Bowles's connection to the Beats is his most significant cultural connection, whereas McCarthy has no such allegiances. Bowles's writing is regarded as part of an existentialist tradition in fiction.[8] McCarthy, however, eludes such literary-philosophical classification.

There is never enough time for the reflective discussion after the theory building exercise, but in discussion students will often begin to see common themes in the works of these authors, such as the effacement of the self, the provisional and temporary nature of the human, the relation between that nature and the vastness and wildness of the desert, and violence. For instance, when students pair the passage in *Blood Meridian* where McCarthy writes of "a man and a rock . . . endowed with unguessed kinship" (247) with the passage in "Baptism of Solitude" (Bowles, *Their Heads* 78–94) where Bowles writes of "a wholly mineral landscape" where "even memory disappears" (129), they identify a link between two authors who might seem at first to be very different.

Both writers treat the desert as an animate force, something that can inhabit in addition to being inhabited. In Bowles's fiction, the experience of the desert leads characters to undergo a process of realignment or rebalancing of the embodied and the intellectual: the landscape enters the individual to create difference in the moment the individual enters the landscape. In the "optical democracy" of *Blood Meridian*'s desert, no one thing can claim precedence: the human is externally, as well as internally, reintegrated (247). But McCarthy's work goes a stage beyond Bowles's: in *Blood Meridian* the human is changed to the extent that it becomes inseparable from its surroundings, and the boundaries between concepts such as self and environment become meaningless. Another example of the shifting boundaries of self comes in Bowles's short story "A Distant Episode" (24–35), in which the Reguibat people capture a professor of linguistics and, in a cruel irony, cut out his tongue. They also fashion for him an exoskeleton of tin cans. He becomes terribly changed. The professor suffers the excision of language, and all that is left to him of self-expression—the phenomenon that, some would argue, defines humanity—is capering in the sand for the amusement of his captors. In the subtraction and addition of parts he becomes a Frankenstein's monster for the posthuman era. More significant, the professor's self or personhood begins to dissolve in the desert. At this point the idea of the desert gothic becomes a useful heading under which to consider Bowles, McCarthy, and other writers in the course such as Silko.[9]

The session on works by Bowles and McCarthy has allowed participants a sense of the ways in which we can be affected as embodied humans by what we read. I hope that, in the process, students have experienced an intensity and openness to the world. Clearly, to have my students dive into the Rio Grande, or any river, would be impractical, even if I could produce the desire in them to do so. When I was based in central England, however, I could take a group of students to the theaters in Stratford or, better, The Globe Theatre in London, where they could be groundlings for a few hours. In a seminar on nineteenth-century poetry, I might take a party to explore the remains of Emmonsails Heath, the fragments of true heath at Castor Hanglands, or the grassland at Barnack Hills and Holes. Maybe in these locations it would be possible to gain an insight into what John Clare might have felt in the countryside that inspired his poetry, and to compare the feeling of being there to the feeling his poetry gives us now. Even if embodied engagement of this kind is not available to teachers and learners, theory building and the associated workshop activities can approximate this kind of experience. To reunite intellect and feelings in response to literature, and even to reconnect mind and body, is part of a powerful learning experience for all who participate.

NOTES

[1] Defined by the *Stanford Encyclopedia of Philosophy* as "a non-intentional, or perhaps pre-intentional, openness to a world" (Wheeler).

[2] This essay is autoethnographic in that it records my own experience and presents that as research. Autoethnography demands that researchers be "vulnerable, forthright in exploring . . . character weaknesses, struggles, and ambiguities" (Anderson and Glass-Coffin 75). Teaching in the way I describe exposes researchers to the skepticism of students and colleagues who are comfortable with the more passive lecture and seminar model of higher education. Such teaching also demands that researchers reflect openly on their own practice as an example to students. Such openness leads, again, to vulnerability. I want to represent this openness and vulnerability in this essay.

[3] The autoethnographic method of research is important because it recognizes ideas of embodiment. Just as the work of a musician is corporeal, an autoethnographer's work also draws on and works from embodied knowledge and experiences. This focus frees the voice and body from the conventional and restrictive mind-body split that continues to pervade traditional academic research and writing.

[4] I first learned of this kind of activity through the work of Jonothan Neelands, now of WBS Create, which is part of Warwick Business School. He and my colleague Jonathan Heron have made my use of embodied pedagogies possible.

[5] The handout includes the complete passages from Cather; McCarthy, *All the Pretty Horses* and *Blood Meridian*.

[6] It is only after careful preparation prior to and during the session that participants will feel confident and engaged enough to work in these ways. This preparation includes the selection of the right space for these activities by the facilitator. See Monk et al. for more details.

[7] Earlier sessions on the course engage with William Faulkner, Ernest Hemingway, Willa Cather, F. Scott Fitzgerald, Shirley Jackson, Nella Larsen, American modernist poetry, and the Beats. Later sessions include work by Toni Morrison, Lorraine Hansberry, Sandra Cisernos, Cynthia Kadohata, Thomas Pynchon, and Don DeLillo.

[8] Bowles's status as an existentialist is a given in both academic and mainstream circles. See Pinsker; Halpern.

[0] Botting notes of the gothic that "[n]ature appears hostile, untamed and threatening: . . . darkness, obscurity and barely contained malevolent energy reinforce atmospheres of disorientation and fear" (4). The desert gothic features, also, as does the work of both Bowles and McCarthy, the ruins of buildings, ghostly presences, blood and violence, loss and nostalgia, the grotesque, and intimations of the eighteenth-century sublime.

Teaching *The Road* in the Context of Apocalyptic Studies

Shayna Sheinfeld

When I first read *The Road* in preparation for a class on post-apocalyptic and dystopian fiction, I listened to the audiobook on my daily forty-five-minute commute. The audio version draws out some of the most terrifying parts of the story; I remember how I had to pull over when I heard the scene in which Papa and the boy discover the cellar full of naked, trembling people who have been locked away by the cannibals for food. I remember, too, thinking about how the post-apocalyptic world in McCarthy's *The Road* is both similar to and wildly different from the ancient apocalypses that are the basis of my research. The book also sits uncomfortably among contemporary post-apocalyptic and dystopian narratives, especially given its ambiguous ending.[1] This essay examines how *The Road* both participates in and redefines the apocalypse genre of fiction through its use of a variety of themes, including dualism, salvation, and the meaning of life. Approaching *The Road* from the perspective of apocalyptic studies creates another way for students to engage with the text—by focusing on the novel's portrayal of end-times and on how McCarthy participates in the apocalypse genre and disrupts it in order to make us, as readers, uncomfortable.

McCarthy's *The Road* depicts a world without hope or security, where there is a clear dualism of good and bad, but the main difference between good and bad is perspective rather than any moral absolute: while most of my students would agree that cannibals are bad, the other characters, especially the man but also the boy, fall into moral ambiguity. McCarthy's novel is clearly set after some sort of massive catastrophe—what we will call an apocalypse—but this event remains unidentified throughout the book.[2] The cause of the catastrophe is beside the point in McCarthy's novel: the consequences of life after this event are key in *The Road*, as is how the characters navigate the challenges of moral decision-making. For instance, while Papa, the man, generally defers to the boy's generosity, one could question whether this deference actually benefits other characters. For instance, is the boy's decision to share food with Ely, and to therefore extend his life, while potentially limiting the boy's and man's own lives, an act of generosity or cruelty? Similarly, although the ending of *The Road* is perhaps one of the more hopeful endings found in McCarthy's works, it is still devastatingly depressing and dissatisfying, especially in terms of the conventions of the apocalypse genre. As I explore in more detail below, this genre has roots in ancient religious worldviews as well as in contemporary iterations of those worldviews. The climax of ancient apocalyptic narratives is always salvation for a select group. The ending in *The Road* misses what, in the estimation of Frank Kermode, is the point of an ending: to connect the beginning, middle, and conclusion of a story in order to satisfy the reader (35–36).

To fully explore *The Road* in the light of this genre, I first discuss the subfield of apocalyptic studies from the broader field of religious studies. Instructors do not need to participate in this discipline, however, in order to teach *The Road* from this perspective. Following an introduction to the field, I give concrete examples of activities and assignments that teachers can bring to their classrooms. After a discussion of teaching apocalypses, I show how *The Road* can be brought into the wider discussion of genre and apocalypse. Finally, I propose some other contemporary popular cultural narratives that could benefit from an in-class discussion similar to the one I describe here for *The Road*. Thus, depending on the interests of instructors, this approach could be no more than a way into analyzing *The Road* with students, or it could be the basis for an entire course examining apocalyptic narratives throughout history and in different mediums.[3]

What Is an Apocalypse?

When I ask my students to define an apocalypse, inevitably the responses center on an apocalypse being the end of the world. After some discussion, this response often gets refined: an apocalypse is the end of *our* world, or at least the end of our world as we currently know it. Movies, books, and other forms of popular culture identified with the apocalypse genre often portray not the end of our world, exactly, but the beginning of a new societal order after the destruction of the current one; in other words, they are often post-apocalyptic instead of apocalyptic. Beyond *The Road*, such works include *The Hunger Games* trilogy of books, which have been adapted into films and which follow their protagonist, Katniss Everdeen, in a post-apocalyptic United States; the television series *The 100*, which follows a group of survivors of nuclear fallout on earth; and the comedic film *This Is the End*, which follows a group of men dealing with the apocalypse.

The Road falls into the category of a post-apocalyptic narrative rather than into the apocalypse genre proper—since it portrays the aftermath of an unidentified apocalypse that leaves the world as we know it barren—but the way the story shifts between the present and the past, as well as the man's hope for the future of the boy, which undergirds the entire narrative, makes this McCarthy novel a valuable example that students can use to explore how apocalyptic studies can be applied to contemporary popular culture.

Apocalyptic Studies

The study of apocalyptic literature has primarily been situated within the academic study of religion, where it has mainly focused on the book of Revelation. While an area of study within the field of biblical studies, apocalyptic literature was often treated as the wicked stepsister: it was usually avoided as a subject, and when it had to be discussed, it was treated with embarrassment and disdain. Two examples highlight this embarrassment: the first comes from the third-century CE church bishop of Alexandria in Egypt, Dionysius, who is quoted in Eusebius:

> Some before us have set aside and rejected the book [of Revelation] altogether, criticizing it chapter by chapter, and pronouncing it without sense or argument, and maintaining that the title is fraudulent. For they say that it is not the work of John, nor is it a revelation, because it is covered thickly and densely by a vail of obscurity. And they affirm that none of the apostles, and none of the saints, nor any one in the Church is its author. (25.1–2)

In this quotation Dionysius is arguing for the rejection of Revelation as an authoritative text. He claims that it is "without sense or argument" and questions whether its author is John, the author of the fourth Gospel.[4] The second example derives from the German biblical scholar Klaus Koch's critical review of scholarly attitudes toward apocalyptic literature, which he titles *Ratlos vor der Apokalyptik*—that is, perplexed or embarrassed by apocalyptic. Koch's title notes the distress that many scholars and theologians feel when they are presented with a work of apocalyptic literature, whose weird visions and proclamations of the end seem to defy interpretation.

While theologians and scholars have referred to texts about apocalypses as a type of literature as early as the third century CE, it was only in the 1970s that the study of apocalyptic literature began to move into more mainstream biblical scholarship, when scholars took an interest in noncanonical texts written by Jews and Christians in antiquity. The study of these texts began with an analysis of the apocalypse genre. Biblical scholars had previously used the terms *apocalypse*, *apocalyptic*, and *apocalypticism* freely without regard to definition or continuity. The word apocalypse comes from the Greek *apokalypsis*, which means "something revealed" and is first found in the title of Revelation, although there is evidence that Jewish texts fitting this literary type existed as early as the third century BCE, the Book of the Watchers being one example. Of course the earliest Christians were Jews, so it should be no surprise that this literary tradition was adopted and adapted within the early Jesus movement. In fact, the undisputed letters of Paul show an urgent apocalyptic expectation. Take, for instance, 1 Thessalonians, where Paul teaches his community at Thessalonica that this world will soon pass, even before his death:

> For this we declare to you by the word of the Lord, that we who are alive, who are left until the coming of the Lord, will by no means precede those who have died. For the Lord himself, with a cry of command, with the archangel's call and with the sound of God's trumpet, will descend from

> heaven, and the dead in Christ will rise first. Then we who are alive, who are left, will be caught up in the clouds together with them to meet the Lord in the air; and so we will be with the Lord forever.
>
> (*HarperCollins Study Bible*, 1 Thess. 4.15–17)

Here Paul writes that those believers who have died before Christ's imminent return will be the first to be resurrected. Likewise, "we who are alive, who are left," will also be taken to heaven to be with the Lord. Of course, this expectation was not fulfilled for Paul or his communities. However, it should be clear that the early Jesus movement was apocalyptic in nature. As the movement developed, Christianity continued to make use of the apocalyptic tradition, as did Judaism, although the genre is not as commonly found in the Jewish tradition. In the late first century, for instance, Christians wrote the Apocalypse (or Gospel) of Peter, a noncanonical work of apocalypse literature that has Jesus take his follower Peter on a journey into hell in order to see how the wicked are being punished (*Apocryphal New Testament*). From rabbinic Judaism there is also a brief example in the Mishnah, codified around 200 to 220 CE. Mishnah *Sotah* 9.15 is often called the little apocalypse in rabbinic scholarship because it traces the decline of Jewish history and includes an extended list of the evils that will occur immediately before the coming of a messiah (*Mishnah*). Islam, too, adopted an apocalyptic outlook, as many verses in the Koran mention the last judgment and resurrection of the dead (e.g., 17.52).

Other religious traditions also contain apocalyptic worldviews. For instance, in Buddhism there is the idea that when the world declines and Buddhist ideas are forgotten, a new Buddha, Maitreya, will appear and offer his teachings to the world. Hinduism has the belief that there are four ages and that we live in the last: following this age most humans will be destroyed, the final incarnation of the god Vishnu will appear to collect the righteous souls, and the world as we know it will be destroyed—and then recreated in a purer form. Of course, in addition to appearing in religious traditions, apocalypses and post-apocalypses are now prevalent in secular forms of literature, movies, and art (Sheinfeld 201–02).

John J. Collins defines the apocalypse literary genre as a "genre of revelatory literature with a narrative framework, in which a revelation is mediated by an otherworldly being to a human recipient, disclosing a transcendent reality which is both temporal insofar as it envisages eschatological salvation, and spatial insofar as it involves another, supernatural world" (5). Collins's definition has served as the foundation upon which subsequent studies of ancient apocalypses have been built and has provided a shared point of departure for the study of apocalyptic literature in the ancient world. Collins's definition breaks down the apocalypse genre into identifiable pieces. First, to call a text an apocalypse, it must be a narrative that includes a secret knowledge revealed to a human recipient through an otherworldly being. This revelation must include some reflection on salvation at the end-times and on God, angels, demons, heaven, hell, or other parts of the supernatural world. This definition makes it relatively easy for one to determine if a text can be called an apocalypse, but it does not take into account texts that do not meet the definition but might still qualify as apocalyptic—meaning that they exhibit apocalypticism (the worldview described below)—or even as post-apocalyptic, and there exists a relation between all three types of texts.

Biblical scholars such as Collins have noted that apocalyptic texts written by ancient Jews and Christians, such as Daniel and Revelation, contain certain generic elements that make identifying the literary type called apocalypse possible. Likewise, scholars have noted that some other ancient texts or parts of texts (e.g., Mark 13) contain strongly apocalyptic language and ideology but do not meet Collins's generic definition of apocalypse; scholars refer to this worldview in such texts as apocalypticism. Apocalypses and apocalypticism exist both within canonical texts such as Daniel and Revelation and also in noncanonical texts from antiquity, such as the Dead Sea Scrolls.

Collins makes it clear that his definition of apocalypse applies only to the particular literary type, and it does not engage with more complex treatments of genre theory, such as that of Alastair Fowler, who notes that genre has primarily to do with communication: "[Genre] is an instrument not of classification or prescription, but of meaning" (22). In Fowler's view, genre should be understood as dynamic and inclusive of variation within a literary type, rather than as taxonomic, or rigid in its classification of a type. Another writer who is critical of the treatment of genre as a classification system—the treatment proposed by Collins—is Jacques Derrida, who argues that a text should not belong to a genre but instead should be considered a participant in it: "a taking part without being part of, without having membership in a set" (230). If we are to take genre theory seriously, we should already be hesitant to simply accept Collins's definition, although in terms of the history of scholarship in religious studies it has proved useful in moving the field of apocalyptic studies forward.

More recently the biblical scholar Lorenzo DiTommaso has developed an approach to the apocalypse genre that involves examining it as a series of works that express the worldview of apocalypticism rather than as a literary type. He defines apocalypticism as "a worldview, a fundamental cognitive orientation that makes axiomatic claims about time, space, and human existence." He further explains that apocalypticism

> presumes the existence of a transcendent reality, which defines the cosmos and everything in it, but remains almost entirely concealed from observation and beyond the grasp of human intellection. It contends that the present reality is constitutionally structured by two antagonistic and irreducible forces, which are typically identified with good and evil. It maintains that a final resolution of the conflict between these forces is both necessary and imminent, and that it is also redemptive, in the sense of a deliverance

> from the present reality. The apocalyptic worldview further assumes that the revelation of these mysteries orients existence, and gives life meaning and purpose. (474)

DiTommaso's approach is considerably more useful than Collins's for instructors who wish to teach *The Road* through the lens of apocalyptic studies and is also used by Stacey Peebles in her comparison of the novel and its 2009 film adaptation. Good/evil dualism is essential to apocalyptic literature and is certainly found in the man and boy's dialogue in *The Road*. The search for redemption as a "deliverance from the present reality," too, is present in both the book and other examples of apocalyptic literature. There is, of course, more to the book than dualism and redemption, but here genre studies is useful as a theoretical model with which to engage the text.

Teaching Apocalypses

When I introduce undergraduate students to apocalypses, I do not shy away from the problem of genre; however, I often begin by discussing other genres that students may be more familiar with (e.g., horror, romance, or comedy). They discuss in groups what movies or books in one of these genres are like, and then they map out that genre on the board. Students understand what a genre is, even if they have not studied it theoretically, and they are often able to express how a movie or book both fits into and redefines a genre. For instance, romantic comedies often play on the attraction and subsequent miscommunication between a man and a woman, who eventually form a union at the movie's end. *The Crying Game*—an example that most of my students now have not seen—falls into the category of a romantic thriller, but with a twist: the woman is revealed to be transgender.

Students learn that understanding the variations within a genre can help them to classify a particular work and to identify what makes it unique, interesting, and surprising. An apocalypse can be examined in the same way, whether it is ancient or contemporary. The majority of ancient apocalypses fit Collins's definition, which we review in class, but we also find ancient literature that clearly has an apocalyptic worldview but does not meet the definition. As a low-stakes assignment, I ask students to write a one- or two-page apocalypse using Collins's definition as a guide. I tell them to be as creative as they would like, and to feel free to engage with a contemporary setting or with contemporary issues. During the next class students share their mini-apocalypses in small groups and discuss how their peers' stories do or, as is often the case, do not meet all the elements of the definition. This is a fun activity (e.g., one student wrote about a meat apocalypse, with meat falling from the sky!), and it allows students to engage directly with the problem of genre. Students follow up with a one-page analysis of how their own story does or does not fit the definition and why—and whether they would still identify their mini-apocalypse as an apocalypse. This final activity helps students bring critical reflection to their own work and develop ways, in terms of writing and argumentation, to offer a defense of their decision-making.

Following the exploration of apocalypses as a genre and the student-produced mini-apocalypses, I make sure students examine at least one ancient apocalypse so that they have a sense of the origins of the genre. It is easy to stick with canonical apocalypses, such as Revelation or Daniel 7–12.[5] Even instructors who are not specialists in biblical or apocalyptic studies can examine the basic narratives with their students, attempt to outline them, and find the elements of the apocalypse genre in each one. If time is a limitation, students can read Daniel 7 in class and analyze it.[6] Doing so will allow them to see the patterns in the ancient texts and to find them in the more contemporary narratives under analysis, such as *The Road*.

What students learn by examining the ancient texts, and what they are then able to see more readily in the contemporary stories that the class turns to, are the ways each story relates directly to its social, political, and historical context. The increased popularity of apocalyptic and post-apocalyptic narratives in contemporary popular culture derives in part from the insecurity that readers and viewers feel about their circumstances, with the result being that authors create the protagonists in these stories to either take action themselves or look to another character, who is often a superhero, for help (Sheinfeld 210–11). This insecurity as reflected in apocalyptic and post-apocalyptic narratives also provides a place for social critique; this critique is especially visible in narratives that relate to environmental concerns (regardless of whether those concerns are natural or caused by humans). For instance, David Williams's recent novel *When the English Fall* explores the environmental consequences of solar flares accompanied by coronal mass ejection on the American population, and in particular, the Amish. Similarly, *The Road* explores the consequences of environmental disaster, and when students read the novel or watch the film adaptation, they can discern that McCarthy is clearly criticizing issues related to societal or consumerist ethics as well as to the environment, although he is not explicit about what causes the environmental issues.[7]

Apocalypse and The Road

Once I have explored the definition of the apocalypse genre, I then pose this question to my students: Is *The Road* an apocalypse? It is a fruitful question for class discussion, and a complicated one. Students can begin to answer it by considering whether the novel meets Collins's definition of an apocalypse. The novel is not revelatory, although it is literature and has a narrative framework. There is no otherworldly being interpreting the situation for the humans in the story—although one might consider the narrator to be a kind of angel, and

Papa might view the boy as one. The novel does not seem to offer eschatological salvation, although the man and boy's trek to the coast in the South is, in fact, a search of a kind of salvation. Last, the novel does not seem to deal directly with God, angels, demons, heaven, hell, or other parts of the supernatural world, except perhaps that it depicts our world as a kind of hell in terms of the clear environmental destruction and the destruction of most humans.[8] While debating the question, students can consider whether Collins's taxonomic approach to genre is useful in a discussion of what McCarthy is trying to do with this narrative, or whether the discussion should move toward a broader idea of genre—more along the lines of Fowler or Derrida.

I now turn the class's attention to DiTommaso's definition of apocalypticism—is the narrative of *The Road* better identified as an expression of apocalypticism? At first glance this identification seems to fit the novel better than Collins's definition of apocalypse does, but take note of a particularly sticky point: The worldview of apocalypticism "contends that the present reality is constitutionally structured by two antagonistic and irreducible forces, which are typically identified with good and evil" (DiTommaso 474). It is unclear if *The Road* makes such a contention. Are the man and the boy good, and is everything else evil? Certainly some of the other humans in McCarthy's novel would qualify as evil, such as the group of people keeping humans locked away in the basement in order to use them piecemeal as food (109–11), or the man from the truck who attempts to kill the boy (62–66). But what about the man struck by lightning (49–50), or Ely, who shares a meal with Papa and the boy (161–75), or even the man who steals their stuff from the beach (253–60)—are they inherently evil or clearly good? What about Papa? The question of good and evil in this book, as in many of McCarthy's works, is complicated, whereas the ancient apocalypses are straightforward in their dualism, such as in Daniel 12.2, where there are only two options for resurrection: the good will be resurrected "to everlasting life," and the wicked will be resurrected "to shame and everlasting contempt" (*HarperCollins Study Bible*).

Viewing DiTommaso's final sentence as descriptive of *The Road* may prove particularly challenging: "the apocalyptic worldview further assumes that the revelation of these mysteries orients existence, and gives life meaning and purpose" (474). If this story does nothing else, it questions the meaning of existence in a desolate world. If Papa lives for his boy until his death, what does the boy live for? McCarthy's descriptions of Papa and the boy carrying "the fire" (83, 128–29, 216, 278) might appear to offer a raison d'être for the two protagonists, but it seems just as likely that carrying the fire is something Papa instructs the boy to do in order to provide him with some meaning in what Papa sees as an otherwise pointless existence.

While students might struggle to make *The Road* fit the categories provided by Collins and DiTommaso, there is no doubt that the narrative takes place in a post-apocalyptic world, and therefore it is useful to discuss some of the elements that are present both in the novel and in apocalyptic literature, which expresses the worldview of apocalypticism as described by DiTommaso. Some of these elements have been mentioned, such as the meaning of life, dualism, and salvation, which are in fact major themes in *The Road*. Other elements might include repentance and obligation to others. If we return to the most basic definition of apocalypse, the one students would have initially come up with—that is, apocalypse as the end of the world as we know it—then the novel certainly fits into apocalyptic studies. Leaving the question open to debate allows space for students to develop their own arguments and provides an opportunity for another low-stakes writing assignment, an essay, or even an in-class debate. These types of assignments help students develop critical thinking, close reading, and creative skills that support the use of high-impact teaching practices by instructors, which in turn promote deeper learning.

Applying Apocalyptic Studies to Other Narratives

Reading McCarthy's *The Road* is an excellent way for students to explore apocalypses in the contemporary period and, more broadly, apocalyptic studies. But the pedagogical tools discussed here are also relevant for other types of dystopian, apocalyptic, and post-apocalyptic narratives from a wide variety of time periods and media. For instance, a class might examine Margaret Atwood's recent post-apocalyptic *MaddAddam* trilogy (which consists of *Oryx and Crake*, *The Year of the Flood*, and *MaddAddam*) with the same tools mentioned above. A class discussion of the differences between Atwood's and McCarthy's stories would offer opportunities to analyze the contexts from which the authors were writing, their concerns, and, as is often the case for this type of literature, the underlying social critiques in their works. Both authors' works happen to highlight criticism of environmental politics, among other things, although Atwood's trilogy is more concerned with human-caused climate change, while McCarthy's novel suggests an event beyond human interference. It is helpful to ask students what this contrast might say about the authors' understanding of their contemporaneous social context.

Using other media, too, is a good way to explore the relation between apocalypse and social critique. If instructors teach the film adaptation of *The Road*, they may ask students how it differs from the book and what those differences say about the kind of critique McCarthy is presenting. Instructors should also consider teaching movies such *I Am Legend*, *Mad Max: Fury Road*, or *This Is the End*, and if they wish to expand the analysis, they should consider graphic novels such as the original series *The Walking Dead*, created by Robert Kirkman and Tony Moore, or *Wasteland*, written by Anthony Johnson and drawn by Christopher Mitten. As with the variations within each narrative, the type of medium chosen by the author or creator affects what messages and social critiques are being presented. For example, *The Giver*, a post-apocalyptic book by Lois Lowry that has been adapted for film, is often known to my students, as it is assigned at many high schools in the United States. This novel criticizes, among other things, the submission of personal freedoms and free will in order to create a supposedly safe state.

Students enjoy reading these texts to engage with ideas about what happens at the end of the world as we know it and to think about ways in which narratives are reflective of the time in which they are produced. In reading these works, students also learn how to critically examine materials created specifically for them—a trailer advertising a movie, for instance, or an Internet ad for a particular product—and come to understand that the creators of these materials, too, have an agenda for their audience, just like the writers of ancient apocalypses and of contemporary novels such as *The Road*. As a genre and a worldview, apocalypse is both ancient and contemporary, and it draws us to think about the present's connection to past and future, notions of what if and if only, what we might lose in the future and who we might become, and who we might already be.

NOTES

[1] I was aware that McCarthy had been no stranger to apocalyptic themes and motifs in his previous work—for instance, White's musings on the end of Western civilization in *The Sunset Limited*, Sheriff Bell's characterization of Chigurh as a "*true and living prophet of destruction*" in *No Country for Old Men* (4), and the imagery on just about every page of *Blood Meridian*—but *The Road* is his most explicit engagement with the idea of apocalypse as a real, global event.

[2] McCarthy has hinted, however, that the environmental devastation described in the book is based on what might happen if a large meteorite hits the earth ("Cormac McCarthy's Apocalypse").

[3] Murphy and Schedtler is a terrific resource for teaching an undergraduate course on apocalypses throughout history.

[4] In fact, the author of Revelation is John of Patmos, who never claimed to be the John who wrote the fourth Gospel. As it is today, the name John was common in Jewish and Christian circles of the first and second centuries CE.

[5] Note that there are actually three apocalypses in this section of Daniel: chapters 7, 8, and 10–12; chapter 9 is a prayer.

[6] I recommend using the *HarperCollins Study Bible* or *The New Oxford Annotated Bible*, both of which use the New Revised Standard Version translation and have excellent scholarly notes. For historical context, instructors can also read, and possibly assign students to read, the section from Collins's *Apocalyptic Imagination* on the biblical text that is being examined.

[7] For more on this, see Dominy; Jergensen; and Scott Yarbrough's essay in this volume.

[8] God is referred to by the narrator and mentioned by characters in *The Road*, but these references are not in conversation with the novel's inherent apocalypticism.

Teaching Style Using the *Cormac McCarthy Corpus Project*: *Blood Meridian* and *The Road*

Delys W. Snyder, Phillip A. Snyder, and Jeremy Browne

The distinctive style of Cormac McCarthy has been present in his writing from the very beginning of his career, giving rise to consistent critical praise but also to the oft-repeated observation that upon first cracking open a McCarthy book, readers will either absolutely love or completely hate his style. This is an overstatement, to be sure, but one that reflects the discomfort some readers may feel initially with his lack of quotation marks to set apart dialogue, his nonchalance in identifying exactly who is speaking, his celebrated eschewal of the semicolon, his penchant for using archaic vocabulary and creating his own words, his frequent and unapologetic use of untranslated Spanish in his southwestern novels, and so forth. Some readers might call his style innovative and engaging, while others might call it unconventional and off-putting. Admiring scholars have commented on the stylistic issues mentioned above and on others in McCarthy's writing such as the overarching narrative divisions, epigraphs and epilogues, italicized lyrical passages, narrative voice, terse colloquial dialogue, and syntactic variety and complexity. In this essay, we consider how teachers can engage student and general readers on both sides of this stylistic binary, in order to help new readers of McCarthy understand and appreciate his style and to encourage seasoned readers to deepen their understanding and appreciation.

To accomplish these aims, we rely on the developing disciplines of digital humanities and corpus linguistics, both of which enable and advocate the use of big data and distant reading and thus give us the ability to do quantitative stylistic analysis in addition to the long-established practice of qualitative stylistic analysis. Specifically, we introduce the *Cormac McCarthy Corpus Project* (*CMCP*), which is hosted by the Digital Humanities Department at Brigham Young University (Snyder et al.). The *CMCP* allows researchers to use search programs such as *Voyant Tools* and *Sentence Structure Search* to interrogate this digital corpus for patterns of structure, syntax, and diction while using as large or as narrow a scope as the researchers desire: from one section of one chapter in one book by McCarthy to the whole of the corpus. The *CMCP* allows researchers to quickly do huge searches that would otherwise be impossible or intensely time consuming. While quantitative analysis may be fascinating in and of itself, its main value derives from our asking what the data mean and exploring their potential implications in a qualitative way. At the same time, qualitative questions can lead to quantitative analysis, including the development of new search tools and other digital innovations. Our investigation into McCarthy's distaste for the semicolon can serve as an example.

With a few clicks of his mouse while using a non-*CMCP* search tool on his computer, Jeremy Browne determined that there are thirty-eight semicolons in *The Orchard Keeper*, McCarthy's first novel; one semicolon in *Suttree*, the big Knoxville novel that marked the end of McCarthy's Appalachian phase; and one semicolon in *Blood Meridian*, the first of McCarthy's southwestern novels, which was published immediately after *Suttree*. We concluded that McCarthy, for some reason known only to himself and perhaps his editor, significantly changed his use of the semicolon after that first novel. Phil Snyder wondered about McCarthy's use of the colon, which immediately inspired another search, the results of which are in table 1.

The colon appears throughout McCarthy's writing with varying regularity, but the semicolon does not. Delys Snyder then suggested that we look at the sentences in which the lone semicolons appear in *Suttree* and *Blood Meridian*, which we did. In those two instances a colon would have been a more appropriate mark of punctuation, at least in our considered opinion:

> "Wanted to trade; two blind crabs for one with no teeth" (*Suttree* [e-book]).
>
> "They rode through regions of particolored stone upthrust in ragged kerfs and shelves of traprock reared in faults and anticlines curved back upon themselves and broken off like stumps of great stone treeboles and stones the lightning had clove open; seeps exploding in steam in some old storm" (*Blood Meridian* [e-book]).

After further research, we found that print editions of *Suttree* differed from the publisher's 2010 e-book, which we had used in our initial search: the print *Suttree* does have a colon ("Wanted to trade: two blind crabs for one with no teeth"; 375), while the e-book has a semicolon. Unlike the e-book edition of *Blood Meridian*, the print edition has a comma instead of a semicolon ("stones the lightning had clove open, seeps exploding in steam in some old storm"; 50),

Table 1. Colons in McCarthy's Novels

Novel	Number of colons	Average number of pages per colon
The Orchard Keeper	69	3.56
Outer Dark	43	5.62
Child of God	31	6.35
Suttree	79	5.96
Blood Meridian	12	28.08
All the Pretty Horses	21	14.38
The Crossing	10	42.60
Cities of the Plain	22	13.31
No Country for Old Men	39	7.92
The Road	18	13.38

so we concluded that the two semicolons were simply errors introduced in the digitalization process and that McCarthy stopped using the semicolon after he wrote *The Orchard Keeper*. This search reminded us that digital corpora are not infallible and that we need to be thorough in our research.

Describing Style in Blood Meridian *and* The Road

Because *Blood Meridian* is probably the McCarthy novel that has received the most critical attention, and *The Road* is the novel most widely read and taught in high school and college, our stylistic examples come from these two texts. Inspired by Samuel Chamberlain's *My Confession: Recollections of a Rogue* and loosely based on historical events and figures, *Blood Meridian* mimics the style of the Old West memoir in its chapter divisions, with headnotes summarizing the narrative to follow, but without the first-person narrator typical of memoirs, and it features some of the most striking and profound descriptive passages in all of McCarthy's works as well as a range of characters, from the kid, whose dialogue is terse and colloquial, to Judge Holden, whose speech is loquacious and erudite. *Blood Meridian* represents McCarthy's style in its full scope, variety, and power, as though it were an amped-up rock performance geared for sold-out stadiums. *The Road*, on the other hand, with its more limited narrative action and range of characters, represents McCarthy's unplugged style, an acoustic performance in an intimate auditorium. Set in an environmentally devastated and depopulated post-apocalyptic Appalachia, *The Road* depicts a desperate but loving father and son who, on their journey to the ocean, face starvation, illness, marauding cannibals, inevitable separation by death, and the impossible call to act ethically in a world devoid of ethics.

However, both novels, like all of McCarthy's works, share exactly the same "stylistics," which Geoffrey Leech and Mick Short define as "language as used in literary texts with the aim of relating it to its artistic functions" (13). McCarthy's style is characterized by "syntax that varies in length and complexity according to narrative and thematic contexts and diction that appropriates and creates words from multiple sources" (Snyder and Snyder 33). One main element of McCarthy's basic narrative style is coordination—the use of a list-like string of simple sentences that are linked together, most often with the coordinating conjunction *and*, which makes each sentence in the list equal. This stylistic privileging of coordination over subordination is a linguistic parallel to McCarthy's descriptive notion of "optical democracy" in *Blood Meridian* (247). Coordination makes everything—thing and spider and stone and grass blade—equal grammatically as well as optically. Nancy Kreml calls McCarthy's usual narrative style his "unmarked" style, which changes to a "marked" style in philosophical, rhetorical, and lyrical narrative passages or dialogue. Kreml argues that McCarthy's marked style forces readers to slow down as the "length and complexity of the sentences literally, almost physically, constrain the reader to find meaning" (46). Kreml adds that McCarthy's style, marked and unmarked, is enhanced by the writer's widely sourced vocabulary—archaic, colloquial, foreign, technical, compounded, blended, and invented—which also tends to slow down readers (46–48). While having to slow down may be frustrating sometimes, it also provides a good opportunity for readers to analyze more deeply the stylistic techniques of a brilliant writer.

Analyzing and Mimicking McCarthy's Style

Even before doing a corpus analysis, a teacher can lead students in a close analysis of a novel's words and sentences to give an initial sense of how McCarthy writes. Pick a paragraph from a novel such as *The Road*, and have students mark the number of words in each sentence, bracket the sentence fragments, circle the unfamiliar or unusual words, underline the word *and*, and put boxes around the dialogue (fig. 1).

When students look this closely at McCarthy's writing, they get a magnified view of the author's style. The word count for the sentences in the paragraph in figure 1 shows that McCarthy changes the rhythm of the paragraph by varying the length of his sentences. The fragments might be hard for students to recognize because the periods make them look like sentences, but they are just pieces of sentences, usually noun phrases missing a verb. Teachers can discuss how McCarthy's copious use of fragments in *The Road* reflects the setting of the

> It was a long night anyway. When it was light enough to see he pulled on his shoes and rose and wrapped one of the blankets around him and walked out and stood looking at the road below. The bare ironcolored wood and the fields beyond. The corrugate shapes of old harrowtroughs still faintly visible. Cotton perhaps. The boy was sleeping and he went down to the cart and got the map and the bottle of water and a can of fruit from their small stores and he came back and sat in the blankets and studied the map.
>
> You always think we've gone further than we have.
>
> He moved his finger. Here then. (195)

Figure 1. Annotated text from McCarthy, *Blood Meridian*, p. 195.

novel, a world that is itself disintegrating into fragmented bits. By circling the unfamiliar words, students begin to see the extent of McCarthy's vocabulary, and they can discuss how this expansive vocabulary shapes the prose and affects reader comprehension. Some words can be understood in context, while others must be looked up to ascertain their meaning. The unique words in this paragraph, "ironcolored" and "harrowtroughs" (*Road* 195), are newly minted compounds created for this passage, and they simultaneously ring familiar and exotic while revealing their meanings through context (if readers know what *harrow* and *trough* mean).

Underlining the instances of *and* in the paragraph in figure 1 illustrates McCarthy's use of several compound verbs in the list-like passage "he pulled on his shoes and rose and wrapped . . . and walked out and stood," which has much the same effect as the compound sentences that incorporate lists and compound verbs: "The boy was sleeping and he went down to the cart and got the map and the bottle of water and a can of fruit from their small stores and he came back and sat in the blankets and studied the map" (*Road* 195). These compound sentences move us linearly and democratically through the story, with little of the hierarchy that complex sentences have because of their independent and dependent clauses.

Although McCarthy sometimes hides dialogue in a descriptive passage, he usually separates dialogue from narration, but he never uses quotation marks. Further, he gives limited introductions to dialogue, infrequently uses speaker tags, and provides few clues beyond the dialogue itself to tell us who is speaking.

This lack of clear speaker attribution turns readers into close textual listeners. For example, even though we know that the father and son are speaking in this passage from *The Road*, the identity of each speaker is not immediately evident:

> Do you think there could be ships out there?
> I dont think so.
> They wouldnt be able to see very far.
> No. They wouldnt
> What's on the other side?
> Nothing.
> There must be something.
> Maybe there's a father and his little boy and they're sitting on the beach.
> (216)

Admittedly, the son usually asks the questions, but readers are not completely sure who is saying what until the mention of the father and the little boy on the beach, which sounds like what a father would say when beginning a story, and which is a longer utterance than almost anything the boy says. In addition to considering their role as close textual listeners, students can also consider how the omission of quotation marks democratizes dialogue and narration by making them visually equivalent. In discussing dialogue, teachers can also explore how the dialogue's syntax and diction indicate the social, educational, and regional backgrounds of the speakers.

After analyzing a paragraph from *The Road*, students are primed to try mimicking McCarthy's style with their own narration and dialogue. Teachers can assign students to write an original paragraph about two people surviving a disaster—maybe even a zombie apocalypse—in the style of McCarthy. Students can create their own versions of McCarthy's style—sparse language, unique words, laconic dialogue, lists of compound sentences linked with *and*, short sentences and fragments, and minimalist punctuation—to both serious and humorous effect.

Overview of the Cormac McCarthy Corpus Project

Researching style becomes even more engaging when students use digital searches to interrogate McCarthy's novels. Although the *CMCP* is user-friendly, the corpus also has tutorials that show users how to explore and use it in a systematic way. We call this corpus a project to emphasize its ongoing, developmental character. Moving forward, we will update the project and add tools and other resources, and we welcome feedback and suggestions from *CMCP* users.

The *CMCP* has two general tools: *Voyant Tools*, which searches the text for words, and *Sentence Structure Search*, which searches for particular syntax structures. *Voyant Tools*, a text analysis suite created by Geoffrey Rockwell and Stéfan Sinclair, can create a word cloud that shows the most-used words in a novel, graph the frequency of a word in a novel (or in all of McCarthy's novels), contextualize a word by showing the five words before and after it, and search dialogue passages separately from narrative passages.

The graphs make more sense if users understand the difference between a word count and a relative frequency. If we simply count the occurrences of a word, we get a word count, but comparing the word counts of novels can be misleading because sometimes the count is high in one novel simply because the novel is longer. To standardize the count, the *CMCP* measures the relative frequency of a word, which is how many times the word appears in every ten thousand words. In *Blood Meridian*, for example, the word *horse* appears 191 times, and in *All the Pretty Horses*, the count is 405. Since horses are part of the plot of each novel, we are not surprised that both novels have many instances of the word, but *Blood Meridian* is longer, so we also look at the relative frequency: *Blood Meridian* 16.42, *All the Pretty Horses* 40.82. The word count shows a rough two-to-one ratio of *horse* in favor of *All the Pretty Horses*, but the relative frequency provides a more accurate comparison of 2.5:1 (see table 2).

Teaching with the Corpus

One easy way to introduce impatient, digitally fluent students to the *CMCP* is to have them simply play with it and find things to explore that may lead them to research and discussion questions. Another way is to guide them with activities that can help them use the corpus to open up meanings in the text, so we have created some corpus activities that work for high school or college students who are reading *Blood Meridian* or *The Road.*

Divisions

McCarthy divides the text in his novels by using parts, chapters, three dots on a line, dropped capital letters, and blank pages or lines between grouped text. *Blood Meridian*, for example, is divided into twenty-three chapters, with further divisions within each chapter. Because we wanted to discover how each chapter might differ, we marked the corpus accordingly in the version "*Blood Meridian* by Chapter." When students open this version, they see the words that are the most used in the novel represented in a word cloud, and a graph shows how the frequency of these words differs across the twenty-three chapters. A quick search for a key word can bring insight about the structure of the novel. The word *judge*, for instance, makes sense as a search word because Judge Holden is the dominant character in the novel. In the search box in the window Words in the Entire Corpus, type "judge" and then hit Return. Clicking on the search result generates a graph of the word's use in each chapter. The graph reveals the

Table 2. Count and Frequency of *Horse* in McCarthy's Novels

Novel	Word count for *horse*	Total number of words in text	Frequency of *horse* per 10,000 words
The Orchard Keeper	4	67,189	0.60
Outer Dark	40	57,480	6.96
Child of God	0	35,924	0.00
Suttree	24	176,143	1.36
Blood Meridian	191	116,338	16.42
All the Pretty Horses	405	99,213	40.82
The Crossing	700	149,993	46.67
Cities of the Plain	293	90,144	32.50
No Country for Old Men	21	69,849	3.01
The Road	0	58,717	0.00

ebbs and flows of the judge's presence in the novel: the peaks and valleys of the graph show, respectively, the chapters in which the judge figures prominently and those in which he is not mentioned.

Students could select other words connected to thematic issues in the novel—such as *rode*, *kid*, *said*, *blood*, *sunset*, and *sat*—and trace their use in each chapter. Even a search for the common word *and* can give insight into the narrative style in the chapters, since the word occurs more often in narrative passages. Students could also create a graph that compares the use of several words, such as *judge* and *kid*, across the entire novel (see fig. 2). When a user clicks a dot on the graph, the window Keywords in Context lists all instances of the search word in the chapter associated with the dot and shows the five words to the left and the five words to the right of each instance. These contexts can give clues as to how the word is used in that chapter. Of course, reviewing these instances in the printed text would provide even fuller context.

Dialogue

After we first presented the *CMCP* at a conference of the Cormac McCarthy Society, we asked our colleagues for suggestions on the next step we should take, and, overwhelmingly, they asked us to separate the dialogue from the rest of the narrative, which we did. Now for each novel we have a corpus that includes the full text and one that separates narration and dialogue. We can now search words and phrases to discover how they are used differently in the narration and the dialogue.

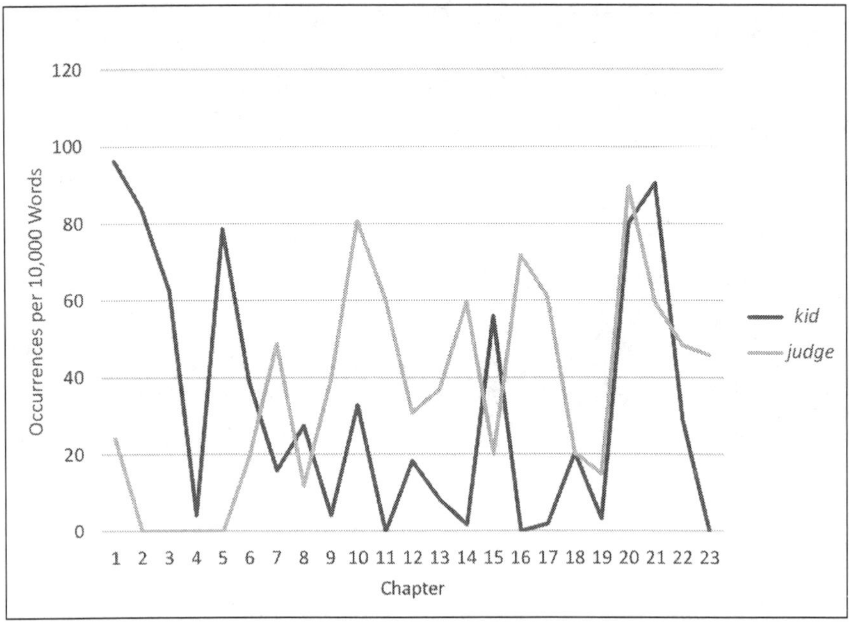

Figure 2. Frequency of the words *kid* and *judge* in *Blood Meridian*, by chapter. Reproduced from Snyder et al.

A search of "*The Road* Narration-Dialogue" corpus, for example, allows students to determine some differences in word use between the novel's narration and dialogue. In the Trend column in the window Words in the Entire Corpus, words that are used more in the narration than in the dialogue have a backslash, while those used more in dialogue than in narration have a forward slash. A graph of the most common words in the corpus has two points for each word on its x-axis, one for narration and one for dialogue. A line connects the narration mark and the dialogue mark for each word in order to represent the difference between the two marks. For example, the most common word in the novel, *the*, is used four times more frequently in the narration than in the dialogue. Students can look at examples of a word in narration and discuss why it does not appear as often in dialogue. Words like *and*, *he*, *of*, and *in* also occur more frequently in the narration than in the dialogue, and words like *to*, *I*, *you*, *we*, and *what* occur more often in dialogue. These word searches can also lead to a discussion about the differences in usage between storytelling and conversation.

Much of the conversation in McCarthy's novels contains colloquialisms, and the *CMCP* can help students examine some of the differences between Standard English and less formal language. In the *Blood Meridian* corpus that separates narration and dialogue, students can easily search colloquial words to find out if McCarthy uses them exclusively in the dialogue or if they appear in the narration as well. For instance, if students search for the terms *aint*, *dont*, and *cant*, they will discover that these contractions, which McCarthy writes without an apostrophe, are prevalent in the dialogue but never occur in the narration. Having no common contractions in the narration makes the narration more formal. Next, students can search for more nonstandard words or swear words, like *em*, *nothin*, *damn*, and *hell*. Again, they will find that these words are found only in the dialogue. McCarthy's vocabulary in the narration is in Standard English, but the conversations are often in a nonstandard dialect.

Syntax

The *Sentence Structure Search*, another tool in the *CMCP*, allows users to analyze McCarthy's syntax. Students can use the tool to determine, for instance, whether McCarthy begins sentences in his novels with coordinating conjunctions such as *and*, *but*, or *yet*. This activity could be especially useful for secondary school students, who are sometimes taught never to begin a sentence with a coordinating conjunction and often have to unlearn this rule in college. To use the *Sentence Structure Search*, students must click on parts of speech in a sequence that will create a complete sentence. Careful use of the Wildcard button as a placeholder makes this tool work more easily. For example, click Coordinating Conjunction and Wildcard to show sentences that begin with a coordinating conjunction. The wild card makes the search possible because it stands in for the rest of the sentence after the opening coordinating conjunction. The results show the number and percentage of sentences in each novel that begin with a coordinating conjunction, and they also show five random example sentences from each novel. McCarthy uses conjunctions at the beginning of his sentences one to three percent of the time.

Teachers often try to help students write sentences with more variety by teaching them to begin sentences in different ways. A *Sentence Structure Search* of McCarthy's novels shows many examples of how the author begins his sentences, which can serve as models for students learning how to vary their own sentences. Not surprisingly, a common way to begin a sentence is with a determiner such as *a* or *the* and a noun phrase. To search for these types of sentences, students should choose the buttons Determiner and Wildcard and then note the results (fig. 3). McCarthy begins his sentences with determiners eleven to twenty-four percent of the time, depending on the novel. If students search for sentences that begin with personal pronouns, such as *he* and *they*, by choosing the buttons Personal Pronoun and Wildcard, they will find that thirty-three to forty-two percent of sentences begin this way. Sentences can also begin with a preposition or a subordinating conjunction, so for this search students can choose the buttons Preposition or Subordinating Conjunction and

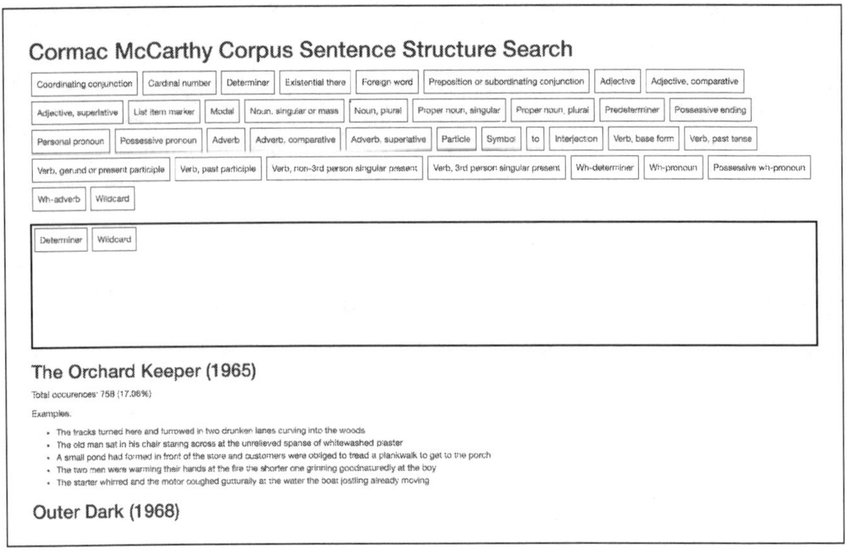

Figure 3. Screenshot of a search for sentences that begin with determiners. From Snyder et al.

Wildcard. McCarthy begins sentences this way three to seven percent of the time. Students can also try the buttons Verb, Gerund, or Present Participle and Wildcard to find more variety, as well as Adverb and Wildcard or Proper Noun and Wildcard. Whether students find themselves inspired or discouraged by reading McCarthy's carefully chosen prose, these syntax exercises can help them look more carefully at the details of this writer's language with an eye toward improving their own.

Diction

Although McCarthy has a massive vocabulary, he generally writes so that literate readers can understand what he is writing about; nevertheless, he sometimes pulls out esoteric and descriptive terms that send most readers to the dictionary for help. Some of these terms are only listed in the *Oxford English Dictionary*, and some of them are too specialized for the *OED*. For example, in *Blood Meridian*, McCarthy uses the term "framestrap" (322) to describe a part of a gun. The word does not appear in the *OED*, but it does appear in antique gun catalogue descriptions.

Students can learn more about diction by searching the corpus using *Voyant Tools*. A search of all the novels by McCarthy shows how many words are in each novel and how many unique words are in each novel. McCarthy's novels contain a total of 920,990 words, many of which are repeated, but his vocabulary of distinct words is 29,938, an astonishing number. Variations of words are counted as separate words, meaning that *horse* and *horses* are counted as two words. Even so, the number of unique words is overwhelming and comparable to the number in Shakespeare's works. The chart in the window Corpus shows the number of tokens (all words counted as many times as they are used), the number of types (unique words), and the density. The density is the number of types divided by the number of tokens times one thousand. The denser a novel is, the more unique words are used in a smaller amount of text. Even McCarthy scholars might be surprised to learn that McCarthy's densest novel is *Child of God*, which has a density of 127.6, and that the least dense is *The Crossing*, which has a density of 64.2. The higher the density, the richer the vocabulary—at least according to this formula. What is the density difference between narrative passages and dialogue passages? It might seem that narration would be denser, but the *Voyant Tools* analysis for *The Road* shows that while the dialogue in the novel is more terse, it is denser (105.6) than the narrative (91.2).

One of the most fun things to do with the corpus is to make a word cloud. *Voyant Tools* automatically creates a word cloud when a user opens a corpus. In *The Road*, the initial word cloud shows the most frequent words in the novel, and these are, not surprisingly, all function words like *the*, *and*, *he*, *a*, *of*, *to*, and *in*. These words, known as stop words, are usually the most frequently used words in novels written in English because the language requires these words to make syntactical meaning. To clear the stop words from the word cloud, click the gear icon, which represents the Options dialog box, in the window titled Cirrus. In the Options dialog box, choose English, check Apply Stop Words Globally, and then click OK (fig. 4). Users can also review the tutorial about how to remove stop words from the word cloud. After stop words are removed, a new word cloud will appear in Cirrus (fig. 5), and a new list of words will pop up in the window Words in the Entire Corpus: both windows will show the words *boy*, *said*, *road*, *looked*, *dont*, *stood*, *okay*, *know*, *sat*, *man*, *yes*, and *went*, among others. The more frequently a word occurs in the novel, the larger it will appear in the word cloud. Students can look at this word cloud and ask why certain words appear and others do not. Clicking a word in Words in the Entire Corpus will display its frequency in the window Word Trends. Students can ask themselves what

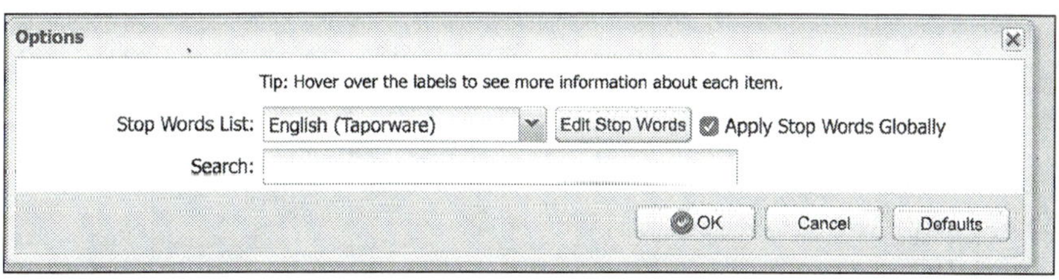

Figure 4. Screenshot of options for managing stop words in a word cloud. From Snyder et al.

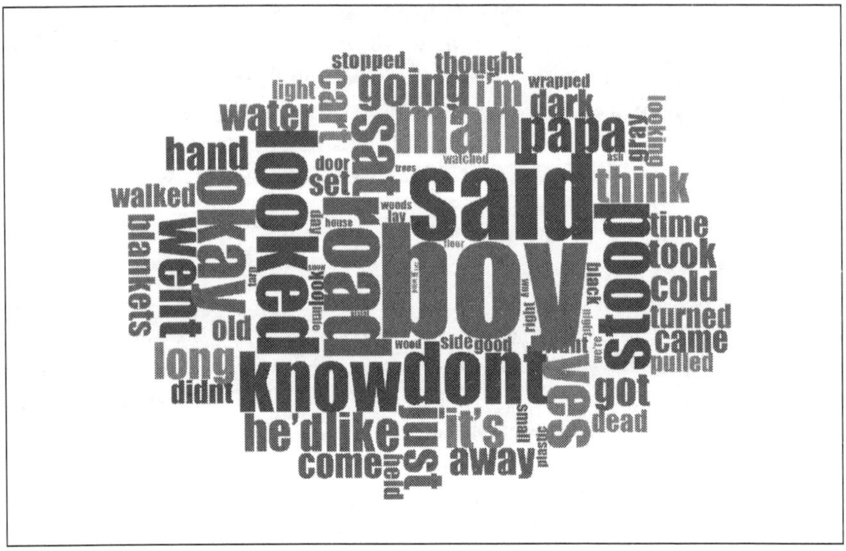

Figure 5. Screenshot of a word cloud of McCarthy's *The Road* with stop words removed. From Snyder et al.

the significance is of the first verbs on the list—*said*, *looked*, *stood*, *know*, and *went*—and how these words match the action in the novel. Word clouds can be created for other McCarthy novels in the same way.

Teachers can also have students search for terms related to gender in the novels by using the search box in Words in the Entire Corpus. A *Voyant Tools* search of the corpora "*Blood Meridian* by Chapter" and "*The Road*" will show that the word *she* occurs only in specific chapters in the two novels. Outside of those chapters, *she* is rarely used. Students can try the same kind of search with the word *he* for a contrast. *She* is used 114 times in *Blood Meridian*, whereas *he* is used 2,519 times. *The Road* has similar numbers, although women figure differently in the plot of that novel. When users click a term in Words in the Entire Corpus, the graph in Word Trends will track the term's frequency in each chapter. This kind of quantitative information can send students back to the novels with qualitative questions to pursue, such as why women are underrepresented in McCarthy's writing. A search of all the novels shows that the words *she* and *woman* are used the least in *Blood Meridian* and *The Road*, and this issue is worth discussing in class. Have students compile their own lists of words that mark gender and see where searching for those terms leads them.

Students can also use *Voyant Tools* to learn about how McCarthy employs metaphors in his prose. Entering the word *like* into the search box in the window

Words in Documents, for example, brings up the ten-word context for many of the instances of the word *like* in a given novel, and those instances will include many of McCarthy's similes. The language in *The Road* seems pared down and leaner than the language in the other novels, but a search for *like* shows that McCarthy still uses plenty of similes in the novel. The similes in this list can serve as mentor texts by showing young writers how effective vivid metaphors can be.

Students should also go beyond the *CMCP* in their stylistic analyses. For example, the excellent concordance "Words Cormac McCarthy Uses in His Novels," created by Christopher Forbis, Wesley Morgan, and John Sepich, lists every word in McCarthy's novels and its frequency in each novel (Forbis et al.). Sepich and Forbis have posted for each novel a concordance that lists the novel's page numbers where each word can be found (Sepich, "All Cormac McCarthy's Words"); this tool will help students find exactly where a word is used.

The *CMCP* can open up McCarthy's writing to reveal stylistic trends within each novel and across all the novels. Supplementing their close readings with distant readings, students can play with the corpus to find patterns, connections, or anomalies that they can see only with a big data search. Searching the corpus will help answer their initial questions about McCarthy's prose and will also provide fertile ground for additional research questions.

Teaching *The Orchard Keeper* to High School Students

Jamie Brummer

Literary landscapes have always been treacherous, brimming with frightful antagonists, disturbing settings, and anxiety-inducing plot lines designed to lure us into them at our own risk. Homer, Dante, Shakespeare, John Milton, William Faulkner, Flannery O'Connor—all the biggies challenge their readers to step beyond the safety of the quotidian and wander into more shadowy and uncomfortable realms. Now consider for a moment the panoply of horrors one encounters in the fictional universe of the contemporary American author Cormac McCarthy. It's easy to quail at their numbers—all those cold-blooded murderers, bloodthirsty cannibals, predatory pedophiles, lurking necrophiles, midnight melon mounters haunting the sleepy hollows of rural America, and sinister drug lords (and ladies) whose reach spans the globe. One quails at the derelict, debauched, and degenerate in McCarthy's novels and at the suppurations, cauterizations, and decapitations, to say nothing of dead babies and the "stinking forms of foetal humans" (*Suttree* 4) floating in rivers, abandoned in forests, found too often around or in campfires, and infamously, unforgettably, suspended from a tree in *Blood Meridian*. It's as if McCarthy's body of work has been designed to assault readers with images of innocence not just lost but ravaged or annihilated and to present for our consideration a legion of morally corrupt characters the likes of which may never before have been assembled by a single author.

Now take a moment to consider a different kind of horror, one that to my knowledge has never appeared in a McCarthy text but that any high school educator who wishes to teach his works must reckon with: the parent-teacher conference. Choosing a McCarthy text to teach when parent-teacher conferences loom on the horizon is a dicey proposition. Teachers could opt to assign *Child of God* to students and hope that the benign-sounding title and deceptively homespun opening will satisfy parents that the novel is appropriate for their children. Or teachers could assign *The Road*, banking on Oprah Winfrey's imprimatur and maternal aura to soften the grisly post-apocalyptic events that the novel relentlessly details. But there is little to satisfy parents in McCarthy's other novels. For instance, they might view *All the Pretty Horses* as promoting running away and premarital sex, *Cities of the Plain* as featuring prostitution and fat jokes, *The Gardener's Son* as having too much class warfare, *The Sunset Limited* as having too much nihilism, *Suttree* as having too much drinking, *No Country for Old Men* as having too much Anton Chigurh, and *Outer Dark* as featuring incest. Parents might respond even more negatively to *The Counselor* and to *Blood Meridian*.

Instructors could simply avoid McCarthy's works and opt instead for a safer voice, perhaps a more mainstream writer who channels the current fascination with wizards, vampires, or teenagers saving the planet from the dystopian meddling of their parents. Or instructors could succumb to the trend of avoiding fictional works altogether and teach only nonfiction pieces that have been scrubbed of anything controversial, constructing a safe space out of so-called informational texts until they have built an unassailable year-long ACT test prep course. Or they could (and this is my advice) draw a line in the sand, stick with McCarthy, and circle back to where it all began—his first novel, *The Orchard Keeper*.

High school students encountering the world of Cormac McCarthy for the first time (in print, if not on the big screen) discover in *The Orchard Keeper* a fertile seedbed of thematic and stylistic elements that the author develops and refines in his later works: a soaring, baroque prose style surprisingly punctured with dead-right colloquialisms, an episodic and recursive plot structure, scenes of searing violence that are also capable of evoking intense beauty, an exploration of the fraught terrain connecting and dividing fathers and sons, a complex celebration and critique of American masculinity, and a haunting, elegiac tone that has become a hallmark of so much of McCarthy's fiction. As such, McCarthy's first novel is an ideal introduction to the author's broader body of work. It also happens to be a fine story.

I teach at Christian Brothers High School, an all-boys Catholic high school in suburban Memphis, Tennessee. The school serves boys in grades 9–12 and has an approximate total enrollment of eight hundred students. Usually I teach the novel during the first semester in the school's Advanced Placement English literature and composition class for seniors. As we explore *The Orchard Keeper*, I ask my students to pay special attention to juxtaposition as one of McCarthy's central rhetorical strategies: the way, for example, an erudite narrator will share the page with illiterate characters, how descriptions of bloodshed and destruction are often evoked through luminous prose,[1] the persistence with which ghosts of dead patriarchs haunt their living progeny, and the abiding sense that the past echoes through and problematizes the present. We challenge ourselves to consider how McCarthy uses these dualities to paint a modernist (sometimes postmodernist) portrait of a country not so much rushing toward its future as having become unmoored from its past. As I emphasize these elements in *The Orchard Keeper*, we also track them back into works by Faulkner and Ernest Hemingway—two authors firmly ensconced in the high school canon—in an effort to contextualize aspects of the novel within modernist American literature.

These are challenging goals, and *The Orchard Keeper* is a challenging and provocative text. In this essay, therefore, not only do I describe approaches that have proved successful in introducing Cormac McCarthy—one of America's finest living writers and a personal favorite of mine—to high school readers, I also acknowledge a few others that have backfired.

Matters of Style

McCarthy has a deservedly renowned ability to locate his characters in time and place, especially in greater Appalachia and in the borderlands of the desert

Southwest and Mexico; McCarthy's evocation of landscape and ear for regional dialects are unsurpassed. Some readers can't help but hear Herman Melville, Nathaniel Hawthorne, Faulkner, or O'Connor in McCarthy's works and thus situate the writer's prose style within the larger context of American literature; such readers view the style as an homage to these predecessors, even as McCarthy composes an unmistakably personal voice. Scholars of McCarthy who read his works in the light of an encyclopedic knowledge of McCarthy criticism might recall "a discourse that is episodic, elliptical, laconic, rigorously metonymic, reliant on serial structures [and] exact in its taxonomic diction" (Bartlett 5). This description is true enough.

Now consider, however, that the predominant aspect of McCarthy's style that high school readers notice is the lack of quotation marks. For readers new to McCarthy, this lack of quotation marks is a vexing and recurring problem that must be addressed. Close readings, character analyses, historical contextualization, structural maps—these will have to wait. Quoting McCarthy on punctuation in general is a good way to start the class discussion: "There's no reason to blot the page up with weird little marks. I mean, if you write properly you shouldn't have to punctuate" (Interview). This quotation usually provides enough of an explanation to allow us to move into more fruitful discussion of such elements of McCarthy's style as its varying sentence length, syntactical complexity, sentence fragments, high and low diction, neologisms and archaic usage, regionalisms, ambiguities, and stream of consciousness.[2] These primary colors in McCarthy's palette are all on beautiful display in *The Orchard Keeper* and help make it not only a wonderful novel to read but also a powerful resource that instructors can use to teach elements of good writing.[3]

Matters of Substance

In addition to studying *The Orchard Keeper*'s stylistic strengths and eccentricities, my students and I also consider the novel thematically. One must be careful treading this ground, however, as high school students have a tendency to read benign morals into the texts they are studying (and may, for instance, view *The Orchard Keeper* as a cautionary tale about the dangers of alcohol use or speeding while driving) or to rely too heavily on Internet sources for their intepretations. So when I challenge my students to consider McCarthy's novel thematically, we go analog—no computers or smartphones. We have just the text, some awkward silences, and our own ideas. And under these conditions, students do great. They appreciate the novel's complex rendering of John Wesley Rattner's journey from innocence to insight (and some students may even trot out the term *bildungsroman*). They see in Kenneth Rattner—his lips "fat as leeches" (22) and "carplike" (36), his "cheesy neck-flesh" (38)—someone they never want to see again. They see in Uncle Ather one of their own elderly relatives, someone desperately trying to hold onto a life that no longer seems to fit or have value in the world, whose cantankerousness functions in part as a defense mechanism against a culture that is changing beyond recognition. In Marion Sylder they see a man alternating between responsibility and recklessness and coming to grips with the consequences of his choices.

For seasoned McCarthy scholars, it's worth remembering that my high school students are encountering *The Orchard Keeper*, and most likely McCarthy's works in general, for the first time. They haven't completed a literature review, studied continental critical theory, or ventured into the publication labyrinth. In other words, they're perfect. What a profound joy it is for a teacher to have innocent readers, students for whom the novel is enough (and more than enough). How often do we teachers conjure up a cacophony of secondary sources before we've allowed our students the chance to converse with the primary text, to laugh at McCarthy's sly humor, to marvel at the epic destruction of The Green Fly Inn, to feel sufficient compassion for (and be slightly creeped out by) Mildred Rattner, and to wander among landscapes so perfectly rendered that they hum with mystery:

> [T]he sun broke through the final shelf of clouds and bathed for a moment the dripping trees with blood, tinted the stones a diaphanous wash of color, as if the very air had gone to wine. . . . [T]he rain still mizzling softly and the darkening headlands drawing off the day, heraldic, pennoned in flame, the fleeing minions scattering their shadows in the wake of the sun. (246)

In his first novel, as he continues to do throughout his body of work, McCarthy mourns the passing of an American way of life even as he acknowledges the complex myths that gave rise to it. High school students (especially the upperclassmen with whom I read the novel) know something about being both created and confined by their past. They live and breathe the tension between a desire to escape their roots and become something new and the palpable fear that this desire creates. The college admissions process looms before them, a daunting rite of passage. Many of them have spent their entire lives trying to meet their parents' expectations and are now confronted with the possibility that their own dreams and desires may no longer sync with those expectations. They may vaguely recall having read somewhere that the "Child is father of the Man" (Wordsworth). Reading *The Orchard Keeper* makes this real.

Other Masters

Most high school students have never heard of McCarthy. Those who know the name at all probably associate it with movies, not books. A good many will have seen *No Country for Old Men*, and a few will have seen *The Road*, *All the Pretty Horses*, or *The Counselor*. Nearly all high school students, however, have heard of Faulkner and Hemingway. Faulkner's "Barn Burning" and "A Rose for

Emily" are fairly standard high-school fare, as are Hemingway's Nick Adams stories or perhaps "A Clean, Well-Lighted Place." This familiarity with two of the masters of American modernism provides instructors with another promising pathway into *The Orchard Keeper*.

I ask my students, for example, to nominate the novel's most Faulknerian moment, and we set about constructing a top-ten list. This eerie passage when Sylder first encounters Kenneth Rattner face-to-face often makes the cut:

> By the phosphorous glow, more like an emanation from the man's face than from the domelight, Sylder froze, his hand batting at the air stirred by the outflung door. The face stared at him with an expression bland and meaningless and Sylder groped for some, not cause or explanation, but mere association with rational experience by which he could comprehend a man sitting in his car as if conjured there simultaneously with the flick of light by the very act of opening the door.
>
> (McCarthy, *Orchard Keeper* 33)

Another contender is this excerpt near the novel's end, when John Wesley returns to the ruined house of his childhood: "About him the tall wheels veered and dished in the erratic parabolas of spun coins unspinning as if not attached to the wagon at all but merely rolling there in that quadratic symmetry by pure chance. He crossed the road to give them leeway and they swung by slowly, laboriously, as if under the weight of some singular and unreasonable gravity" (244). Such passages represent perfect close-reading opportunities. They allow me to ask students what it means to write in a Faulknerian mode; why McCarthy uses inversions, qualifications, and negations; and whether the passages reveal a writer succumbing to self-indulgence or whether they work in concert with other elements of the text. We also wade into Uncle Ather's stream of consciousness and consider whether these italicized passages are triggered by previous events or conversations in the novel, whether the text as a whole repays the reader for the considerable effort required to read the stream of consciousness, and who Ellen is and what happened to her. Teachers might be surprised by how capably high school students handle such questions.

Echoes of Hemingway resound throughout the novel as well, and students can profitably search for passages built largely from monosyllables, where the diction is more acoustic, more muted, driven by old, Saxon verbs and concrete nouns, as in this scene when Sylder is taken to jail: "The patrolman returned to his post at the door. From the cells to the rear of the building came bits and pieces of a sad voice singing. The sergeant turned papers over. In the outer corridor men were coming in, stamping their feet and rattling their raincoats, cussing the weather. A furnace pipe clattered" (McCarthy, *Orchard Keeper* 209). Consider also this simple description of Uncle Ather: "The old man came awake late in the afternoon and ate some cold cornbread, sharing it with the hound. He did not eat much and the cornbread was enough. Then he started down the mountain, trucking behind him his sorry chattel, picking a course through the small trees and laurel jungles" (190). I ask students how the rhythms created in the first example resonate within the larger context of Sylder's imprisonment, and how the distilled diction of the second example captures something about Uncle Ather that a loftier, more elevated style might miss. And we consider what to make of a novel that, often on the same page, mixes and matches, blends and blurs two so dissimilar narrative styles. I've found *The Orchard Keeper* to be an ideal text with which to explore these connections; to trace their roots back into earlier works by the likes of Hemingway, Faulkner, Melville, and Hawthorne; and to challenge my students to unpack McCarthy's famous dictum that "the ugly fact is books are made out of books. . . . The novel depends for its life on the novels that have been written" ("Cormac McCarthy's Venomous Fiction"). Those bitten by the McCarthy bug during our study of *The Orchard Keeper* (which includes a surprisingly high number of students) can go on to test this dictum as they trace echoes of his first novel through much of his later work: *Child of God*, *Suttree*, *The Crossing*, and *The Road*. They can also remain on the lookout for McCarthy's influence on a new generation of authors that includes Charles Frazier, Jeffrey Lent, and Daniel Woodrell. Thus students learn not only to enter into conversation with the text they are reading but to tune into how one author is influenced by, and influences, others.

Matters of the Heart

One thing high school teachers soon come to learn is that no subject—no matter how emotionally toxic, transgressively sexualized, graphically violent, or politically subversive—is off limits as long as it's in a work by William Shakespeare. But if instructors try to teach contemporary American literature, then any topic addressed in class that even borders on the subversive will anger students' parents and lead them to engage in fiery tweetstorms, write a slew of angry e-mails, and call the principal's office.

This essay opens with the suggestion that the bulk of McCarthy's work may simply be too controversial for the high school classroom. But that is far from what I believe. It's true that McCarthy's works are profoundly controversial, challenging, and guaranteed to assault their readers' comfortable sense of self—but giving students that experience is what studying great literature in the classroom is for. Years ago Leslie Fiedler proclaimed that our national literature is a literature for boys, an adolescent literature whose funky mix of Gothic and Romantic tropes provides cover for a host of deeper insecurities. And the high school classroom is the perfect arena in which to explore these anxieties through challenging stories such as the ones that McCarthy has been telling for over half a century now. Furthermore, it has become abundantly clear that this generation of young men will be asked to reexamine issues of masculinity. What better way to do so than by reading texts that shed light on our assumptions about race, class, gender, and a world of other ideas that we too often relegate to the shadows? Yet despite the benefits of reading controversial texts, there's a disturbing trend not only at the university level but also increasingly in secondary education that would purge uncomfortable material from the syllabus and leave behind a sterilized set of texts collectively deemed to be safe.

Our students inhabit a complex, rapidly changing world—hadn't we better prepare them to deal with the chaos? Writers like Cormac McCarthy and works like *The Orchard Keeper* can help us do just that. *The Orchard Keeper* has too long been something of a critical ugly duckling. Fifty plus years after its initial publication it deserves renewed interest, in the high school classroom and beyond. Yes, it will challenge students' assumptions. It will breed awkward and anxious moments in the classroom. It will prompt thoughtful consideration of class issues in American culture, of gender constructions, and of regional stereotypes. It will also provide a perfect opportunity for young people to grapple with controversial ideas, to stand up for their opinions while respecting those of others, and to listen (to writers, teachers, and one another) with big hearts. Great literature has the potential to counter a tendency toward intellectual and emotional tribalism that has become more prevalent in contemporary discourse, in and out of the classroom. When we choose to lose ourselves in a fictional world, sure, there's risk, but there's also the chance that we might end up discovering something new about ourselves. Isn't that what works of the imagination are about? Aren't they about placing us smack in the middle of unfamiliar places, surrounded by strange people, and forcing us to come face-to-face with something other—and to deal with it? There's danger in reading such works, but there's magic as well. It's the magic that has kept me in the classroom for my entire adult life.

NOTES

[1] Consider the description of the destruction of The Green Fly Inn in McCarthy, *The Orchard Keeper* 47–48.

[2] The *Cormac McCarthy Corpus Project*, a Web site hosted by Brigham Young University, is a phenomenal resource for exploring a wide range of stylistic elements in McCarthy's fiction and a fine way to introduce students to a more quantitative approach to literary research. See the essay by Delys Snyder, Phillip Snyder, and Jeremy Browne in this volume.

[3] McCarthy's fast-and-loose attitude toward punctuation, however, has also been known to inspire a similar free-spiritedness among student writers—something for instructors to keep in mind when they assign analytical essays.

"Green Hair and Bones in Their Noses": Teenagers' Appreciation for *No Country for Old Men*

Kristy Wilson

In 2007 I started assigning *No Country for Old Men* as summer reading for my fall composition class, in which high school students earned college credit through the State University of New York, New Paltz. The composition class allowed students who were successful during their junior English class to take a more difficult class while still earning credit for senior English, which they need to graduate. The novel worked well enough, but I hadn't really taught it—on the first day of class students handed in papers about their summer reading, and we only spent a few days discussing their summer work before we moved on to other readings. That changed three years ago when I started teaching senior English and decided to make *No Country for Old Men* one of the core texts for that class.

Half of the senior English classes I have taught in the last three years have been inclusion classes, meaning that many of the students in the class are classified as special education students with one or more learning disabilities. In such classes, I could have students who will go on to attend some of the finer universities in the Northeast sitting next to students whose goal is to become diesel mechanics. Many of my students come from homes well below the poverty line. Last year forty-five percent of my students were eligible for free or reduced lunch. To complicate that picture further, every year some of my students have parents in prison.

One of the best things about teaching *No Country for Old Men* is that it works on so many different levels. On its surface, it is a thrilling read with a premise that any teenager could find intriguing. My struggling readers, once they've managed to move beyond the novel's lack of quotation marks, are bolstered by their understanding of the exciting plot, which, for some of them, is enough to sustain their attention. I have found that the language of *No Country for Old Men* makes it much more accessible to my students than that of other McCarthy works.

My stronger readers not only are excited by the plot line but also stop at every page to discuss the novel's events, make connections to what we have read or discussed earlier, or discover new things in the text that I haven't led them to or new analyses that they come to themselves. They question Llewelyn Moss's motivation, they laugh and widen their eyes at Anton Chigurh's audacious persona, they have sympathy for Sheriff Bell, and they admire Carla Jean.

Many of my students know far more about the Middle East than they do about the border between Mexico and the United States, which is the setting for the novel. If they know that the border is violent, then they likely believe that the only people affected are the narcos warring against each other. To introduce them to border issues, I have them watch the first episode of HBO's documentary *Witness*, which follows the photographer Eros Hoagland in Juárez, Mexico. After that, the class is divided into two groups: one reads and discusses an article released by the United States Overseas Security Advisory Council that offers advice to government workers about how to avoid the violence raging through Nuevo Laredo, a city on the Mexican border ("Travel Advisory"), while the other group reads an article that details how dangerous it is to merely report on the violence on the border, especially on the Mexican side (Gallón). Once these groups have read and discussed the articles, they report what they've learned back to the rest of the class.

At the conclusion of our discussion about border issues, students are given five images, all photographs that originally accompanied news stories about violence in Nuevo Laredo. In small groups, they must order the images and create a story around them. One image depicts uniformed school children fleeing a building under a police escort, one shows a Mexican police truck ablaze in the middle of the street with bodies around it, one shows a US Border Patrol truck alongside the wall separating Mexico and the United States, one depicts two blood-covered children walking out of a building, and one shows a woman, aghast, being held back by police officers from a shooting in the street.

Students say that they get the most from this last exercise in the lesson on the border. The exercise effectively demonstrates that the violence of the region is so pervasive that it affects everyone, not just the narcos. Writing from the images also helps students temper their response to the gruesome opening of *No Country for Old Men*: while Chigurh's ruthless murder of the deputy sheriff may initially be entertaining to my students, they instinctually side with Bell, and their enjoyment of the scene is moderated by the knowledge that they gain from the five photographs and by their new understanding that border violence is ripping communities apart. Students' study of the border fosters a sense of maturity and gravity they might not otherwise bring to the start of the novel.

Right before we begin the book, I give students a list of statements to gauge their ideas about some of the more important concerns that we'll consider in class. They have to decide whether each statement is true or false, then we discuss their ideas. Three of the statements are as follows:

> The world is becoming an increasingly dangerous place.
> People are usually rewarded for doing the right thing.
> Money is money and it doesn't matter where it came from.

We revisit these ideas as we progress through the novel. Many of my students have been confident enough to admit that some of their ideas about the world have been changed by this book. For example, before they read the novel, students say during class discussion that the world is obviously getting more evil every day—and they cite the current underclassmen as an example! When I share with them the last epigraph in *Blood Meridian*, which reports on a 300,000-year-old skull that had been scalped, they tend to disregard my argument that the world has always had an element of darkness in it. But when they reach the end of *No Country for Old Men* and have read Uncle Ellis's assertion that the Southwest has always been a dangerous landscape, many of them accept that maybe this degeneracy of the world is not something new.

The novel also challenges the idea that people are usually rewarded for doing the right thing. Some students might initially believe that this idea is true, but when they read that Moss gets "caught" because he returned to bring the dying "dopedealer" water (McCarthy, *No Country* 26), some of them reflect that the idea may just be something they were told as children. To further explore the idea, I give students a writing assignment in which they must contrast two very similar scenes in *No Country for Old Men*. They pair up to examine the scene where Moss crosses the bridge after being shot by Chigurh and asks some teenage boys for a shirt, and then the scene in which Chigurh's truck gets T-boned and Chigurh asks another group of teenage boys for one of their shirts to use as a sling (116–17, 261). After studying these scenes, students, with their partners, write two paragraphs discussing their conclusions. They usually determine that McCarthy is telling readers in a not-so-subtle way that he does not believe that people get rewarded for being good, and that one is just as likely to be punished for good behavior. The assertion that people are rewarded for good behavior is something my students are used to hearing, and they realize by the end of the novel that the truth is not that simple. Strangers do not, as it turns out, treat our hero, Moss, better than they do the villain in the story. My students appreciate these realistic claims that McCarthy makes, and they often say that this is one of the first books they've read that tells them the truth.

The Common Core Learning Standards for New York State indicate requirements for the study of literature in each grade, and I write many of my assignments with these requirements in mind. For instance, one reading standard calls for students to consider why an author makes certain decisions, then to determine how those decisions affect a novel's overall meaning. For one assignment that addresses this standard, I ask students to form small groups and to examine similar lines of dialogue that Moss and Chigurh say in McCarthy's *No Country for Old Men*. The groups must then discuss how the quotations bear on the characters' current predicaments. The quotations we analyze, while spoken by different people, sound as though they could have been said by the same person. Moss, for example, tells the hitchhiker that there is no such thing as a clean slate. "It's not about knowing where you are. It's about thinkin you got there without takin anything with you. . . . You dont start over. . . . Ever step you take is forever" (227). Later, Chigurh tells Carla Jean something very similar: "Every moment in your life is a turning and every one a choosing. Somewhere you made a choice. All followed to this" (259).

When they complete this exercise, students arrive at a problematic conclusion: Moss seems to have a lot more in common, at least philosophically, with Chigurh, the novel's villain, than with the other protagonist, Bell. Students come to admire Moss's brave—if foolhardy—decision to accept the consequences of his actions instead of somehow atoning for his sins and begging, on his knees, in front of Chigurh. And while students certainly recognize the ruthless cruelty that allows Chigurh to murder Carla Jean in order to keep his word to a dead man, they also, when pressed, can now admit that Chigurh is at least honest about who he is.

The novel leads us to speculate about the impact of personal decisions on our world. We discuss how Moss endangers Carla Jean because he feels he can successfully navigate the situation he's in. We also examine the moment in the novel when an elderly woman is shot above the Aztec Theatre. She is accidentally murdered as a result of Moss's shootout with Chigurh, and Carson Wells declares that Moss is responsible for her death. While the chances are good that Moss did not kill her, Wells's claim leads my class to consider personal responsibility, luck, and fate, among other ideas. As Bell later says to Uncle Ellis, "When you're called on like that you have to make up your mind that you'll live with the consequences. But you dont know what the consequences will be" (278).

Some of the students' favorite assignments are geared toward determining characters' motivations. After reading chapter 5, for example, I ask students to write a letter from Bell to Moss, explaining why Moss must give up the money. Even though students don't yet know of Bell's inability to resolve his feelings about his mistake during the war, the best of these letters underscore the fact that Bell is scared for Moss and Carla Jean and seems to have experienced disappointment in the past, which serves to make him more determined to safeguard them. Even if students haven't yet read the story that Bell relates to Ellis, they understand that he is unlike some cops who may have pulled them over for speeding. They know that there is a lot at stake for Bell in protecting Moss and Carla Jean. One of the best letters written last year featured Bell telling Moss what a wonderful and loyal woman Carla Jean was, how much she loved Moss, and how incredibly selfish Moss was for putting her life in jeopardy.

When I first started teaching *No Country for Old Men* to my composition class, the students' ideas about whether Moss should take the money were largely philosophical. Many students in the composition class came from wealthier families, and the money Moss stumbles upon, while it sounds as though it could signify a change for him, did not draw the visceral reaction from those students that it does in my senior English class. Many of the students in senior English are not as privileged as those in the composition class; as a result, they react in markedly different ways to his discovery of the money. On the one hand, they understand that this money represents complete and sudden freedom from financial worry for Moss. He can allow Carla Jean to retire from Walmart. He can provide for her as he never dreamed he'd be able to. In discussion these students say that of course he should take the money. On the other hand, students in senior English who have a parent in prison tend to see the issue differently. When we discussed the scene in one class, these students shook their heads and told the rest of us that nothing good would come of Moss's decision and that the money wasn't worth the trouble it would bring. They believed that there were several warning signs Moss should have heeded, and they intuitively understood the line, "Moss absolutely knew what was in the case and he was scared in a way that he didnt even understand" (17).

Because it prompts so much debate, the scene where Moss decides to take the money ends up taking a half hour or more to discuss in my senior English class. The arguments can be passionate. The kids get upset, tell each other that the money isn't worth it, worry about the villain at the start of the novel, and fret over Moss's safety in the middle of the West Texas desert where he has no one to help him. Other students, especially those who have experience hunting, argue that Moss can obviously fend for himself. They cite his skills as a hunter and his weaponry to prove to their classmates that this is a man who is in his element, is a skilled—albeit cocky—marksman, and is familiar with the country in a way that the "drugrunners" are not (73).

By the time we're midway through the novel, the kids are typically really invested in the story. One day I came into class to see that one of my seniors had written "SOCKFEET" in huge letters across the chalkboard—referring to the compound neologism McCarthy uses to describe how Chigurh and Wells approach people stealthily by first taking off their shoes. Chigurh ultimately kills Wells, but before he does they have an interesting exchange—readers get to know Chigurh a bit better and consider his motivations. Once he kills Wells, I frustrate my students beyond all reckoning by stopping our progress in the novel. We pause to read an article entitled "What 'Psychopath' Means" (Lilienfeld) and discuss whether they feel Chigurh would be classified as a psychopath. After this discusson, students pair off to complete a cursory survey—the Levenson Self-Report Psychopathy Scale, which can be found online (openpsychometrics.org/tests/LSRP.php)—and to answer each question as they feel Chigurh would. In the survey, students are asked to respond to statements such as "For me, what's right is whatever I can get away with," "Most of my problems are due to the fact that other people just don't understand me," and "People who are stupid enough to get ripped off usually deserve it."

After students complete this twenty-six-question survey in pairs, we, as a class, complete the survey again; for this second round, the entire class has to agree on the answers. We view each statement on the projector screen, and students must make text-based arguments to defend their assertions about how Chigurh would respond. This activity takes forty-five minutes, or more if I have particularly opinionated kids in the class. The results of the test are provided to us on two scales: primary and secondary psychopathy. In each class that tests Chigurh, he always scores ninety percent higher than other test respondents, at least on the primary scale, and his high score indicates that he is indeed a psychopath.[1]

Students often change their answers based on the class discussion, and once that is done, they must write argumentative essays about whether Chigurh is indeed a psychopath. Even though there is ample evidence that he is one, without fail, the best, most provocative essays posit that Chigurh is not a psychopath; indeed, his behavior in *No Country for Old Men* does not match what the article suggests is typical psychopathic behavior. Students must cite evidence from both the novel and the article to back up their claims. Often, they will begin drafting the essay and then realize that they want to argue the opposite position.

One of the things that differentiates high school students from students in college is that high school kids tend to react viscerally to what they read.[2] This tendency has provided me with the means to approach some of the more powerful scenes in the book from a critical perspective. In the past, I would assign critical essays in my classes to show students exemplars of the analytical essay, but I did not have much success engaging my students with this method, in part because the material I chose was too difficult for them, but also because they just didn't care enough about the text they were reading to invest in what someone else had said about it. However, that all changed with *No Country for Old Men*. When the students grow concerned about the conflicts and characters in the novel, their emotional investment makes it easier to engage them in more challenging discussions of critical theory.

Once students have read the scene in which Moss dies, they write about McCarthy's decision to kill this character they have so much admiration for, and I try to interject as little as possible while they work their way through the writing exercise. Once we finish the novel and watch the film adaptation, directed by Ethan Coen and Joel Coen, my students are already so disappointed by what happens to Moss that when they read Dennis Cutchins's essay "Grace and Moss's End in *No Country for Old Men*," they are pleasantly surprised to find that a writer not only agrees with them but also takes their ideas and expounds upon them. Their fiery emotional response to Moss's death in both the novel and the film provides the means for them to engage in more cerebral criticism. They are willing to navigate Cutchins's essay, and they feel as though they have a stake in the conversation. The students agree with Cutchins when he writes, "I found myself disappointed by the film's insistent portrayal of the world as a meaningless place in which the lives of human beings are dictated solely by fate or happenstance" (156). Even before my students read the essay, one of them wrote that "Moss' death was different . . . the movie did not give his death any meaning. He originally died for being a good person, and in the novel he was shooting back at the Mexican [while attempting to defend the hitchhiker], while falling down the stairs." In general, the students feel that Moss's death in the novel is more tolerable because he dies a hero. They are troubled by what they perceive as the decision by the film's directors to strip Moss of his poignant and noble end.

Cutchins asserts that the film's "changes represent the Coens' rejection of McCarthy's notions of grace as well as his portrayal of a meaningful world"

(163). My students may not say it as eloquently, but they already lean toward the same interpretation when they watch the film. They feel that because the Coens eliminate the hitchhiker, Moss's character is not as well-developed in the film. Moss cannot reveal his philosophical beliefs in his advice for the hitchhiker. He cannot attempt to save her, and so he doesn't die a hero. Many students have difficulty enjoying the film for this reason. On the other hand, some of them struggle to accept that they are not being unfaithful to the novel if they also like the film. Many of my seniors have a very strong sense of justice and are powerfully affected by the Coens' decision to change this critically important detail of the novel.

Similarly, my students are surprised and disappointed that in the film adaptation Bell never shares his war story with Uncle Ellis. They feel that those two details—Moss's death while saving the hitchhiker and Bell's failure to stay with his troops during the war (McCarthy, *No Country* 237, 277–78)—are completely central to what McCarthy articulates about these characters in the novel. Bell's cowardice is the background upon which Moss's remarkable bravery plays out. Each character's actions amplify the other's. Students also notice and remark on less conspicuous issues in the text and the film. In the film, when Moss is speaking to Carla Jean on the phone while he's in the bus station, he checks out a random woman who happens by. One of my female students made a disapproving sound at that point, and later, when students had to contrast the two versions of *No Country for Old Men*, she wrote: "Moss would have never done that [in the novel]."

One of the fun discussion points in the novel stems from the leap that Bell makes when he posits that the criminal behavior in his county, and in the nation more broadly, originates in bad manners in young people with "green hair and bones in their noses" (McCarthy, *No Country* 295), even though, as Sonya Topolnisky points out, "[n]o people with green hair, under the influence of outside forces, enter into the plot" (121). As teenagers, my students are used to being viewed suspiciously: for instance, by shop owners who follow them around a store and wait for them to shoplift. Although they are on board with much of what Bell says until his explanation of criminal behavior, after reading this and similar statements, my students begin to question his misguided ideas about the state of the world.

However, despite their gradual realizations that Bell does not have the world figured out, my students still really like him. Perhaps they appreciate the fact that he is imperfect, that he tried to save Moss and Carla Jean, or that he has, for his entire life, attempted to atone for his actions in the war. The attachments that students form to the characters help them enjoy this novel more than any other that I've taught. Ironically, teaching *No Country for Old Men* for the first time to my senior English classes three years ago was an experiment that I did not expect would succeed. Indeed, I thought that students would more easily relate to *All the Pretty Horses*, even though it's more difficult to read, because the novel is a bildungsroman. But the experiment with *No Country for Old Men* was a success. And instead of attempting to teach a different text, I am content to take my cues from my students. It has been thrilling to teach a novel by my favorite author to a group so receptive to his work.

Last year after I finished teaching the novel, one of my classes was handing in their copies of the book. The students know where this text is shelved, and some of them have noticed that there is a class set of another McCarthy title in the cabinet. As they were handing in their copies of *No Country for Old Men* and taking copies of Jon Krakauer's *Into the Wild*, one of my students suggested that a revolt was in order because he had seen copies of another McCarthy book in the cabinets. He actually did take out a class set of *All the Pretty Horses*, before we all laughed, and he realized that he had to let McCarthy go.

Teaching *No Country for Old Men* has made me critical of all the other books I teach and the way I teach them. Its success in my senior English classes has challenged me to seek out this level of engagement and excitement in everything I do in my classroom.

NOTES

[1] Respondents generally take this cursory test because they feel as though they have psychopathic tendencies or because a psychotherapist has asked them to take it as part of an evaluation.

[2] Senior English students are often devastated when they learn that Moss gets killed in *No Country for Old Men*. One was so affected that the student's basketball game later that day was ruined. Another student cried. A few students in my classes last year slammed their books shut and declared that they were done with the novel and would not read any further.

Cosmology in *Outer Dark*

Christina Bieber Lake

Hans-Georg Gadamer writes, "The art of questioning is the art of questioning even further—i.e., the art of thinking" (84). Following Gadamer's lead, I believe that teaching in the humanities should be about opening up enduring questions for our students—the questions that drew many of them to college in the first place. Why are we here? What is the nature of existence? Why are we often inclined toward evil behavior? And most of all: what are we to make of our world? If helping students think deeply about such questions is the goal of teachers, then the work of Cormac McCarthy is a perfect fit for the classroom. Here is a contemporary American novelist who trades unflinchingly in the realities of evil and violence, but whose explanation for their existence cannot easily be pinned down. His cosmological imagination has been variously described as Gnostic, materialist, sacramental, postsecular, and nihilistic—among other things.

In literature, philosophy, or general education classes, teaching McCarthy's novel *Outer Dark* provides an exemplary way to host a structured and dynamic conversation on these issues. Coming in at a terse and suspense-filled 242 pages, it gives instructors the much-needed space to provide context, approach larger questions of form, and teach close reading skills—all while maintaining strong student interest in an exciting story. This essay suggests how instructors can set up a productive class discussion centered on cosmological questions raised by *Outer Dark*.

Setup and Structure

As James Lang argues, the difficulty with teaching anything, especially the more abstract questions of cosmology, comes down to context (91–111). We professors forget that students lack the dense connective tissue that years of advanced study have provided us. Often questions like "Is McCarthy's vision primarily Gnostic?" seem to them to come out of nowhere. The students can sense that the questions are large and important, but they can't find a way to grab onto them. Literary study as a discipline appeals to students in large part because the story's connection to real life gives them those handles.

Setting a basic philosophical foundation is thus critical to a cosmological discussion of *Outer Dark*. In an ideal world, students would have read (and be able to draw on) the Gnostic Gospels and the work of Augustine, Thomas Aquinas, Nietzsche, Darwin, and Hans Jonas—but the classroom is not an ideal world. I recommend using a handout that sets up the various metaphysical systems most commonly referred to in McCarthy's fiction. The appendix shows my version of this handout. After spending adequate time setting up the categories of metaphysical interpretation, I emphasize that these are not the only interpretive possibilities for this novel. The scholarly conversation surrounding McCarthy's work is dynamic, and we are getting just a glimpse of that conversation. To get students to work and to move around the classroom a bit, I ask them which of these cosmologies best describes *Outer Dark*, and then, depending on how they respond, I direct them to move to one of three places in the classroom. After the groups are in place, I deliberately sit in the least occupied section, which has a wonderfully unsettling effect on the students.

Then we set up some ground rules for how the discussion will proceed. On the board I write the following.

> What kind of story is *Outer Dark*? Is it an existentialist novel, a fable, a parable, a myth, or something else? What does its setting, structure, and point of view lead you to conclude?
>
> Which cosmology best explains the novel's opening, the ferry crossing, the act of cannibalism at the campfire, the pigs driven over the cliff, the murder of the infant, or any other scene you want to discuss?

The first set of questions will work only if the students have long been primed to think deeply about form. In all of my classes in recent years I have introduced a kind of mantra: literary studies exists as a discipline in part because we know that forms are never neutral. They make an argument, reflect a worldview, impose an order, or habituate individuals in some way. While in literature these forms go by terms like genre, structure, style, and plot, forms exist everywhere and do the same kind of work.[1]

Before we begin, I remind students to ground their arguments in the text. Students usually do well on their own at this point, but this discussion format can be modified according to their skill level and confidence. I sometimes have students write answers to the above questions before moving to their assigned spots, since doing so forces them to take a position without being influenced by their peers. Depending on the class dynamic, students can be asked to move during or at the end of the conversation if their original opinion changes. If the conversation gets stuck, instructors can stir the pot by referring to some of the arguments below. At the end of the conversation, students should be given the opportunity to reflect together on what arguments they found most persuasive and why.

The Naturalistic Interpretation

While *Outer Dark* sometimes seems like a fable, its depiction of the physical world is decidedly naturalistic. Culla and Rinthy Holme do not reside in hell, but in the rugged and unrelenting landscape of late-nineteenth- or early-twentieth-century Appalachia. Nothing that happens to them is either supernatural or mysterious. Their fate is determined by the accident of their births:

born into poverty, seclusion, and ignorance, they find an animal comfort in each other. But the laws of society oppress them with a profound moral guilt, and Culla is simply surviving the best he can when he abandons the product of their incestuous relationship in the forest. McCarthy emphasizes that the child's birth is an accident in the chilling paragraphs at the end of the first chapter, in which the baby "howled execration up on the dim camarine world of its nativity wail on wail while he lay there gibbering with palsied jawhasps, his hands putting back the night like some witless paraclete beleaguered with all limbo's clamor" (18). Culla falls down in the swamp, and like a bird coming out of its shell, he sees the hostility of the world this baby has been thrown into. The baby itself is a "shapeless white plasm" that struggles "like a lank swamp hare" and, from the perspective of the universe, is fundamentally no different from a hare (17). While McCarthy's diction makes the scene feel ancient and important, this is simply the move we've grown accustomed to from this postsecular writer. As Amy Hungerford might argue, the words "nativity" and "paraclete" give the text the feel of scripture, but without any of its authority or content.[2] The infant, like all of us, comes unbidden into this world and is wailing out a protest to its very existence.

Similarly, chance brings the tinker to this spot, just as chance dictates every encounter the main characters have from beginning to end. Rinthy is left without her baby. Culla is left wandering in the same swamp he started in, following a blind man. He has no hope for healing or redemption. The novel begins in spring and ends in spring, but this structure is emptied of any symbolic significance of new life or a new beginning.

The scene that makes the naturalistic case most decidedly is the one in which Culla crosses the river on the ferry (McCarthy, *Outer Dark* 165–67). Culla winds up alone, fighting helplessly against a seething, swallowing river and a screaming horse. The black fog needles his face and eyes. It is only luck that enables him to escape the ferry and end up nearer to the shore, where he can hear the river whispering, as if it were looking for him after having just missed its chance to kill him. When he calls out, no one answers, and there is not even an echo.

It is a part of the logic of naturalistic fiction that Culla would escape a furious river only to wash up on shore in the worst possible place: at the campfire of the three killers. The men have proved to be closer to animals than to human beings—one of them does not even have a name—and they are eating human flesh, which they offer to Culla. They steal the boots that Culla had stolen from the squire, proving that Culla is clearly not the fittest in this competitive world.

In this Darwinian landscape, the best explanation for Culla's general feelings of guilt and for his behavior toward his baby is the incest taboo, which is so powerful within Western culture that Culla has internalized it unconsciously. He knows that the baby must not live and that it is the necessary sacrifice for his sin—not against God, but against nature. The natural world is unforgiving to the weak. He should have known better than to leave the baby's death to chance; he should have killed and buried it.

Finally, critics as diverse as Vereen Bell and Hungerford have illustrated that McCarthy's metaphysical-sounding prose invites allegorical interpretation only to thwart it. Culla and Rinthy's ultimately fruitless quests prove only that meaninglessness is humanity's true condition. The scene in the swamp that ends the novel brings Culla and the readers back to the beginning. Culla has lost everything and has gotten nowhere.

> Late in the day the road brought him into a swamp. And that was all. Before him stretched a spectral waste out of which reared only the naked trees in attitudes of agony and dimly hominoid like figures in a landscape of the damned. . . . A stale wind blew from this desolation and the marsh reeds and black ferns among which he stood clashed softly like things chained. He wondered why a road should come to such a place.
>
> (McCarthy, *Outer Dark* 242)

Culla is left in a "spectral waste," and the narrator tells us not to expect anything more: "And that was all." As Bell argues, this return to the swamp highlights "the prevailing gothic and nihilistic mood of all of Cormac McCarthy's novels" as it "contributes an appropriately unaccommodating resolution to an otherwise inconclusive and highly unconventional narrative" (1). Human lives in the real world have similar endings, with no greater meaning or purpose.

The Gnostic Interpretation

The mythic form and feel of *Outer Dark* resolutely prevents a merely naturalistic reading. Though the setting can be identified as Appalachia, the novel gives no sense of time or place—it could be happening anywhere at any time. McCarthy's novel seems to be set in the outer dark itself—a place full of malevolent, spiritual forces, with no light to be found.

It would be difficult to conceive of a world more bereft of goodness than the one that McCarthy creates here. The baby is born, through an act of incest, to a completely ignorant and isolated couple. They have no community, real or imagined, to share their burdens or lead them out of ignorance. The birth seems to be part of a dark scheme that prompts Culla to do something, and the only thing he seems able to do is to reject life itself by abandoning his child. Indeed, Culla lives in such complete darkness that he cannot even get away from the scene of the crime. The world is itself bereft of moral guidance or direction:

> With full dark he was confused in a swampy forest, floundering through sucking quagmires and half running. He did not come upon the river but upon the creek again. Or another creek. He followed it down, in full flight now, the trees beginning to close him in, malign and baleful shapes that reared like enormous androids provoked at the alien and substantiality

> of this flesh colliding among them. Long and long after he should have reached the river he was careering through the woods with his hands outstretched before him against whatever the dark might hold. (16–17)

Culla, like Rinthy, has never been anywhere but lost in a darkness bent on providing him no escape. McCarthy's bizarre image of the trees as "enormous androids" emphasizes that human beings are utterly alien here: this world was never meant to be a home, and we are lost in it. It is no surprise that Culla finds himself back at the spot from which he was trying to escape. We are all thus imprisoned—as the text reads, everything is chained in the "landscape of the damned" (242). Any pity we might feel for Culla and Rinthy is for their ignorance of their true condition, an ignorance that all humans share. As Dianne Luce explains: the "Holme siblings together evoke the dualistic gnostic attitude: contempt for the ignorant principal in humankind and in the world, deep pity for the captive Divine spark in humanity" (*Reading* 105).

Since Gnosticism teaches that human reproduction is evil, it is no surprise that Rinthy's longing for the baby "imprisons her, as any obsession would," and that she gains nothing in her pursuit of it (Luce, *Reading* 102). Though the baby is saved by the tinker, we know this to be a temporary delay of its destiny, as the cosmic structure of the novel leads the tinker to an inexorable meeting with the demonic trio who roam the earth with no other purpose but to do evil. McCarthy emphasizes the spiritual quality of this meeting in the italicized sections that he uses to trace the characters' movements:

> *What discordant vespers do the tinker's goods chime through the long twilight and over the brindled forest road, him stooped and hounded through the windy recrements of day like those old exiles who divorced of corporeality and enjoined ingress of heaven or hell wander forever the middle warrens spoorless increate and anathema. Hounded by grief, by guilt, or like this cheerless vendor clamored at heel through wood and fen by his own querulous and inconsolable wares in perennial tin malediction.*
> (*Outer Dark* 229)

The passage takes as real the ghostly "old exiles" that it compares to the tinker here. The earth, like Dante's inferno, consists of spirits both living and dead who "wander forever the middle warrens" completely "spoorless," cheerless, and damned. The tinker meets his fate in this scene with the "grim triune" of evil men that readers meet before they meet anyone else in the novel, men who "moved in shadow altogether which suited them very well" (129, 3). The baby is never named—making it the parallel to one of these evil men, who does not need a name—and is abandoned, tortured, murdered, and possibly eaten. It has lost an eye, prompting Culla to remark that "he ort to have two," and one of the men to reply: "Maybe he ort to have more'n that. Some folks has two and cain't see" (232)—a clear reference to Culla himself.

The ending paragraphs of the novel emphasize that Culla's problem in this cosmos of the "outer dark" is primarily a spiritual one. He is led by a blind man on a road that goes back to where it all started—the swamp. Luce explains that "this appalling swamp, then, is the cosmos itself, depicted in imagery that is Dantean with a gnostic overlay: the cosmic underworld, stagnant water and wind, imprisoned beings. The sexual paranoia of the scene links it even more explicitly with the gnostic vision" (*Reading* 85). There is no growth, no change here. Culla is doomed to wander without purpose and without salvation.

The Augustinian Interpretation

Outer Dark is primarily a parable. Its effects depend on the biblical view of creation and incarnation that its structure and imagery deliberately invert. McCarthy sets the action in a hell-like world—the outer darkness where there is weeping and gnashing of teeth (Matt. 25.30)—in order to emphasize that evil is the absence of good. In a universe ordered by God, evil is the result of willful disobedience and leads inevitably into contempt for human life.

Treating *Outer Dark* like a parable, rather than a myth, novel, or allegory, best accounts for its placed placelessness.[3] Parables, as Sallie McFague has argued, are extended metaphors, not allegories or "example stories." In a parable, meaning is found within the story but not exhausted by it. A parable's purpose is to expand awareness (McFague 13). McCarthy's parable inverts the biblical story of the Incarnation of Christ in order to draw attention to, and speak prophetically against, humanity's potential for evil. The novel begins not with three magi following a star and visiting a Christ child but with the three marauders following the sun as it sets in the west. As they walk in the afternoon sun they can be seen "*pausing and grouping for a moment and going on again strung out in silhouette against the sun and then dropping under the crest of the hill into a fold of blue shadow with light touching them about the head in spurious sanctity*." They move until the sun goes down to "full dark." Then they start again the next day (*Outer Dark* 3).

After we witness these men moving across the landscape, a child is born. This child is not heralded but abandoned. He is fated to meet with the perverted magi who, instead of bringing gifts, serve to fulfill Herod's command to kill newborn sons.[4] Either these men or the tinker have wounded the child first such that it "had a healed burn all down one side of it and the skin was papery and wrinkled like an old man's. It was naked and half coated with dust so that it seemed lightly furred and when it turned to look up at him he saw one eyeless and angry red socket like a stokehole to a brain in flames" (231–32). This innocent child's death has no power to save and is the inevitable result of a world that has turned its back on God. The child's grisly murder has its closest analog in the fiction of Flannery O'Connor, in which any murder is meant to be understood literally first and symbolically second. The three marauders in *Outer Dark* are what the absence of the good looks like.[9] Culla, having already decided to kill his own child, and now wandering around supposedly looking for his sister, will be witness to the unavoidable outcome of his evil will. Just prior to the child's throat getting slit, Culla and the bearded man have this exchange:

> The bearded one was tunneling gouts of mud from the welt of his boot with a stick. Well, I see ye didn't have no trouble findin us.
>
> I wasn't huntin ye.
>
> You got here all right for somebody bound elsewhere.
>
> I wasn't bound nowheres. I just seen the fire.
>
> I like to keep a good fire. A man never knows what all might chance along. Does he?
>
> No.
>
> No. Anything's liable to warsh up. From nowheres nowhere bound.
>
> Where are you bound? Holme said.
>
> I ain't, the man said. By nothin. He looked up at Holme. We ain't hard to find. Oncet you've found us. (McCarthy, *Outer Dark* 232–33)

Culla, choosing to wander aimlessly in darkness instead of seeking the light, will find nothing but darkness and the men who are bound by it. Read parabolically in Augustinian terms, these men, who choose not to be bound by any moral law, are choosing a life bound by sin. No one is truly free from sin, and evil is not hard to find again, after you've chosen it once.

While this scene seems to express the Gnostic rule of *heimarmene*, or "universal Fate" (Jonas 43), that reading doesn't hold up well when considered alongside another parabolic biblical inversion, the scene with the hogs. Structurally unnecessary, the scene is symbolically central. The biblical story of the Gerasene demoniac appears in all three synoptic Gospels. The longest of these stories is in Mark, where we learn that the possessed man lives in the tombs and is so far gone that he cannot be restrained by chains (5.3). Christian tradition holds that the scene is given so much narrative weight because it is about revelation and recognition. Jesus recognizes that evil spirits are corrupting an otherwise good man. Similarly, the demons recognize that Jesus is the son of God. They thus appeal to him not to send them away but to cast them into the herd of hogs. In a moment not without irony and humor, Jesus obliges them, and the herd runs violently into the sea, where the hogs drown, destroying the demons when they could have been exiled instead.

McCarthy's scene also seems concerned primarily with recognition—but in this case Culla is falsely accused of inciting the herd to panic and rush into the river, carrying the drover Vernon to his death. Yet readers—the only witnesses to all of his actions—know that Culla is guilty of far worse. "Everybody seen what he done, Billy said. You all seen it" (*Outer Dark* 222). The dark humor of the scene pays homage to O'Connor's vision, and functions the same way. Culla deserves the sentence that the preacher (who just happens to be walking by) apophatically suggests to the men. "The preacher had begun to gesture inanely with his cane. Boys I believe he's plumb eat up with the devil in him. But don't hang him" (223). Faced with being hanged or flung into the river, Culla is forced to jump, and the river leads him back to the grim triune and the grisly murders of the tinker and the baby.

Jesus sees the good in the demoniac, exorcises his evil demon, and returns the man to health. "Clothed and in his right mind," the man then becomes a witness by spreading the word about what Jesus has done for him (Mark 5.15). An Augustinian reading of *Outer Dark* requires that witnesses—readers—similarly recognize evil as evil, judge accordingly, and be challenged to see the goodness in every human being. McCarthy's novel would be emptied of its power if its writer could not count on the reader's horror at the murder of the innocent infant. Rinthy elicits our empathy because we recognize that her instinct to protect her child is good. As a character in a parable designed to feature the corrupting absence of good, Rinthy will not be able to save the child. But as Matthew Potts insists, "her love—even in all its ignorance, trauma, and weakness—cannot be denied either, nor can the feeble, frail, frank holiness of it" (186). Thus we finish reading *Outer Dark* confronted with a picture of the damning effects of our own depravity as humans, and with the wisp of an idea that this story is not the final word on it.

As I mention above, it is wise to leave space at the end of the conversation to discuss where students end up with their thinking about the novel, and why. Although I argue for the naturalistic, Gnostic, and Augustinian interpretations of *Outer Dark* as if they could be conclusive, the students quickly discover that a definitive interpretation may not exist and that what they have instead is more questions. They leave the class with a productive confusion and, if all goes well, a strong desire to return to McCarthy's fiction.

NOTES

[1] Levine's work can help students understand the importance of form. Levine borrows the concept of affordance from design theory, where it describes "the potential uses or actions latent in materials and design. Glass affords transparency and brittleness. Steel affords strength, smoothness, hardness, and durability" (6). When carried over to literary forms, this concept helps students see that identifying the genre, style, structure, and other formal elements is essential to understanding how any text does its work.

[2] Hungerford reads *Blood Meridian* and *The Road* as strong examples of a belief in belief itself. She views *Blood Meridian* as a sentimental novel, "designed to make us feel, above all, like God is speaking, but to leave us in possession only of the unreadable aesthetic object, like the illiterate kid clutching his Bible" (95).

[3] See Hillier, "In a Dark Parody," for an argument that the novel should be read allegorically.

[4] Reading the three men as an unholy trinity, as Spencer does, also supports the position that *Outer Dark* is an inversion or parody of biblical ideas.

[5] There are similarities between this approach to reading the novel and that of Metress, who suggests that McCarthy has a largely apophatic theological vision—in which we can know spiritual truths only through a *via negativa*, a way of unknowing.

APPENDIX
Metaphysics in *Outer Dark*

To help students consider whether McCarthy's cosmological vision is primarily naturalistic, Gnostic, or Augustinian, the following handout provides background on these three metaphysical systems and on how they have been used by scholars to interpret the novel.

Naturalism

In philosophy, naturalism has an ontological and a methodological component. According to the *Stanford Encyclopedia of Philosophy*, "the ontological component is concerned with the contents of reality, asserting that reality has no place for 'supernatural' or other 'spooky' kinds of entity. By contrast, the methodological component is concerned with ways of investigating reality, and claims some kind of general authority for the scientific method" (Papineau).

In literature, naturalism reached its height in the late nineteenth century in the works of Émile Zola, Stephen Crane, Frank Norris, and Theodore Dreiser. Though it takes a variety of forms, it can generally be defined by the idea that one's fate is determined by heredity, environment, and chance. Human behavior, according to this idea, is almost entirely determined by forces outside our control.

Naturalism in literature often depicts nature as hostile to humans and the universe as indifferent to human fate. There is often a Darwinian component to human and animal behavior in this literature, which highlights the fight-or-flight instincts of characters and showdowns that result in the survival of the fittest.

Naturalism views death as the natural end of everything and as offering no redemption.

In *The Achievement of Cormac McCarthy* Vereen Bell argues that *Outer Dark* is "as brutally nihilistic as any serious novel written in this century in this unnihilistic country" (34). McCarthy's novels invite but thwart allegorical interpretation; the writing in them foregrounds the "episodic nature of experience itself" over "what it leads to or how our moral natures are shaped by it or what principles might be inferred from it" (5).

Gnosticism

Quotations and ideas below are from Hans Jonas, *The Gnostic Religion*.

Gnosticism is syncretistic, and there are many versions of it in ancient cosmology, which have been perpetuated through myth. These versions share discernible principles.

Gnosticism is fundamentally dualistic: the cosmos is dark and alien to God, who is light. Gnosticism therefore has contempt for nature: creation means existing in a fallen state, and God is unknowable through it.

The Archons (sadistic rulers) created humans to keep them imprisoned in the cosmos. "Outer dark" is thus the whole cosmos and the human condition (43).

The goal of the Gnostic religion is to transcend to the true light that is God through knowledge (gnosis) of our condition and how we are trapped in it, knowledge that others may be numb or asleep to. "The Soul slumbers in Matter" (69). We are to be led by an "Alien Man" (Jesus, in the Gnostic Gospels) who can show us the way out our condition. Each person contains a divine spark that longs for reconnection to the light.

The Gnostic response to the guilt and ignorance at the center of our experience is to replace the concept of sin with the concept of ignorance, so that gnosis is the solution.

Asceticism is encouraged because the "reproductive scheme is an ingenious archontic device for the indefinite retention of souls in the world" (145). In the Valentinian version of Gnosticism, the first children were the products of rape (205).

Gnosticism is a repudiation of the Greek idea of order in the cosmos as a positive concept. "Order and law is the cosmos here too, but rigid and inimical order, tyrannical and evil law, devoid of meaning and goodness, alien to the purposes of man and to his inner essence, no object for his communication and affirmation. A world emptied of divine content had its own order: an order empty of divinity" (250).

Dianne Luce in *Reading the World* has called *Outer Dark* a "gnostic nightmare," arguing that Gnosticism is the most consistently evoked metaphysical system in McCarthy's work that is avowedly syncretistic (92). Luce's basic idea is that the novel reflects not a modern conception of Gnosticism but an ancient one that is more Manichaean, in which an original principle of darkness animates every part of creation.

Augustinianism

Quotations below are from Augustine, *The Enchidiron on Faith, Hope and Charity*.

The basic idea of Augustinianism is that evil is not being but the privation of good. We recognize evil because we have a sense of the goodness of creation.

All things have been created by a divine trinity who is supremely, equally, and unchangeably good—but all other beings are not supremely, equally, or unchangeably good (40).

The universe is well ordered to reveal the goodness of the good by contrast with evil. God would not allow any evil to exist if God were unable to bring good out of it (41). "If there were nothing good, there would be nothing that could be called bad" (43).

You can corrupt a thing almost completely, but for it to be completely evil it would have to cease to exist. Therefore if something exists, there is still some good in it. "Corruption cannot consume good without consuming the thing itself" (42).

God is the only cause of good, "while the cause of our evils is the will of the changeable good falling away from the unchangeable good, first the will of an angel, then the will of a human being" (57).

Why does evil exist? God "judged it better to bring good out of evil than to allow nothing evil to exist" (60).

To be free to do good, one must be redeemed by God. "We are truly made free when God makes us, that is, forms and creates us, not that we may be men, which he has already done, but that we may be good men: this he does now by his grace, that we may be a new creation in Christ, according to the saying, create a pure heart in me, oh God" (64).

Matthew Potts argues that McCarthy's debt to "Augustinian semiotics and the theology of the cross" means that goodness is often best revealed negatively (10). McCarthy's novels mean to defy the cruelty that they portray. Signs of sacrament exist, as do acts of goodness and love, and such acts, "as rare and as futile as they sometimes are in these novels, do not fail to be real or worthwhile because of their rarity and futility" (14).

The Road, Consumerism, and Consumption

Scott D. Yarbrough

I would guess that *The Road* is the most read and the most taught of all of Cormac McCarthy's novels and that it has been for a number of years. There are a number of reasons why this might be the case: The prose in *The Road* is more approachable than that of some of McCarthy's more difficult works, and although the circumstances of the plot are abhorrent, they are no more so than in earlier novels such as *Child of God*, *Outer Dark*, and *Blood Meridian*. Readers of those three novels may find little sympathy for their protagonists, whereas readers of *The Road* can easily and without equivocation root for the wandering man and his son. Furthermore, the apocalyptic quest narrative in *The Road* seems firmly rooted in literary and religious imagery that invites close readings and engenders class discussions. The novel has received both critical acclaim, as demonstrated by its winning the Pulitzer Prize, and popular approbations, represented by its selection for Oprah Winfrey's book club.

Course Framework

I teach the novel every semester and have found that it works best in my Survey of American Literature class. Typically the survey is a sophomore-level course; I've taught it both in a two-semester format (in which the first part of the course loosely follows the chronology of North American colonization through the Civil War, and the second part runs from the post–Civil War era through the present) and a one semester format. *The Road* acts as a capstone to the course, which briefly considers the view of colonial expansion as self-interest in John Smith's *A Description of New England*; the origination and codification of the American dream in *The Autobiography of Benjamin Franklin*; and the dark side of capitalist greed and American expansionism in narratives by Frederick Douglass, Harriet Jacobs, and Henry David Thoreau. Students examine what happens when the American dream becomes not a quest for economic fulfillment in *The Great Gatsby* but a means by which one's worth is determined by one's material accumulations and societal status.

And finally, following all this, we have the grim apotheosis of *The Road*. The novel not only presents a biblical apocalypse but also stands as a stark warning of what may occur when unchecked consumerism and consumption reach their ultimate end. The only way the father and his son can survive is by scavenging for packaged goods and the other scattered remnants of a culture obsessed with consumption rather than sustainability, and these two protagonists in turn become commodities that are in danger of being consumed.

The American Dream

In my surveys, we spend some time discussing the notion that national identity is less about birthplace and more about the ideas and cultural practices that people participate in both knowingly and subconsciously. Accordingly, one of the earlier assigned readings in my surveys is Smith's *A Description of New England*.[1] In this report, published in 1616, Smith extolls the virtues of the New World in order to convince Europeans, and particularly the English, to immigrate to and colonize North America.

We consider in class how two common themes present themselves in *A Description of New England*. The first theme is of the New World as an escape from the rigid class strictures of the Old World. As Smith says, he is "not so simple to think, that ever any other motive than wealth, will ever erect there a commonwealth." However, immigrants will find in North America that

> [h]ere nature and liberty affords us that freely, which in England we want, or it costeth us dearly. What pleasure can be more, than (being fired with any occasion a-shore, in planting vines, fruits, or herbs, in contriving their own grounds, to the pleasure of their own minds, their fields, gardens, orchards, buildings, ships, and other works, &c), to *recreate* before their own doors, in their own boats upon the sea. . . . (71; emphasis added)

Present in the writing of one of the earliest English explorers and colonizers, then, are the germs of what much later became a significant component of the American dream: the idea that no matter who you are, how rich or poor your family is, or where you come from, you can come to this wondrous place and recreate yourself. You can determine your own destiny. Smith's efforts to entice his audience to immigrate to the New World were aided by the development of nascent capitalism in seventeenth-century Britain, brought on in part by the growing practice of enclosure, which limited peasant access to lands for feeding livestock and farming and allowed the aristocracy to capitalize its holdings. Enclosure reduced access to land, and the new stress on landownership would make Smith's vision of a fertile New World more appealing to his English readers.

The second common theme that presents itself in *A Description of New England* is the assumption that North America exists as something to be consumed; this theme perhaps operates as a sad counter to the optimistic notion of the germinal American dream expressed above. We consider in class Smith's claim that in the New World a man is a "very bad fisher [who] cannot kill in one day with his hook and line, one, two, or three hundred cods: which dressed and dried . . . [could] be sold . . . for ten shillings the hundred"; Smith goes on to note that if "a man work but three days in seven, he may get more than he can spend, unless he will be excessive" (71). And so, from the very founding of the

English colonies, the search for financial gain to change one's place in life was one of the primary lures used to bring Europeans to North America, but so too was the notion that the New World provided an inexhaustible bank of natural resources to be harvested.

With Smith behind us, we examine in class how Benjamin Franklin codifies this idea that one can shape one's own destiny and can, with sufficient hard work, change one's economic status and place in society. A printer, author, scholar, scientist, inventor, diplomat, and statesman, Franklin creates in his autobiographical portrait a symbol for what the new nation might offer. In my class we focus less on how historically accurate *The Autobiography of Benjamin Franklin* is and more on the way Franklin uses events from his life to illustrate certain ideas that came to represent the American dream even as the nation was founded. He informs readers that his family came from "Ecton in Northhamptonshire" and had been there for some "300 years" on a "freehold of about 30 acres, aided by the Smith's Business which had continued in the Family" (249).[2]

Franklin, we are to understand, was no aristocrat but instead was lowborn. He tells how his father had seventeen children, of whom he remembers thirteen "sitting at one time at his table," Franklin himself being "the youngest Son and the youngest Child but two" (251). So, not only was he born to working-class parents, but he was also the youngest son and fifteenth out of seventeen children. At a time when even the poor often observed the practice of primogeniture, he stood to inherit very little from his father's candle-making business.

Franklin describes his younger self as a kind of model for the Enlightenment: he taught himself to improve his writing and to tackle difficult texts, and he strove to improve his proficiency in such areas as mathematics and geometry. Aflame with intellectual curiosity, he read more and more complicated materials. I like to tease my students, pointing out that he wasn't getting any college credit or a new car for good grades. He worked so hard (if we can believe him) because of an earnest desire to learn and to improve himself.

We discuss Franklin's move to Philadelphia, where the writer arrived with virtually no money and was "very hungry," his "whole Stock of Cash consist[ing] of a Dutch dollar and about a shilling in copper" and his pockets "stuff'd out with Shirts and Stockings" (263). From this origin, however, grows the legend of Franklin: armed with this desire to learn, with this need to improve himself and thus his place in life, he found amazing success. He published great advances in the physics of electricity, he invented the lightning rod, he became a well-known printer, and he invented bifocals. He aided Thomas Jefferson in writing the Declaration of Independence, and as a diplomat he helped convince France to join the Revolutionary War on behalf of the colonies. Although he was not a signatory to the United States Constitution, he was present during the framing of the document.

But I remind students that, as many writers have pointed out over the years, there was a serpent in the American Eden from its very inception, a fatal flaw in the heart of the American dream: slavery. The horrors of what nineteenth-century writers sometimes called the peculiar institution are well documented in Douglass's *Narrative of the Life of Frederick Douglass, an American Slave*, published in 1845, and Harriet Jacobs's 1861 book *Incidents in the Life of a Slave Girl*. These stories are telling indictments of the transgressions and failures of the founding leaders of the republic. In a nation that allowed the lawful practice of slavery, slaves and fugitive slaves like Douglass were not full-fledged consumers but were instead commodities, something to be consumed.

At the same time, Douglass's life paralleled Franklin's in a few interesting ways. Working with obstacles the likes of which Franklin never faced, Douglass, too, privileged education in his life and struggled to learn to read and write, having to overcome the rules of his owner, who forbade him to be taught. But having taught himself, he eventually picked up a book of short essays for recitation titled *The Columbian Orator*, just as Franklin famously discovered an "odd Volume of *The Spectator*" (256). Reading *The Columbian Orator*, Douglass found in an essay by the Irish writer Richard Sheridan a "bold denunciation of slavery, and a powerful vindication of human rights." Reading this and other essays gave Douglass a perspective and understanding of his status as a slave and changed his life forever. Going forward, he writes, the "silver trump of freedom had roused my soul to eternal wakefulness. Freedom now appeared, to disappear no more forever" (963). Douglass went on to become one of the nation's most significant activists against slavery and became such a prominent leader of the African American community that he met with Abraham Lincoln to discuss the plights of African American soldiers fighting for the Union during the Civil War.

The context of these and other slavery narratives are in the minds of my students when we discuss Thoreau's "Civil Disobedience" ("Resistance") and its reaction to President James K. Polk's push to realize manifest destiny through the Mexican War of 1846–48.[3] Despite Thoreau's and others' resistance to the war, the United States carried it out and soon annexed California, as well as New Mexico, Utah, Nevada, and Arizona. These territories were, in a sense, consumed by the growing American state.

The Great Gatsby *and Background Readings*

In preparation for reading Fitzgerald's 1925 novel *The Great Gatsby*, the class discusses background readings on modernism. What happens, I ask my students, when American culture judges people based on how much money and how much property they have managed to accumulate—in short, how much capital they've assembled and consumed? In the version of this course that is for sophomores, we mostly deal with critical theory loosely, in conversation, whereas in upper-division classes I assign essays and book excerpts to help provide an overview and some examples of the critical theory in practice. In both lower- and upper-division versions of the course, though, I provide students with chapter 4 of Thorstein Veblen's significant 1899 book *The Theory of the Leisure Class* (49–69). In this work, Veblen coins the term "conspicuous consumption" (49), and we read how

> [t]he quasi-peaceable gentleman of leisure . . . consumes freely and of the best, in food, drink, narcotics, shelter, services, ornaments, apparel, weapons and accoutrements, amusements. . . . Since the consumption of these more excellent goods is an evidence of wealth, *it becomes honorific*; and conversely, *the failure to consume in due quantity and quality becomes a mark of inferiority and demerit.* (64–65; emphases added)

I also make available for students two chapters from Raymond Williams's *Marxism and Literature* (75–82, 108–14) and chapter 10 from John Kenneth Galbraith's *The Affluent Society* (114–23). Armed with these readings, we move on to *The Great Gatsby*, a novel that shows the dark side of a dream based on gain and consumption. I require students to write a short response to the novel (twelve hundred words) using two of the three provided background readings (Veblen, Williams, or Galbraith).

The school of theory that my students generally find most relevant and easiest to apply to *The Great Gatsby* is literary Marxism. Again, in lower-division courses I don't overstress the theoretical approach, but I do make use of the perspectives from Williams's chapters as well as the more general economic points in the works by Veblen and Galbraith. As we delve into the novel, I remind students of Galbraith's observation in *The Affluent Society*:

> Yesterday the man with a minimal but increasing real income was reaping the satisfactions which came from a decent diet and a roof that no longer leaked water on his face. Today, after a large increase in his income, he has extended his consumption to include cable television and eccentric loafers. But to say that his satisfactions from these latter amenities and recreations are less than from the additional calories and the freedom from rain is wholly improper. (121–22)

As Galbraith notes, affirming Veblen's ideas in the passage quoted above, it follows that once a "society sets great store by the ability to produce a high living standard," that society will then evaluate "people by the products they possess" rather than by other more ephemeral standards, such as their character and aspirations (Galbraith 126).

In the novel, Jay Gatsby is perhaps as much to blame as Tom Buchanan for the dashing of Gatsby's dreams and for the trap Gatsby sets himself and willingly enters into, but he is churned up in the gristmill of American affluence after the Great War. During the climatic gathering in Tom's town apartment, Tom rebuffs Daisy's request that he show restraint. Tom says, "I suppose the latest thing is to sit back and let Mr. Nobody from Nowhere make love to your wife. Well, if that's the idea you can count me out" (Fitzgerald 130). His remark suggests that Gatsby's blue-collar roots are as much a problem as his wife's retributive affair with Gatsby. Indeed, from the start Tom seems to be on to Gatsby's connections to bootleggers. When Tom examines Gatsby's house and the trappings of conspicuous wealth after one of Gatsby's extravagant parties, he asks Nick Carraway, "Who is this Gatsby, anyhow? . . . Some big bootlegger?" Tom explains, "A lot of these newly rich people are just big bootleggers, you know" (107). Tom, as a scion of an upper-class family, a man who owns capital handed down to him from previous generations and whose "freedom with money was a matter for reproach" (6) even in college, appoints himself as a kind of gatekeeper: since Gatsby is new money, he isn't worthy of joining the upper class. Tom's belief in rigid class boundaries frustrates Gatsby's ambition to achieve a higher social status through acquisition, an ambition that Daisy inspires in Gatsby: as a poor young officer with no past, Gatsby wasn't worthy of her; when he becomes a man of wealth, on the other hand, she finds him suitable.

The Road *as the Apotheosis of Consumption*

Like *The Great Gatsby*, *The Road* may seem to be a simple novel on the surface, but in fact it is complex enough to inspire readings from a diversity of perspectives. Among the more pervasive readings are ones that identify the novel's setting as the aftermath of a nuclear war that has left civilization in ruins. Equally popular are ecocritical readings that focus on the human despoliation of nature and its horrific apotheosis in *The Road*. I talk about both approaches in the class, and I spend a good amount of time discussing the messianic, Christological, and Catholic imagery that is layered throughout the book.[4] For our purposes, the Christian imagery is most significant for the way it coincides with the novel's other pervasive motif, cannibalism, which provides an entry into discussion of an intratextual theme in McCarthy's work: the Eucharist.

The more common term for the sacrament of the Eucharist is *communion*. According to the *Oxford English Dictionary*, communion also means "[t]he fact of being associated in one's actions or relations" or "sharing or holding something in common with others" ("Communion *N.*," defs. 1a and 1b). The ritualistic breaking of bread that recurs in McCarthy's texts operates as a Eucharistic signifier, evoking yet repudiating the cannibalistic perversion of the sacrament. Scenes depicting the sharing of meals and drinks occur repeatedly throughout McCarthy's body of work and almost always take on a symbolic resonance. There are significant communal meals or drinks in *Suttree*, *All the Pretty Horses*, *The Crossing* (where they are especially frequent; see Arnold, "McCarthy"), and *The Sunset Limited*. As is the case in these other works, the shared meals in *The Road* have a ritualistic quality, whether they are between the man and his son or they also include Ely, whom the man and boy offer sustenance. These acts of breaking bread evoke in all these books the taking of bread and wine, the figurative act of entering into communion with Christ, God, and other members of the faith.

In communion, taking and eating the bread or host acts as either the literal or symbolic consumption of the flesh of Christ; drinking the wine signifies the consumption of Christ's blood. Between this ritualistic observation of Christ's sacrifice and the perversion of it in McCarthy's *The Road* by cannibalistic predators, we see a transformative rupture. The reasonable fear that the father holds for other travelers, and his lack of willingness to feed or trust others, demonstrates how removed he is from the communion of believers and the fellowship of humankind, just as he is divorced from communion with God. When he thinks of God he angrily wishes to "throttle" God and, failing the test of Job not to succumb to desire, he damns God (11).

The Bible says that Christ offers himself to be consumed because "God did not send his Son into the world to condemn the world, but in order that the world might be saved through him" (*Holy Bible*, English Standard Version, John 3.17). Christ rejects consumption in order to be consumed. On the other hand, the roving bands of cannibals in *The Road* take rather than offer. They seek not to enter into communion with their fellow humans but to reduce them to the status of a consumable commodity.

As we discuss these motifs, I ask my students how we might tie them more deeply to the themes discussed all semester. We note that the landscape of McCarthy's *The Road* is an "ashen scabland," which is "[b]arren, silent, godless" (17, 4). Atmospheric ash seems to have permanently blocked out the sun's nourishing rays, and nothing can be grown or harvested. In fact, throughout the novel, we find evidence that nothing in the post-apocalyptic milieu is produced at all. Instead, materials and food are only consumed. The implication is that all the people in the novel spend all their time in an ongoing search for food. Given the destruction of the natural world and the attendant disappearance of livestock, which has presumably been eaten or has starved to death for lack of grazing, humans have two choices for survival: subsistence by cannibalism or by scavenging the comestible remnants of the consumer society that has disappeared. In an essay I make available to students on reserve, Jordan J. Dominy draws connections between cannibalism and consumer culture, writing that

> *The Road* is cannibalism as a critique of unchecked consumption of environmental resources and the products made with them. Images of marketing, branding, and shopping have survived the catastrophe and serve as markers of past consumption that have outlived its own heyday. The landscape of the novel features "billboards advertising motels. Everything as it once had been save faded and weathered" (8). In some towns the pair travel through, bill-boards are painted over to create a clean space to write warning messages, but "through the paint could be seen a pale palimpsest of advertisements for goods which no longer existed" (127–28). The communication that endures is the plea to purchase a product.
>
> (Dominy 147–48)

Dominy points out that the only brand name in the novel is Coca-Cola, which is first mentioned in the scene where the father manages to extract a can of soda for his son from an old vending machine. In another article that I place on reserve for students, Brian Donnelly examines the use of Coca-Cola and notes that "[t]he novel describes the demise of humanity in the same terms as those articulated in the Coke incident: a detrimentally excessive consumption finds both its apotheosis and its apocalypse in cannibalism, the utter and abject dissolution of recognizable society" (72).

Coca-Cola shows up a second time in McCarthy's *The Road* when the father and son are holed up in a bunker (in both scenes the drink is referred to by its full name and not by the abbreviation Coke). The father refuses to drink much of the soda, preferring the boy to have it. In one of his typical flashes of insight, the son asks, "It's because I wont ever get to drink another one, isnt it?" (22). The scene is telling because it reinforces at an early stage in the novel how much the world has changed; additionally, the scene provides us with a profound sense of loss. I ask my students to consider, despite all the shortcomings of modern civilization, how bereft they would feel if we lost so many of our modern conveniences: not only fast food and sodas but also modern printing processes, telecommunication, antibiotics, and laser surgeries.

It is important for instructors to warn students that McCarthy is much more given to describing and questioning in his novels than he is to proselytizing. Ascribing to this famously reticent author a point of view presented in one of his texts is always a significant example of the intentional fallacy. Although *The Road* demonstrates a failed consumerist society, McCarthy still understands the value, convenience, and ease of modern civilization. When the novel's two protagonists find the bunker, the "richness of a vanished world" (147) rendered in a small oasis, we again see all that is lost: the certitude of a next meal, comfort, convenience, and safety. And although the boy earlier assumes that they will never again have a Coca-Cola, in the bunker he and his father are able to share mugs of the soda. The father rightly understands, however, that the soda is simply a remnant of what has been lost. Upon finding a "double handful of gold krugerrands" hidden in the bunker, he "kneads" them a moment and then returns them to where he found them. They no longer have value, their worth having vanished with our modern world (151).

The connection in the novel between cannibalism, consumerism, and lack of production is made most clear when the father and son find the remains of a cooked newborn infant. The horrific scene recalls lines from W. B. Yeats's poem "The Second Coming," "The blood-dimmed tide is loosed, and everywhere / The ceremony of innocence is drowned," and it also evokes Jonathan Swift's 1729 essay "A Modest Proposal." Just as that essay uses a bloody and satiric proposal of legal societal infanticide and cannibalism to offer a commentary on the British treatment of the Irish, McCarthy's depiction of the desecration and eating of infants show a grim furtherance of *The Road*'s theme of consumption: nothing is grown, only consumed.

As my students like to point out in our class discussion, the consumption theme meshes entirely with the novel's other primary themes. The ecocritical readings of the novel are even further supported by the inability of humans in the novel to quit consuming in the face of disaster. To further build context, we discuss how in American literature the wilderness has often proved a place of respite wherein a protagonist can gain perspective and seek renewal. I remind students how in Mark Twain's *The Adventures of Huckleberry Finn*, the river and eventually the untamed territories allow Huck to grow free of the contaminating restraints of society. In a number of Ernest Hemingway's works, including *The Sun Also Rises* and "Big Two-Hearted River" (parts 1 and 2), nature provides a sanctuary wherein men who have been wounded (emotionally as well as physically) can be healed in some sense. In William Faulkner's novella "The Bear," Ike McCaslin enjoys such communion with nature that he comes to reject all material things that have been handed down to him and that carry the sinful taint of slavery (*Go Down, Moses* 109–206).

In McCarthy's *The Road*, however, nature provides no respite. All the animals are dead. Trout no longer dart by in streams. Deer, which might sustain a hunter and his family, no longer linger in the deep woods. The sun cannot break through the ashen skies to nourish the desiccated lands. Even when the father and son seek refuge in a forest, they're awakened when the burned-out trees begin falling about them until, rising the next morning, they find that "the cedar trees lay about in hillocks of snow and broken limbs and a few standing trunks that stood stripped and burntlooking in the graying landscape" (98). There is nothing left in nature; all has been consumed by humanity and by whatever event has precipitated the end of civilization—everything, that is, save the remnants of a consumer culture: canned foods and a can of Coca-Cola.

In essay questions on the final exam, I ask students to reconcile the various readings with the themes we have discussed throughout the semester. The more astute students note that the readings based on the abundant Christological imagery throughout *The Road* also dovetail with a discussion of consumption and consumerism. Christ famously rids the temple in Jerusalem of money changers and merchants, telling them that they have made of God's house a "den of robbers" (*Holy Bible*, English Standard Version, Matt. 21.12–13). Earlier in Matthew, a wealthy young man comes to Jesus, explains that he has done all that is required by the Jewish holy laws, and asks, "What do I still lack?" Jesus replies, "If you would be perfect, go, sell what you possess and give to the poor, and you will have treasure in heaven; and come, follow me." The gospel passage continues, "When the young man heard this he went away sorrowful, for he had great possessions" (19.20, 19.21, 19.22). In essence, Christ calls upon him to reject consumerism and consumption and to instead sacrifice of himself. The disciples, following Christ's crucifixion and eventual ascendance to heaven, follow these words, and Acts has it that "[t]here was not a needy person among them, for as many as were owners of lands or houses sold them and brought the proceeds of what was sold and laid it at the apostles' feet, and it was distributed to each as any had need" (4.34–35). The son, McCarthy's stand-in for a messiah or Christ figure in *The Road*, refuses to hoard his or the father's food—practical and necessary as it is to do so—and repeatedly wishes to enter into sacrificial communion with others whom he and his father encounter: the man struck by lightning, the lost boy, the thief, and Ely. After Ely has departed, the father regrets having shared food with him and tells the son, "When we're out of food you'll have more time to think about it." The son responds, after a while, "I know. But I wont remember it the way you do" (174).

In Hemingway's "Hills Like White Elephants," first published in 1927 and now widely anthologized, the young woman nicknamed Jig, who is the lover and probably the wife of "the American" who is her traveling companion, stares over the Ebro river to where there are "fields of grain and trees" and where life prospers (298). The American, unnerved at the thought of how having a child would change their lives, wishes for her to have an abortion. But seeing these signifiers of life blooming and growing across the river, Jig says, "And we could have all this. . . . And we could have everything and every day, we make it more impossible" (298). Like so many people of their generation, they've lost track of what life is supposed to hold for people and have tried to drown it out in travel, sightseeing, drinking, and excess.

Jig and her lover see their world from different points of view. In a similar vein, the ending of the *The Road* offers clashing perspectives. Proponents of a cynical reading of McCarthy's novel are right to focus on the final passage and its warning that there are things "which could not be put back. Not be made right again" (227). But the preceding section shows a family that is willing to forego its own increase of capital and its own ability to consume enough in order to take in and care for the boy. Its members have learned the lesson that the world in *The Road* has taught them: if humans have any chance for survival, meager as that chance might be, surely they must cleave together and struggle alongside, rather than against, one another. This is the lesson that Jig, in "Hills Like White Elephants," has understood and wishes her companion to understand. If we can learn to live within our resources, and not engage in a Darwinian struggle to constantly increase our status and capital through consumption, we might transcend to a place where we can plumb the mysteries of the old places of the world.

NOTES

[1] In my survey course I generally use the *Norton Anthology of American Literature*. In the single-semester version of the survey course, I always use the shorter editions.

[2] Purportedly, the first section of *The Autobiography of Benjamin Franklin* was intended as a guiding missive for Franklin's son, William, who was then governor of New Jersey, but the book soon outgrew its epistolary origin.

[3] Thoreau's essay was originally published as "Resistance to Civil Government" and is still listed as such in some anthologies.

[4] *The Road*'s rich and cohesive references to biblical figures such as Abraham, Job, Jonah, and Elijah and its evocation of the son as a Christ figure are well discussed in many essays, including Josephs; L. Cooper, "Cormac McCarthy's *The Road*."

Ethical Leadership and Historical Reflection: Teaching McCarthy at The Citadel

Lauren Rule Maxwell

When I joined the faculty of The Citadel, The Military College of South Carolina, in 2008, I didn't realize the degree to which the institution's mission of achieving excellence in the education and development of principled leaders would affect my own teaching. That mission has come to influence what works I choose for my courses, the assignments I give my students, and the opportunities I create for them to connect what they learn in the classroom to the world outside The Citadel's gates. Fostering principled leadership has become part of my own teaching philosophy, a goal for both my undergraduate and graduate classes, whether they focus on writing, pedagogy, or literature.

I came to The Citadel from Emory University, where I received my doctorate, and I encountered a very different student body when I arrived. Most of the undergraduates I teach are cadets, students who have chosen a structured military environment for their studies and live on campus in barracks. These cadets are not required to serve in the US military after graduation, but about a third of them do. In addition to the Corps of Cadets, both veteran and active duty students can take day classes. The undergraduate and graduate students who choose to come to The Citadel do so with an understanding of the college's commitment to principled leadership. Most of these students earnestly believe that they can better themselves and the world around them by undertaking a course of study based on this commitment, which is undergirded by the college's key values of honor, duty, and respect.

During my time at The Citadel, I have observed that students invest in their reading of Cormac McCarthy's works to a greater extent than in their readings of other assigned texts. Instead of reading McCarthy's novels merely to fulfill an academic duty, students pursue a deeper, more sustained engagement with the works because they enjoy them and find them relevant. I've taught McCarthy's works in many sections of two different courses: a lower-level composition class that teaches students how to write about literature, and an upper-level course on twentieth- and twenty-first-century American fiction. I use different books and have different modes of teaching in these two courses, but both courses to some degree involve thinking critically about ethical dilemmas in the literature and about relating characters' choices to broader discussions of principled leadership.

In the composition course, I introduce students to literary terminology and analysis by teaching selections of fiction (short stories and one novel), poetry, and drama. At the end of the semester, students apply and extend their knowledge by writing a research paper about *All the Pretty Horses*. I chose this novel in part because I believed the students would like it—and they have liked it. But selecting *All the Pretty Horses* also allows me to use the events in the journey of John Grady Cole, the book's protagonist, to highlight the intersection of moral courage, ethical leadership, and growing up. By teaching this novel, I can stimulate freshmen at the beginning of their college careers to think critically about the importance of ethics. The unit on *All the Pretty Horses* spans three weeks; classes during this time consist primarily of in-class guided discussion but also include brief reading quizzes, small group exercises, minilectures (on McCarthy's biography and oeuvre, historical contexts, Spanish-language terms, etc.), student-led vocabulary reviews, a critical research presentation, peer-review paper workshops, and clips from the 2000 film adaptation *All the Pretty Horses*.

After the students have read part 1 of the novel, we outline what happens at the outset of the novel and consider how those events set the stage for the journey that follows. I ask the students to discuss the following two questions: "Where are John Grady and Lacey Rawlins headed, and what do they hope to find there?" These questions encourage the students to consider the choices that the young men make in leaving home and the motivations that spur their actions. In these conversations, students sense the importance of John Grady's relationship with his father and recognize the novel's foreshadowing of the trouble that follows the boys' encounter with Jimmy Blevins. The relationships between characters remain in focus as students discuss mentoring and leadership in the novel. With the ethical-reasoning training cadets receive (which has now been formalized in the Freshman Ethical Fitness Seminar), students can readily identify the question of whether to leave Blevins as an ethical dilemma. They consistently point out an important moment in the text: when Rawlins says, "Ever dumb thing I ever done in my life there was a decision I made before that got me into it. It was never the dumb thing. It was always some choice I'd made before it" (McCarthy, *All the Pretty Horses* 79).

For part 2 of the novel, we discuss the encounters that take place on the hacienda and the importance of horses as both actors and symbols in the novel. We talk at length about John Grady's connections with horses and about the breaking of horses—how they are broken, by whom, and whether the breaking is different when it is a spectacle. Focusing on John Grady, we examine his actions in this part to discuss whether he is admirable and deserves to be respected. We scrutinize him much as Don Héctor Rocha and Dueña Alfonsa do, while considering why he fails to tell Don Héctor about Blevins and what the implications of that decision might be. We also consider his blossoming relationship with Alejandra. I ask students to debate whether his choices in each case are unethical. Is he being brave or foolhardy? How are his choices related to growing up?

The arrest of John Grady and Rawlins and their jailing in part 3 provide opportunities for the class to discuss authority and different styles of leadership. We contrast the codes of honor of Blevins, John Grady, and the captain and question the ethics of their choices. I ask students how they feel about the execution of Blevins and whether it is just. In small groups, students do a close reading of the following quotation and reflect upon its significance: "Yet the captain inhabited another space and it was a space of his own election and outside of the common world of men. A space privileged to men of the irreclaimable act which while it contained all lesser worlds within it contained no access to them. For the terms of election were a piece with its office and once chosen that world could not be quit" (179). I encourage students to look closely at the syntax, punctuation, and word choice of this passage, to characterize the "space" that is mentioned, and to consider the words "election" and "piece." Afterward, we discuss John Grady's knife fight. Is there anything he could have done to avoid it? Does he exhibit moral courage by fighting?

These in-class discussions and group work with close readings of the text help prepare the students for presenting their own literary analysis in the final paper. Because this class introduces students to the act of writing about literature, many come not really knowing how to identify and locate sources or how to use them to contribute to the broader critical conversation. One of my tasks is showing them how to use quotations from these sources to enrich their own arguments and how to properly cite others' works. I relate this to The Citadel's core values by explaining the ethical imperative of properly attributing others' work. The Citadel's honor code—a cadet does not lie, cheat, steal, or tolerate those who do—is familiar to all Citadel students. The stakes of following the honor code are high, because, if students are convicted by the student-led honor court of plagiarism, they will be expelled. I explain that plagiarism is a type of stealing of others' ideas, a dishonest representation of one's own work, and that one can avoid this with proper citation practices.

I give students a great deal of freedom in choosing the topic of their essay on *All the Pretty Horses* because I want them to write on something that interests them. I have been surprised, however, by the degree to which students' final papers focus on ethical considerations and, more specifically, on principled leadership. The guided discussion about ethical dilemmas in the novel appears to affect the students' reading of the novel more than other discussions do. I would have expected more papers on the role of horses or death in the novel or on religion, which is important to many of our cadets. The vast majority of the papers, however, have been about morality and leadership. Typical paper titles include "The Things That Make Men Who They Are," "Bad Decisions," "Maturity through Hardship," "A Man Ought to Do What He Thinks Is Right," "From a Boy to a Man," and "Lawmen of the West."

What emerges in these papers is the recurring theme of maturing through conscious pursuit of ethical behavior. The following quotation from one student's paper illustrates how students map this theme onto John Grady's journey within the novel: "Cole, though skilled in most aspects of ranching, horses, and self-sufficiency, lacks the necessary mental and moral maturity that goes along with such an undertaking. Throughout the novel the reader sees a shift in his character as the chapters of his life are mixed together, with [his] coming full circle at the end as a changed man." The "shift" in John Grady's moral maturity is also noted by other students, one of whom starts out by claiming that "[t]he protagonist of the story, John Grady, is without a doubt, the most dynamic of all of the characters."

In tracing John Grady's progression in their essays, some students assert that the character always has good intentions, and one surmises that "John Grady's qualities of honesty and sense of duty to do the right thing must have started at a very young age" and that "honesty and duty were the only pure things he had." Students complicate this claim about John Grady, though, by acknowledging that his understanding of what it means to be duty-bound to others changes over the course of the novel and that this change takes place, in part, because he learns better what not to do as a man and leader by observing others' failings. After discussing John Grady's honesty and sense of duty, the student quoted above contrasts John Grady's behavior to that of other characters, including Rawlins and the captain: "[John Grady] actually kidnaps the Captain and holds him hostage while taking back the horses, which were essentially stolen from him, Rawlins, and Blevins, but he does not kill the man even though the Captain had shot and killed Blevins earlier and sent him and Rawlins to prison for no reason." This student ultimately argues that John Grady matures because he develops principled leadership and that he refines his sense of justice by observing the missteps of those who exercise power over him.

Another student claims in his final paper that, instead of having a sense of duty, "John Grady appears isolated and self-centered" at the beginning of the novel. "John Grady never told his parents that he was leaving," the student explains, "or urged Rawlins to stay because Rawlins's family needed . . . help on their ranch." The student suggests that meeting Blevins is the turning point in John Grady's moral education: "After meeting Blevins, John Grady became concerned about someone other than himself; he accepted the responsibility of Blevins's wellbeing." Other students focus in their papers on caring as a key marker of John Grady's moral development and suggest that care-based thinking should be used to resolve ethical dilemmas. One student explains that "John Grady learns the loss of innocence and the gaining of experience, especially the experience of caring" throughout his journey, but "[h]is care of Blevins and his care of Alejandra are brought to an end by forces that were more established, complex, and powerful than John Grady could ever control." This student highlights that, although John Grady "fought and killed a man[, he] found that he cared about his nameless [would-be] assassin because the killer was another human being." The paper concludes: "John Grady proves that becoming a man is not always about achieving the dream, but [about] persistently caring and trying to achieve even when the dreams remain elusive." This paper identifies, explains, and even idealizes care-based ethics.

In addition to centering their final papers on ethical analyses, the composition students tend to return to this focus in the essay portion of their final exam, which has this prompt about McCarthy's *All the Pretty Horses*: "Dueña Alfonsa tells John Grady that '[s]cars have the strange power to remind us that our past is real' (135). What is the significance of this quotation for the novel as a whole?" In answering this question, most students discuss the emotional and physical scars that mark these characters, concluding that these marks remind the characters of the consequences of their choices and prompt them to lead more upstanding lives. Some students return to a care-based focus here as well, suggesting that the scars lead these characters to do what they can to minimize harm to others—that the scars give rise to empathy.

Although the course on twentieth- and twenty-first-century American fiction differs greatly from the composition course, students in the fiction course also consistently view the texts we read through an ethical lens, though the scope of the course is broader; instead of considering the fictional world of one novel, students consider a range of novels and short stories and also the role of narrative in the history of the United States. This upper-level course, taken primarily by junior and senior English majors, asks students to consider how masterworks of American fiction both reflect their own times and serve as meditations on American history. During the semester, we consider the significance of these works: Why are they so widely read, and what do they tell us about how our understanding of what it means to be an American has changed over time? As with other novels we read (e.g., *The Great Gatsby*, *Light in August*, *Beloved*), we focus on the ways in which McCarthy's works depict the social, cultural, intellectual, and political realities of the time. In discussion of *Blood Meridian*, for example, I detail some of the history of the Southwest during the period in which the novel is set, using excerpts from Samuel Chamberlain's *My Confession* (1–6, 86–88).

When I first taught this class in 2008, of McCarthy's works I included only *Blood Meridian*, but in the three sections I've taught since, I've added another McCarthy novel and the film adaptation of either *No Country for Old Men* or *The Road* because students asked for more of McCarthy's work. At the end of the semester in any course I teach, I give the students an informal questionnaire that asks them to provide me with feedback about the course: What did they like, and what do they wish had been different? How can I improve the course the next time I teach it? Students who enroll in this course on fiction typically do so because they love reading American literature; that this group would enjoy reading *Blood Meridian* is to be expected. When I first taught the course, though, I didn't anticipate the fervor with which students would engage the novel or their appetite for more exposure to McCarthy's oeuvre, which they repeatedly made clear on the questionnaire.

In addition to adding another McCarthy novel, which replaced selections of short stories at the end of the course, I've adapted my original design of the upper-level course to allow students more opportunities for critical conversations about the texts that we read outside of class. Like my composition course, my upper-level courses are primarily discussion-based, but I wanted to give students other modes for engaging both the class material and their classmates. To this end, I created a site on *Wikispaces* to serve as a discussion board, resource center, and creative workplace for students. Much to my delight, students have dived into this virtual platform to take ownership of their class experience. For example, on the *Blood Meridian* wiki I created for the 2015 class, students demonstrated a deep engagement with areas of the text that we discussed only briefly in class, providing rich expositions of biblical allusions, discussing the meaning of various tarot cards, and offering definitions of words. Students also posted to the page videos they recorded of themselves giving critical readings of the novel in a style similar to that of a TED Talk. What I liked most about this virtual space was the excitement it created among the students for a more sustained and thoughtful engagement with the novel.

This high level of engagement by students has translated to thoughtful writing about this novel and others that we read in the course. Even the informal reading posts, which students have to write prior to each class in response to a reading assignment, evince higher-level thinking about the novels. Students have the freedom to write about the aspects of the text that confuse them or that they want to talk more about in class. The titles of posts by students in the 2015 course, progressing from the first to last reading assignments for the unit on *Blood Meridian*, include the following: "'Instruments of Liberation in a Dark and Troubled Land,'" "Violence of Man and Nature in the West," "Grit, Gore, and Beauty," "Who's Judging?," "Morality in the West," "Will the Real West Please Stand Up?," "A New Judge or Failed Disciple," "Uncovering History," "New and Old Westerns," and "No Nations. No Borders." As the titles suggest, students progress in their reading of the novel as their focus expands to include comparisons with narratives outside the novel and broader conceptions of history, race, nationality, and place. This focus inevitably incorporates the moral imperative of remembering and accounting for the human costs of past events, a focus that sharpens during our discussion of the next novel in the course, Toni Morrison's *Beloved*.

One reason for the expanding scope of the students' analytical focus is my introduction of literary criticism about the novel. Students read Mark Eaton's article "Dis(re)membered Bodies: Cormac McCarthy's Border Fiction" as well as excerpts from the work of other critics, including Harold Bloom. For these and other works of literary criticism, I tell my students to consider not only what the authors argue but also how they formulate their arguments. I ask them to evaluate each piece and discuss its strengths or weaknesses. Because these are upper-level students, they come to this course knowing how to write an English paper, but one of my goals is to foster a more sophisticated engagement with the body of critical work.

Because this course centers on literature, not composition, both my writing instruction and the assignments themselves differ from those of the composition course. There are two major types of writing assignments in the upper-level course as I've designed it: essay exams and a ten- to fifteen-page research paper. Over the years, I have varied the exam questions on *Blood Meridian*. I've provided quotations from the judge, for example, and asked students if they agree with Bloom's assertion that *Blood Meridian* is "the ultimate Western" (v).

For the purposes of this essay, I focus on one exam prompt that requires students to extend their analysis of the text to discuss its moral and historical implications. The directions for this part of the test ask students to identify the work from which an excerpt is drawn and its author, to write a paragraph that analyzes the passage, and to provide an explanation of the significance of the passage to the overall work. The quotation from *Blood Meridian* is a diatribe in which Captain White asks, "What kind of people are these?" (33). Student responses consistently and correctly attribute the quotation to the captain, situate it in the action of the novel, and discuss the heavy irony of what he says. Although the responses align in these ways, they demonstrate a rich and varied approach to closely reading the passage and contextualizing it within the rest of the novel. One student focuses in her exam answers on the captain's word choice and highlights words like "captain" and "God" that denote authority and words like "barbarian," "cowardly," and "heathen" that connote negative judgment. "The word 'biased' is interesting because this whole speech [is] biased as it is the captain's perspective," she writes, asking, "what makes him an authority to make such judgements?" She goes on to explain:

> The entire novel is concerned with the question of authority and judgement, especially concerning the judge, his actions, and his ledger. He, too, plays God by documenting in his ledger and destroying the original, physical object. It is conquest, and those that conquer wrote the history that gets read. The other sides are destroyed, wiped "clean" and forced to melt into the dominant culture, if even given the chance.

Other student responses contextualize this passage in a discussion of race. One veteran student writes:

> The character of Captain White is likely a representation of "white culture" and racial thought during the US expansion westward. The captain's xenophobic rant indicates the common American conception that Mexicans were considered a mongrel race, and, thus, deemed unable to govern themselves or support any sort of real civilization. Indeed, as the novel suggests, much of the policy regarding Manifest Destiny was centered in racial subjugation and ideas of white supremacy in order to help justify the expansion and acquisition of Western lands.

Other students place White's war within a broader context of conflict in the West, as in this response: "This passage is significant because it shows how everyone in the West is fighting a separate type of war. . . . For the Apaches, it is a war for their homeland. For White, it is a war for supremacy. This passage indicates the many different agendas that scattered and tore the West—hardly any of which were for man's common good."

In addition to pointing out that White's army does not serve the best interests of humanity in the novel, students also underscore that White is not acting under the authority of the United States government. The preoccupation of students with characters' veteran status, military affiliations, and uniforms is something that becomes evident in earlier units on Hemingway's short stories and on *The Great Gatsby* (see Maxwell), but students' attention to false claims in this regard is heightened when they read *Blood Meridian* after our discussion of Percy Grimm at the end of William Faulkner's *Light in August*. One student, who himself had a United States Army contract, highlights the captain's false posturing in his response: "This passage is the captain's pitch for the kid to join his army. It is assumed that the captain is still a part of the military since he still wears his uniform. However, the captain no longer represents the United States government or military. Instead, the captain is on his own, forming a group of rebels in a continued fight against the Mexicans." He goes on to explain: "Much like the captain is no longer a part of the U.S. Military or its ideals, neither are the other members of the group. Their violent acts do not represent American values [but] the violent truth that forms American identity."

The questions of what American values are and how they inform American identity intrigue students as they choose their final paper topics. For their final papers, students are free to write on any work we read over the course of the semester, but they more frequently elect to write on *Blood Meridian* than on any other single work. To highlight what is unique about how Citadel students use their ethical and historical readings of *Blood Meridian* to find meaning for their own lives, I focus on two papers, both of which were written by students contracted by the US Army to become infantry officers. One student was in my upper-level class my first semester at The Citadel, in 2008, and is now a Green Beret. The other graduated in May 2018.

For his paper, the student from my 2008 class expanded on his study of *Blood Meridian* during my course. His paper focuses on the theme of work and is entitled "The Ultimate Trade Awaiting Its Ultimate Practitioner: An Analysis of Cormac McCarthy's (De)Mystification of the History of Manifest Destiny and the Martial Code." He opens the paper by characterizing the point of view of the narration as that of "a soldier for hire".

> *Blood Meridian* is a novel that forces the reader to re-examine America's foundation. Although the hurricane of violence has long settled, McCarthy re-imagines the storm from the perspective of the soldier for hire. He is an unwittingly patriotic mercenary, a scalp hunter of the American West. Judge Holden, the embodiment of the Enlightenment and American Manifest Destiny, asserts during one of his characteristic speeches that, "All other trades are contained in that of war" (249). In the mid-19th century American West that Cormac McCarthy presents in his novel, the Judge's statement concerning war holds undeniably true. The land is inextricably tied to violence, and war dominates all aspects of life.

The student goes on to assert that "[a]lthough the body of critical response has touched the issues of Manifest Destiny, violence, and the profession of soldiering within *Blood Meridian*, this information has not yet been synthesized into a coherent theory about McCarthy's use of work as a vehicle for demystification of American history." I won't outline his ideas about demystification here—it is still my hope that he will present his own work at a conference on McCarthy someday—but I will gesture toward some of the disconnects that he identifies. He notes, for example, that in the novel, "what is considered transgressive behavior in civilian life is often both endorsed and encouraged for soldiers," adding that "a known murderer would encounter considerable difficulty trying to apply for most jobs . . . [but that identity] is a prerequisite for membership in Captain White's gang." He contrasts Judge Holden's notions of work and war with those of the American Romantics, including Henry David Thoreau. The juxtaposition of these voices in the essay reflects its author's introspection about the purpose of work, specifically the work the author will do in a life of military service. He points out that McCarthy's depiction of the kid "suggests that, in the American West, soldiering provided an ideal fit between man's natural propensities and society's priorities," and he concludes that in "presenting the Kid as representative of mankind, McCarthy identifies an aptitude for soldiering in all men."

In explaining the utility of this aptitude, the student quotes McCarthy in an interview with Richard Woodward: "There's no such thing as a life without bloodshed. . . . I think that the notion that the species can be improved in some way, that everyone could live in harmony, is a really dangerous idea. Those who are afflicted with this notion are the first ones to give up their souls, their freedom. Your desire that it be that way will enslave you and make your life vacuous" ("Cormac McCarthy's Venomous Fiction"). The student asserts that, given the human propensity to violence, we need people who will protect freedom, who will approach the martial profession from a standpoint of principled leadership and not exploitation. "McCarthy highlights the exploitation of the individual and forces a confrontation with a demystified past to caution his readers and shock them from the complacency of the modern world," the author concludes, explaining that this "[a]cknowledgement of the bloodshed that was integral to the events of our nation's communal past frees the [reflective individual] from the hazards associated with ignoring mankind's true nature."

Ten years later, another student with a US Army contract similarly deconstructs *Blood Meridian*'s violence in a final paper entitled "The Enduring Reality of Violence as Seen in McCarthy's *Blood Meridian*." This essay, which was selected as Best Undergraduate Paper in The Citadel's 2018 *Gold Star Journal*, begins by describing the human fascination with violence and its central place in *Blood Meridian*:

> There's a particularly thrilling sensation that comes with the shock we experience when we see blood. The intrigue, the mystique, the color—it all compounds to feed our imagination, oftentimes with more questions than answers. . . . Fascination with the macabre is perhaps just as human a reaction as our revulsion to it. . . . Cormac McCarthy illustrates this

> concept and charts man's grim hypnosis with it throughout his literary career, and isolates it with disturbing precision in *Blood Meridian*.

The student identifies various ways in which *Blood Meridian* captures our preoccupation with violence, including the novel's use of language. He explains that "[t]he chaotic, ambiguous nature of the novel's syntax in many ways parallels the violence and concerns of the universe in the novel: a cruel, numb, untampered churn forward, completely unheeding to the greater concerns which lie in its path." Though it might not be paramount in the novel itself, the "preservation of . . . humanity" is a concern for the student, who notes that this concern fades for the novel's characters: "As the characters are baptized through blood throughout the novel's progression, their cynicism and weariness of this world appear to grow as well, and the indelible hold, if not euphoria, that violence has over them appears to turn them into something other than man, into creatures transformed by violence." In reflecting on the novel, the student notes that readers "grasp for a motive, a meaning, for something behind the senselessness of it all" and may realize "that violence itself dehumanizes man" but also that "we cannot force ourselves to look away." Closely reading statements by the judge, the student surmises that "his central point [is] that the only cycle man knows is no cycle at all, but its natural, unlearned progression . . . followed by the inevitability of its own violent end, destruction, and rebirth."

As one who actively considers the consequences of violence, the student, in a concluding section of his paper entitled "What It All Means," muses: "Violence as a means of controlling the seemingly uncontrollable, of affecting one's own wills and desires with the power of life and death, appears to be the mechanism with which humanity resorts to making civilizations, settling scores, carving out a countryside, and coping with being forgotten." In his final paragraph, the student spells out the significance of *Blood Meridian*'s message to the reader:

> [W]hat it all means is that we . . . are forcing ourselves to acknowledge the unacknowledgeable: that we not only engage in violence as a tool, but we revel in it and have and will continue to for time eternal. Faced with the unanswerable questions of our lives, . . . we resort to the animalistic tendency for violence as our chisel to make the marks on the world in a vain effort to discern a greater meaning. . . . McCarthy does not go so far as to condemn, or to espouse, violence as a solution, . . . but rather brings it into focus as a reality and an enduring truth that we must engage in our lifetimes, lest we ignore it to our detriment.

In this paper and the other writings discussed above, students use McCarthy's fiction to reflect on both the world around us and how we shape it with the work we do and the stories we tell. In this way, the students learn to contextualize the past, to contemplate the marks they will make on the world, and, wielding a drastically different chisel, to inscribe greater meaning.

The Cormac McCarthy Journals: The Single-Author Graduate Course

Jay Watson, Robert Briggs, Andrew Thomas, and Josh-Wade Ferguson

The Value of Reader-Response Journals, by Jay Watson

In spring 2014, I taught a graduate seminar at the University of Mississippi on the writings of Cormac McCarthy. Over the course of fourteen weeks, nine students and I read everything McCarthy had published to date, from the 1959 short story "Wake for Susan" to the 2013 screenplay *The Counselor*, with the exception of *The Gardener's Son*, which was between printings and unavailable to us during the term. In addition to an orthodox, article-length research project due at semester's end, the major writing requirement for the course was a series of weekly reader-response journal entries posted to group discussion boards on *Blackboard*, our online course environment. In this essay I make a case for the pedagogical value of these journal assignments as an approach to teaching the works of Cormac McCarthy. I do this primarily by drawing liberally on my students' journals, and my responses to them, to illustrate the potential of this exercise as an incubator for student ideas, a relatively informal, low-risk, and public forum for brainstorming about a historically rich, philosophically dense, aesthetically innovative, and affectively intense body of writing.

Starting the second week of class, when we were reading *Outer Dark*, the students were asked to submit 350- to 500-word journal entries the evening before each week's class meeting. The journals were posted to the discussion board designated for each week, where they could be read by the other students and by me. I did not supply prompts for these weekly installments; students were invited to post on any aspect of the week's assigned reading that they found intriguing, problematic, mysterious, difficult, or otherwise thought-provoking. Students were allowed to extend, complicate, or contest a classmate's thread for journal credit as well as to initiate their own threads. Each week I posted at least one journal entry of my own, and occasionally two or three, in response to student posts. I did this in part to demonstrate my own belief in the value of journaling and to signal to the students that I wasn't asking them to do anything pedagogically that I wasn't prepared to do myself. Finally, although I posted a weekly assessment of student posts to the *Blackboard* grade center and gave each post a plus, a check, or a minus, I did not provide written evaluations because the primary aim of the journal requirement was not simply to create another graded assignment, as I discuss in more detail below.

Some of the pedagogical advantages of this exercise will be obvious. Setting the posting deadline for the night before class helps insure that students have completed the reading assignment when we sit down to explore it together. It's one thing for a student having an off week to keep a low profile during class discussion, but it's another and more embarrassing thing to come up short on a written assignment that becomes a public artifact perused by one's classmates. The scheduling has the added benefit of priming the pump for the next day's seminar. Because the students have already shared key ideas, questions, or concerns about the reading material with one another and with me the night before class, discussion has in effect begun before we even meet, so we enter the classroom more thoroughly attuned to one another's interests and needs.

Moreover, the journal requirement gives less dynamic contributors to class discussion a chance to shine: to exchange views and try out approaches in writing on a weekly basis without having to wait for the research project at semester's end to showcase their writing and critical thinking abilities. This opportunity helps diversify the skills that the course rewards. By the same token, the journals give me as the instructor another forum in which to provide feedback by responding directly—and typically in some depth—to a limited number of student posts. Though I interact with the students in class each week, consult with them in individual conferences, and provide copious notes and commentary on their seminar papers, my own journal entries represent an opportunity to encourage and challenge them in their written work and to collaborate with them throughout the term, beginning nearly right away. With the students' help, my entries also enable me to push my own thinking, often in exciting and unexpected ways, which I believe some of the examples below will attest to.

Finally, because there's so much going on in McCarthy's oeuvre, I think students benefit not only from developing in their research projects the article-length arguments that McCarthy's work so richly invites but also from opportunities to work in a shorter form: to experiment with different theoretical frameworks, to think provisionally, and to go out on a limb in a relatively low-stakes forum that can nonetheless deliver exciting intellectual yields. Cultivating adventurous, out-of-the-box thinking in these more bite-size installments also gives the students confidence in their ability to take critical risks in their research projects to come. Few bodies of work are as intellectually suited to the brainstorming process, or reward critical daring with such pleasure and profit, as McCarthy's. The journaling requirement is especially valuable for PhD, MFA, and even MA students in their capacity as apprentice teachers building a skill set to take into their future classrooms. Whether or not their journal ideas become the germs of conference papers or published essays, the work and play of generating them is intimately related to the process that yields talking points for lecture material or lesson plans, questions for class discussion, paper and exam topics, and writing prompts for students.

What follows are four student journal entries and my responses, exchanges that follow the pedagogical model sketched above and that illustrate some of its virtues, possibilities, and, no doubt, drawbacks. These exchanges focus on four texts by McCarthy. Each exchange appears beneath a subhead listing the journal due date and the primary and secondary reading assignments for the next afternoon's class. The entries have been lightly edited, but otherwise the students and I speak in our own voices, out of the exigencies of the course and in response to the readings.

By not commenting on these exchanges, I want to show the pedagogy of journaling by letting the entries themselves play the starring role and to avoid pontificating about their significance with the artificial clarity that hindsight always provides. For the same reason, I have not fortified the discussion with scholarly source material on pedagogy, graduate education, or other subjects. I want this contribution to have the immediacy, the authority and authenticity, and the pragmatic value of something more experiential, from the trenches. My hope is that in the weave of these voices readers may find new aperçus into McCarthy's work and new ideas about how to teach it.

Journal Assignment of 18 March 2014

Primary Reading: McCarthy, *The Stonemason*
Secondary Reading: Edwin Arnold, "Cormac McCarthy's *The Stonemason*: The Unmaking of a Play"; excerpt from John Cant, *Cormac McCarthy and the Myth of American Exceptionalism*, 122–35; and J. Douglas Canfield, "Oedipal Complexities in Cormac McCarthy's *The Stonemason* and *The Gardener's Son*"

"Soldier: Soldier," by Robert Briggs

The first scene of *The Stonemason* begins in February 1971, which falls in the midst of the Vietnam War. Scanning back through the screenplay, I cannot find any explicit mention of the war in Vietnam, but I would like to argue that its presence in *The Stonemason* exists. To get the most obvious symbol out of the way, as John Cant asserts, "The fourth generation is represented by Soldier" (128). Case solved: his name is Soldier!

Not until the sixth-to-last page do we find out that the name Soldier is a nickname. Ben calls the police (presumably) and confesses to discovering the body, "He was my nephew, Telfair. *His* name. Benjamin. His name was Benjamin" (McCarthy, *Stonemason* 127). Therefore, excluding the page listing the cast of characters that precedes the screenplay, from the moment Soldier is introduced on page 13, until we discover on page 127 that his real name is Benjamin, the audience must receive every action, mannerism, and spoken word through the lens of his nickname as a combatant, Soldier. Names, as we know from McCarthy's previous novels and Cant's essay, are significant to McCarthy because of his consistent focus on namelessness. "Naming relates word to thing, calls it into consciousness but at the same time limits it and, ultimately, remains its double, its other, necessary but not sufficient" (Cant 133).

Soldier, as a representation of his generation, is another symbol that suggests war's presence in the screenplay. Intergenerational conflict is a staple of the southern narrative, and because we find the Telfair family in Louisville, Kentucky, we are justified, as Cant asserts, to include "the text in the 'Southern' category" (126). We can infer that, because *The Stonemason* is a southern text and because it spans four generations, America's history of war remains on the horizon of each generation. Additionally, as Matthew Guinn states in his book, *After Southern Modernism: Fiction of the Contemporary South*, "The Civil War has been nearly ubiquitous in southern fiction" (161). Because Soldier is only fifteen years old, we know that he cannot serve in the Vietnam War, and by the time he does come of age for service, the Vietnam War will be drawing to a close. Therefore, I recognize that my claim that Soldier represents the Vietnam generation cannot be completely founded on textual evidence. However, after Soldier returns from his absence of several years (a hypothetical tour of duty), Ben visits him in a hotel room. After Ben returns home, Maven and Ben have the following conversation:

> MAVEN. Somewhere else is where he got the way he is now.
> BEN (*shaking his head*). No he didnt. He got that way right here. In this family. Nowhere else. (McCarthy, *Stonemason* 120)

This conversation about Soldier speaks to the debate on post-traumatic stress disorder, a term that the Vietnam War, as Michael Bibby suggests, "introduced . . . into our national lexicon" (159), and a health issue that soldiers returning from Vietnam were struggling to cope with and overcome. In addition, soldiers returning from Vietnam were also struggling with the drug addictions they brought back with them from overseas. Soldier's death from a heroin overdose harkens to this common stereotype of returning Vietnam veterans.

Finally, and I have no reputable source to back this up, I felt like there was some significance to the three pigeon calls when Ben discovers Soldier's dead body. The best answer I could come up with is that the pigeon call was a common sound that drug dealers mimicked when the police or danger was present. Any thoughts?

Watson's Reply

I think there was a sense among many Vietnam-era Americans that the soldier figure might be less readily linked with the warrior's role than with that of a casualty. And I think that sense in turn links up with the significance of Soldier's nickname, which is otherwise never really explained or addressed in the play. The name is certainly significant in deferring our awareness of the boy's incredibly portentous actual name of Benjamin. But any nickname could have served as placeholder and postponement in that way. So when it comes to the positive semantic content of Soldier, does he really come off as an aggressive or martial figure in the play? Or does he come off more as a victim, the truest casualty of a war perpetuated by his elders in the heart of the home place? Look at how casually everybody knocks him around and discounts and low-rates him, from his first appearance in the drama. As a soldier he is more acted-upon than acting, and that particular image of the soldier has its origins in Vietnam-era America's deep ambivalences toward the (mainly) working-class troops, most of them men, whom it was sending overseas to fight its dirty little neocolonial war. Within the Telfair family unit (such as it is), Soldier is pretty much a throwaway figure, less tragic than pathetic. Many Vietnam veterans felt similarly about their role within the bosom of the nation.

And yet on another level, and within the play's central masonic tropology, Soldier is arguably the keystone of the Telfair family structure and indeed of the play—the stone that keeps the entire arch in place and that, when removed, brings the structure down around it. Ben does his best to assign that role to Papaw, but the play knows better, as its plotline reveals. Everything really begins to fall apart following Soldier's mysterious disappearance: then Papaw dies, Big Ben commits suicide, and Soldier returns . . . and dies. Ben's most terrible human error may lie in mistaking this keystone for one of the hewn stones that Ben casts aside and refuses to incorporate into his masonry.

Indeed, this fate of being displaced and discarded has arguably been coextensive with Soldier's entire life. If he's fifteen years old in 1971, then he was born in either 1955 or 1956. Recall that Papaw moved in with the family at the age of eighty-five—that is, in 1955—and it's pretty obvious that despite his age he has been anointed the family's real golden boy, a role that Soldier therefore seems destined never to enjoy at any point in his life. It's like he's being crowded out of the family structure from the moment Papaw arrives to displace him, perhaps before he is born. Not that Papaw would have intended any of this, but the family's veneration of him is a crippling, destructive thing, and Soldier and Big Ben, in their different ways, are the casualties who prove it.

So does the resonance of any of this material point outward to an actual generation of Vietnam-era soldiers coming home in the period encompassing 1971–72? Maybe—but at least for now I'll admit to feeling more secure in viewing the Vietnam context as a way to think about Soldier than in viewing the Soldier character as a way to think about Vietnam.

Journal Assignment of 1 April 2014

Primary Reading: McCarthy, *Cities of the Plain*

Secondary Reading: excerpt from Lydia Cooper, *No More Heroes: Narrative Perspective and Morality in Cormac McCarthy*, 76–109; excerpt from David Holloway, *The Late Modernism of Cormac McCarthy*, 103–44; and Robert L. Jarrett, "Cormac McCarthy's Sense of an Ending: Serialized Narrative and Revision in *Cities of the Plain*"

"The Body as Witness," by Andrew Thomas

Given our discussion last week, we know that the act of witnessing in McCarthy's fiction also entails an act of telling, of narrating, of composing a corrido. "Acts have their being in the witness," the caretaker of the ruined church claims in *The Crossing*. "Without him who can speak of it? In the end one could even say that the act is nothing, the witness all. . . . If the world was a tale who but the witness could give it life?" (154). Comparing this to the final scenes of *The Crossing* couches all historical knowledge within the art—craftsmanship even—of storytelling. The gypsy responsible for the caravan relocating the plane relates to Billy the third and final history of the aircraft: "La tercera historia . . . es ésta. Él existe en la historia de la historias. Es que ultimadamente la verdad no puede quedar en ningún otro lugar sino en el habla" ("The third history . . . is this. It exists in the history of the stories. It is that ultimately truth cannot remain in any other place but in the speaking"; 411; Thomas's trans.). It is the history that each man makes alone out of what is left to him.

Within this interpretive framework, the witness is everything, making McCarthy's magic number three. Regardless of whether this is a literal rendering or more abstracted understanding of three persons, history seems to be the procession of two distinct actors or group of actors (human or nonhuman) that is observed by a witness or audience whose story is then perpetuated (or not). I am reminded of Toadvine in *Blood Meridian* making a mark on the sand with three fingers and then turning his hand and imprinting the mirror image. It is within the context of three that perpetuity, replication, or repetition is possible. And of course one is capable of being witness to one's own actions. Robert L. Jarrett points out—and this is something we definitely do not get in *The Crossing*—Billy's ability to finally narrate and, in so doing, work through the character's past: "Much of Billy's behavior within *Cities of the Plain* seems motivated by a paradoxical attempt to exorcise the trauma of his past through repetition and renarration. . . . Billy enacts the role of novelist by renarrating *The Crossing* and his past" ("Cormac McCarthy's Sense" 334–35). Jarrett also keenly points out that in *Cities of the Plain* John Grady and Magdalena exchange their own historical narratives as acts of intimacy, Grady drawing on his *All the Pretty Horses* days. I am not sure, however, how to totally reconcile this understanding with McCarthy's epilogue in *Cities of the Plain*, where Billy's interlocutor claims that "in dreams there can be no witness" (284). While this may only be the case for dreams, this statement seems to have an eerie resonance with the world we experience apart from dreams. Given this statement, it becomes clearer as to how Jarrett arrives at what might be considered a kind of solipsistic witnessing: the "individual is the author who acts as both witness and narrator of his own dream tale and whose dream world, through writing, intersects the dream world of the reader-witness" ("Cormac McCarthy's Sense" 338).

Is witnessing therefore a form of autopoiesis? And what if all individuals are not literal writers or songsters? Perhaps another way in which narratives are retold is through their being encoded on the physical body. That is, they are written in blood. John Grady's death in *Cities of the Plain* is horrific because of the abuse that his physical body endures; its violence rivals only that of episodes in *Blood Meridian*. And yet, Eduardo's physical prowess and verbal exhibition during what is partly a dialogue and partly Eduardo's dramatic monologue illustrate McCarthy's narrative artistry at its tops. In this scene, McCarthy places the abstract notion of language and verbal communication through Eduardo's eloquent prose alongside the brutally material and embodied evisceration of a silent witness, John Grady, who is reduced to the level of Boyd's dog: by the end of the scene, neither Eduardo nor John Grady can cry out, as they have both been reduced to mute, physically scarred bodies. They merely act as silent witnesses to what is being done. And yet, the scarred body is a legible, historical even, text. John Grady's scar on his cheek not only recalls a past of violence but also acts as an identifier in his present: this scar is used to mislead Magdalena, ultimately to her death. Furthermore, John Grady's self-cauterized bullet wound stands as incontrovertible witness to the character's testimony at the end of *All the Pretty Horses*. Perhaps even alluding to the violence that language engenders, Eduardo carves the letter *E* onto John Grady's body. While it is ultimately left to the person bearing the scars to tell the tale of their origin, the scarred body is itself a witness, albeit a mute one. John Grady's hunting knife mutes Eduardo's elevated prose in an instant, and all that is left to testify are mutilated bodies.

Watson's Reply

Then there's also what Betty witnesses in Billy's corporeal hand, a few paragraphs from the end of McCarthy's *Cities of the Plain*: "Gnarled, ropescarred, speckled from the sun and years of it. The ropy veins that bound them to his heart. There was map enough for men to read. There God's plenty of signs and wonders to make a landscape. To make a world" (291). There would certainly seem to be some sort of reply here to the freeway stranger's thoroughgoing critique of the representational enterprise of mapping a human life—and perhaps, on another level, a reply to the stranger's ethos of the witness as well. Does this scene at all illuminate or complicate the kinds of witnessing that John Grady's body performs (maybe along the lines of what Elaine Scarry calls "analogical verification" in *The Body in Pain* [14; see 13–14, 124–27])? Are these bodies, and their scars, signifying along similar lines or along different ones?

Journal Assignment of 15 April 2014

Primary Reading: McCarthy, *The Sunset Limited*
Secondary Reading: Lydia Cooper, "'A Howling Void': Beckett's Influence in Cormac McCarthy's *The Sunset Limited*"; Bryan Giemza, "Toward a Catholic Understanding of Cormac McCarthy's Oeuvre"

"If It Can't Get Any Worse, Let's Talk about 9/11," by Josh-Wade Ferguson

In reading Bobby's post concerning the value of human life and his allusions to mass human trauma, I wonder if we could also consider a more recent traumatic event that took place in New York City, 9/11. Last week we mentioned that *No Country for Old Men* was McCarthy's first book published after 9/11, and we began to allude to the change in the writer's prose style as perhaps being symptomatic of living within the postevent space. Given that *The Sunset Limited*, a novel in dramatic form, was both published in 2006 and set in New York City, it is not out of the realm of possibility to think that its events take place after 9/11. Also, we see McCarthy's text published among others that directly discuss the experience of surviving 9/11 in New York City. I am thinking specifically of Art Spiegelman's graphic novel *In the Shadow of No Towers*, Jonathan Safran Foer's novel *Extremely Loud and Incredibly Close*, and Don DeLillo's novel *Falling Man*. So, within the post-9/11 literary space, what happens if we think of *The Sunset Limited* as a dialogue between 9/11 survivors? Perhaps, through this lens, we can start to parse together the presentation of human experience "in the shadow of no towers": that is, elucidate how people think and react when they have witnessed one of the most mediated events in world history, and, more important, understand how those who witnessed the event (live in New York City, for the purposes of this post) interact.

Part of White's desire to commit suicide (physical in this case; I'm sure there is an already-made case that he has committed philosophical suicide, which Albert Camus defines in his *Myth of Sisyphus*) is because White sees the world as a "saga of bloodshed and greed and folly the import of which is impossible to ignore. And yet we imagine that the future will somehow be different," and he goes on to claim that he has "no idea why we are even still here but in all probability we will not be here much longer" (McCarthy, *Sunset Limited* 112). He tells us too that the "things I believed in dont exist any more. It's foolish to pretend that they do. Western Civilization finally went up in smoke in the chimneys at Dachau but I was too infatuated to see. I see it now" (27). Although White claims that Dachau was the destruction of Western civilization, he is initially unable to see it. However, if this novel is set after 9/11, then that event may be what enables him to see it now. White's world was forced into the real when the planes hit the towers, the people leaped from the burning buildings, and the towers crumbled. White sees his role as that of a witness; he tells us, "I think it odd that I should be present to witness the death of everything and I do think it's odd but that doesnt mean it's not so. Someone has to be here" (26). What begins to develop is that White perceives life in post-9/11 New York City as without value because everything is dead.

Black, however, seems to find value in human connection (albeit through God) and believes that it is the "pure ore. That forever thing" (95). However, his concern beyond saving White from throwing himself in front of the Sunset Limited is the experience of the witnesses of White's suicide. Black asks if White has considered the other commuters, to which White responds, "I try not to think about them at all" (87). Later Black pretends to read from the newspaper detailing White's suicide and calls the commuters "bloodspattered spectators" (114). Finally, Black asks, "You dont think you might view them other commuters from a certain height?" (115). The other commuters effectively become the communal witnesses of White's death. His blood will spatter over them and stain them with the experience of seeing unmediated death. Black's use of "height," I argue, allows for the image of White jumping from above. The image in the post-9/11 space that sticks in my mind is that of the man who was captured on film as he plummeted to his death (this image is on the cover of and is the inspiration for DeLillo's *Falling Man* and is represented in Foer's *Extremely Loud and Incredibly Close*).

Although I am aware that much of my attempt to understand *The Sunset Limited* [is] part of the post-9/11 literary space, I do think that the novel has cultural and traumatic resonances that allow for such a reading. The form itself is an attempt to take two media to help articulate an event that is beyond verbal expression. Foer's novel too works to express meaning through pictures, art, and letters within the novel's structure in order to help articulate the fractured human experience and the need to have multiple media (voices) to articulate, or at least attempt to articulate, an experience of the real.

Watson's Reply

Black frames White at several points as a leaping man: "You mean when you took your amazin leap?" (McCarthy, *Sunset Limited* 22; see also 10, 127). Now of course there's a whole philosophical and theological discourse organized around the concept of the leap, though if we are to see White's plunge as the proverbial existential leap of faith, it's surely a strange kind of faith that he's leaping toward, or from. What might it mean to reframe White as a falling man, rather than a leaping man? How would doing so make a difference in a reading of the text? And by the same token, what might it mean to reframe the 9/11 figures alluded to in DeLillo and Foer as leaping, rather than falling, men? How would the recontextualization (of agency, purpose, subjective intent) change our response to these characters, their texts, and their 9/11 moment?

Journal Assignment of 29 April 2014

Primary Reading: McCarthy, *The Counselor*
Secondary Reading: excerpt from Jay Ellis, *No Place for Home*, 1–38; and Stacey Peebles, "McCarthy and Film"

"McCarthy's Bad Career Move: 'Help Me, Help You,'" by Robert Briggs

I would like to suggest that McCarthy published his last four projects out of order. If I can be so bold, I would like to offer McCarthy an opportunity to reconsider his decision to write each piece in the order that he did. Instead, I offer the following order to make for a more teleological reading experience that will help the reader better understand McCarthy's oeuvre: *No Country for Old Men*, *The Counselor*, *The Sunset Limited*, and *The Road*. Ultimately, I am simply asking McCarthy to publish *The Counselor* after *No Country for Old Men*. Just think about the fruitful discussion we could have had as a class in contrasting Moss in the latter novel, who makes a greedy decision after stumbling across a bag of money from a drug deal gone bad, and Counselor, in the former novel, who actively pursues an illegal opportunity to capitalize on a drug deal.

Placing the works in the order I suggest would show a clear decline narrative over four works. By decline, I mean that each piece reaches a deeper level of depravity and despair than the one that precedes it. However, reordering the works does more than simply benefit the reader. If McCarthy would take my advice, I believe his screenplay and film *The Counselor* would not have received the poor reviews that followed their publication and production, respectively. Honestly, how could McCarthy follow up *The Road*—a Pulitzer Prize–winning novel whose characters in a post-apocalyptic wasteland tug on your philosophical and emotional heartstrings—with a screenplay that seems bent on shocking the reader with scenes that reach deeply into the genre of the violently and sexually grotesque? I have a suspicion that if McCarthy could answer me, he would echo Malkina's assertion, "I could imagine that my dark and your dark are different darks" (*Counselor* 168).

But, alas, McCarthy has chosen to enact his artistic license, and he continues to ignore my suggestions. What, then, does McCarthy accomplish with the order of his works if not to illuminate the decline of the human condition? It might be worth considering that McCarthy has used his last four texts to illuminate an escalating erasure of borders (maybe not in the same way that *The Road* erases borders, but I believe *The Road* is a cautionary tale). By borders, I am not speaking solely about geographical borders, but I believe that McCarthy is showing how all borders—international, economic, political, spatial, and so on—are eroding as globalization changes the way we as humans interact with the world and each other.

At the beginning of the screenplay *The Counselor*, McCarthy provides vague descriptions of the setting that allow readers a chance to place the text: "*Mexican garage*" (10), "*A street in Amsterdam*" (11), "*A small Mexican port town on the Gulf of California*" (12), "*Southwestern desert*" (13), and "*Northern Mexico at US border*" (49). Toward the end of the screenplay, the clues become less and less descriptive and tied to a region: "*Garage*" (152), "*Desk at a major hotel in a world city*" (161), "*A major street, world city*" (166), "*City street*" (173), and "*World city, apartment in a high rise building*" (174). In this way, McCarthy demonstrates how crime and evil have evolved to the degree that they transcend borders.

One of the examples that demonstrates evil transcending borders develops from the discussion between Counselor and Reiner on the topic of the "bolito" (35). After the gruesome description of how the bolito works, Counselor asks, "Where's all this beheading shit come from? You never used to see that," to which Reiner responds, "Yeah. It's blown in here from the East" (39). As we mentioned in our discussion on *No Country for Old Men*, the appearance of heroin at the border between Mexico and the United States indicates the transfer of a drug trade that followed the soldiers home from Vietnam. Following this trend, McCarthy may be demonstrating how the beheadings that were and are prevalent in the wars of the Middle East are becoming part of the global crime repertoire. Furthermore, the term "blown" suggests that the wind has carried beheadings across the ocean, which is a physical impossibility (*Counselor* 39); however, in a way, McCarthy is hinting at a form of travel that could plausibly "blow" beheadings across an ocean: technology. Here I am thinking about how technology has changed the way in which humans interact and communicate. Evil acts existed long before the Internet, but with the *YouTube* generation's desire to capture everything on camera, dark material is getting more exposure and, as a result, is more accessible (168).

Watson's Reply

Okay, I don't know for sure the time line along which the four most recent McCarthy texts became available for publication, which is to say I don't know in what order McCarthy wrote *No Country for Old Men*, *Sunset Limited*, *The Road*, and *The Counselor*. But for the sake of the thought experiment I will suggest, contra Bobby, that *The Counselor* belongs where it is in the larger sequence.

More specifically, in the same spirit in which I suggested that the other three texts constitute a post-9/11 trilogy (which another student has expanded into a tetralogy by including *The Counselor*), I want to suggest that we should view *The Counselor* as McCarthy's first post-2008 narrative. What this would mean is that we have another apocalyptic context, in addition to 9/11, to which the narrative can be seen as an imaginative response: the subprime mortgage crisis that nearly took down the whole financial sector in the United States in 2008–09 and that created ripple effects that extended at least as far as Europe, where a banking crisis beginning in 2009 nearly toppled the monetary integrity of the Euro and nearly brought down the European Union (perhaps prompting Malkina's diagnosis near the screenplay's end that "[t]here's not going to be a Europe" [177], with the emphasis on the "a," the singular indefinite pronoun indicating a union). For many Americans, the 2008 financial bubble, far more than 9/11, has been a truly apocalyptic scenario.

So in that light let's think for a moment about the crisis at the heart of *The Counselor*. An ambitious young contemporary American professional, at the point of embarking on married (and possibly family) life with his beloved, makes a huge, life-altering financial decision, only to lose his entire investment thanks to an unanticipated circumstance—a risk he was utterly unaware he was even taking when he put his money up. What I'm referring to here is how the Counselor is unaware of the implications of the favor he does for Ruth: he springs her son from jail only for the son to be killed, the septic truck stolen, and the Counselor and his group of investors held accountable for the loss. As a result, his life is ruined and his relationship destroyed, and he is plunged into poverty and radically unhomed, losing his expensive, elegant condominium and winding up alone in shabby, transitory housing. Not only are the investors themselves brought down by their scheme, the collateral damage extends outward into other, innocent lives: Laura and the woman who lends the Counselor her cell phone being perhaps the two most prominent examples (122, 127–28).

Cocaine, beheadings, diamonds, and septic trucks aside, isn't that an all-too-familiar scenario in post-2008 America? And if so, shouldn't we see the anxieties engaged by the narrative not only in terms of the national and geopolitical anxieties of the post-9/11 dispensation but also in the more immediately financial context of the subprime mortgage bubble? Admittedly, the screenplay gets at all of this indirectly, or allegorically (it's about drugs, after all, not derivatives or other complex financial instruments)—except, perhaps, for one brief, seemingly gratuitous moment when the economic subtext or context of the narrative comes out in the open:

> *Back yard of* a suburban middle class home. *The two cheetahs are walking along the edge of the swimming pool. One stops to sniff at the water. In the pool are two boys, aged eight and ten. They stand frozen. A man reclining in a poolside canvas chair lowers the paper he is reading to see what the silence is about. He freezes, holding the paper at the level of his chest. The cheetahs amble slowly along the edge of the pool and out across the lawn. The man lowers the paper into his lap. The two boys turn to look at him.* (McCarthy, *Counselor* 139; emphasis added)

Whereupon the man "closes his eyes and raises one hand palm-out. Almost as if in blessing" (140).

With all due respect to the narrator—this beleaguered father and householder is throwing out a hand not in blessing but in desperation, "as if" to ward off the swift, exotic, predatory forces (the cheetah equals speed plus predation plus exogeny) that have descended invasively and menacingly upon his idyll of domestic home (and pool!) ownership in twenty-first-century middle America. It's a last-ditch gesture to keep his house from going the way of the Counselor's condo. (But what would you bet that this guy is mortgaged to the absolute hilt?)

Not yet having paid a visit to the McCarthy archive in San Marcos, Texas, I can neither confirm nor deny that McCarthy composed his 2013 screenplay after the global financial debacle. But much as Richard Ford's 2006 novel *The Lay of the Land* (about a real estate salesman, among other things) offers an uncanny premonition of the coming mortgage crisis, *The Counselor* makes a lot of sense as a postmortem engagement with the latest in a long string of American apocalypses.

NOTES ON CONTRIBUTORS

Robert Briggs completed his MA at the University of Mississippi and has taught composition and literature at the United States Military Academy at West Point. His essay "There Is No Place (Like Home): Craig Santos Perez's Poetry as Military Strategy" can be found in *Green Letters: Studies in Ecocriticism*, and his short story "Service with a Smile" was published in *War, Literature, and the Arts*. Briggs is currently a student at the Command and General Staff College.

Jeremy Browne is an associate research professor in the Office of Digital Humanities at Brigham Young University. His responsibilities include coordinating the digital humanities and technology program, collaborating on digitally concerned research within the College of Humanities, and teaching classes on Web development, text analysis, and other digital humanities skills. While his first research interest is in nineteenth-century French literature, he has recently published and presented on topics ranging from Victorian short fiction to archiving the Quechua language of Northern Ecuador.

Jamie Brummer teaches English and coaches soccer at Christian Brothers High School in Memphis, Tennessee. He holds a BA in great books from the University of Notre Dame and a PhD in American literature from the University of Memphis. His dissertation explores issues related to masculinity in Cormac McCarthy's western novels. Brummer has contributed to *Callaloo*, *The Cormac McCarthy Journal*, *The Explicator*, *Gothic Studies*, and the book *Bonds of Brotherhood in Sons of Anarchy: Essays on Masculinity in the FX Series*.

Lydia R. Cooper is associate professor of contemporary American and Native American literature at Creighton University. Her book *Cormac McCarthy: A Complexity Theory of Literature* is forthcoming. She is also the author of *Masculinities in Literature of the American West* (2016) and *No More Heroes: Narrative Perspective and Morality in Cormac McCarthy* (2011). Her work on McCarthy and on other modern and contemporary American and Native American writers has appeared in *Modern Fiction Studies*, *Studies in the Novel*, *Contemporary Literature*, *Studies in American Indian Literature*, *Western American Literature*, and *Interdisciplinary Studies in Literature and the Environment*, among others.

Josh-Wade Ferguson is a scholar of African American, southern, and multiethnic literature. His current book project investigates how literary representations of blues music access a Black historical past as well as provide a contemporary means to express systemic social precarity across ethnic, cultural, and national borders. He has interviewed the award-winning writer Kiese Laymon for *New Ohio Review*, and his written work can be found or is forthcoming in *The Journal of Popular Culture*, *Swamp Souths: Literary and Cultural Ecologies*, *The Global South*, and *Langston Hughes in Context*.

Steven Frye is professor of English and chair of the English Department at California State University, Bakersfield, as well as president of the Cormac McCarthy Society. He is the author of *Understanding Cormac McCarthy* and *Understanding Larry McMurtry* and editor of *The Cambridge Companion to Cormac McCarthy*, *Cormac McCarthy in*

Context, and *The Cambridge Companion to the Literature of the American West*. He has done work on numerous authors, including Herman Melville, Edgar Allan Poe, and F. Scott Fitzgerald.

Alex Harmon is assistant professor of American studies at Montana State University. Her primary scholarly and teaching interests engage colonial and postcolonial literatures of the Americas, federal Indian law, critical race theory, and literature and film of the American West.

Christina Bieber Lake is the Clyde S. Kilby professor of English at Wheaton College, where she teaches classes in contemporary American literature and literary theory. Lake is the author of *The Incarnational Art of Flannery O'Connor* (2005) and *Prophets of the Posthuman: American Fiction, Biotechnology, and the Ethics of Personhood* (2013). Her latest book, *Beyond the Story*, examines the theological moorings of contemporary American literature.

Benjamin Mangrum is assistant professor of English at the University of the South. He held previous appointments with the Michigan Society of Fellows and the Departments of English and Environmental Studies at Davidson College. Mangrum is the author of *Land of Tomorrow: Postwar Fiction and the Crisis of American Liberalism* (2018). His essays have appeared in *PMLA*, *New Literary History*, *American Literature*, *Contemporary Literature*, and *Genre*.

Lauren Rule Maxwell is a professor of English at The Citadel, The Military College of South Carolina, and the author of *Romantic Revisions in Novels from the Americas* (2013). Her publications include essays in *A History of Virginia Literature* (2015), *Margaret Atwood's Apocalypses* (2015), *Teaching Hemingway and Modernism* (2015), and *F. Scott Fitzgerald in Context* (2013). She teaches American literature, advanced composition, professional writing, and business communications. She serves as the director of the Lowcountry Writing Project, the Charleston-area site of the National Writing Project, and as president of the Margaret Atwood Society.

Nicholas Monk is director of the Center for Transformative Teaching at the University of Nebraska, Lincoln, and holds a courtesy position there as professor in the Department of English. His monograph, *True and Living Prophet of Destruction: Cormac McCarthy and Modernity*, appeared in 2016. He is the editor of *Intertextual and Interdisciplinary Approaches to Cormac McCarthy* (2011). Monk's other principal research interest is interdisciplinary and collaborative pedagogy, and he is lead author on *Open-Space Learning: A Study in Transdisciplinary Pedagogy* (2011).

Rafael Acosta Morales is an assistant professor at the University of Kansas and regularly teaches courses in hemispheric studies about the frontier, as well as courses in Latin American literature. His research interests relate to political theory, Latino studies, comparative literature, and Mexican studies. His previous work has appeared in *Revista de Estudios Hispánicos*, *Latin American Research Review*, and *Comparative Literature*. His current book project, *Frontier Affects*, studies how affective structures represented in stories illustrate the substrata of political behavior.

Stacey Peebles is Marlene and David Grissom Professor of Humanities, associate professor of English, and director of film studies at Centre College in Kentucky. She is the author of *Welcome to the Suck: Narrating the American Soldier's Experience in Iraq*

(2011) and *Cormac McCarthy and Performance: Page, Stage, Screen* (2017), as well as editor of *The Cormac McCarthy Journal* and vice president of the Cormac McCarthy Society. With Aaron DeRosa, she edited a special issue of *Modern Fiction Studies* titled *Enduring Operations: The Wars in Afghanistan and Iraq*.

Shayna Sheinfeld is an honorary research fellow at the Sheffield Institute for Interdisciplinary Biblical Studies. Sheinfeld's research focuses on ancient Jewish and Christian conceptions of authority and community, especially in apocalyptic texts. In addition, she explores the representation of scripture in popular culture today. She is cowriting a textbook on gender and ancient religions. She teaches on a variety of topics related to antiquity, gender, Judaism, and apocalyptic thought.

Delys W. Snyder uses corpora to study American language usage and American authors, especially Cormac McCarthy. She teaches classes in writing, civilization, pedagogy, and women's studies in the English Department at Brigham Young University. She oversees advanced writing courses and coordinates all activities for the Writing across the Curriculum Program. Snyder has published several essays about language and style in McCarthy's novels. Her most recent article, published in *Foreign Language Annals*, is about the success of using writing fellows in Portuguese classes.

Phillip A. Snyder teaches contemporary literature and western studies in the English Department at Brigham Young University. He has presented and published on Cormac McCarthy for many years. His collaboration with his wife, Delys, in studying McCarthy's style began with "Modernism, Postmodernism, and Language: McCarthy's Style" in *The Cambridge Companion to Cormac McCarthy* (2013). Recently, he has published creative nonfiction essays, including "Rental Horses" in *Sport Literate* (2015) and "Chew the Coca, Take the Valium" in *American Literary Review* (2017).

Mark Steven is lecturer in twentieth- and twenty-first-century literature at the University of Exeter. He is the author of *Red Modernism* (2017) and *Splatter Capital* (2017), as well as of articles in *Modernism/Modernity*, *Postmodern Culture*, *Screen*, and *Substance*.

Nell Sullivan is professor of English at the University of Houston, Downtown, where she teaches courses in American literature and the literature of the South. A former editor of *The Cormac McCarthy Journal*, she has published extensively on gender and class representation in McCarthy's novels and on Katherine Dunn, William Faulkner, and Nella Larsen, among others. Her work has appeared in numerous anthologies and in such journals as *Genre*, *Critique*, *The Southern Quarterly*, *Mississippi Quarterly*, and *African American Review*.

Andrew Thomas is a PhD candidate in literary studies at the University of Wisconsin, Madison. He studies twentieth-century American fiction with an emphasis on post-1945 war literature, gender and sexuality, trauma theory, and the ecological effects of war.

Kevin Trumpeter is associate professor of English at Allen University in Columbia, South Carolina. His research focuses on environmental issues in modern and contemporary literature, and he has articles published in *American Literature*, *Modernism/Modernity*, and *The Journal of Ecocriticism*.

Jay Watson is Howry Professor of Faulkner Studies and professor of English at the University of Mississippi. He is the author of *William Faulkner and the Faces of Modernity*,

Reading for the Body: The Recalcitrant Materiality of Southern Fiction, 1893–1985, and *Forensic Fictions: The Lawyer Figure in Faulkner*, and the editor or coeditor of eleven published or forthcoming collections, many of them also on William Faulkner. He has additionally contributed essays on McCarthy to *You Would Not Believe What Watches:* Suttree *and Cormac McCarthy's Knoxville* and *Cormac McCarthy in Context*.

Benjamin West is associate professor of English at the State University of New York, Delhi, where he consistently offers the course Great Writers: Cormac McCarthy. He is the author of *Crowd Violence in American Modernist Fiction* (which concludes with a chapter on *The Road*) and has published on authors such as Willa Cather, Herman Melville, and Virginia Woolf.

Kristy Wilson has been teaching at Ellenville High School in upstate New York since 2002. She enjoys teaching nonfiction, as well as American literature, to juniors and seniors. She shares her life in the Hudson Valley with her husband and daughter.

Scott D. Yarbrough is professor of English and associate vice president of academic affairs at Charleston Southern University. He is the coauthor of *A Practical Introduction to Literary Study* (2004) and has published articles on William Faulkner, Ernest Hemingway, and Cormac McCarthy, who are also his favorite authors to teach. He and Rick Wallach are editors of the Cormac McCarthy Society's two casebooks on *The Road*.

Gene Young is professor of English and former department chair and dean at Sam Houston State University. He has published and presented on, and taught, twentieth-century American literature, the literature and culture of the southwest and Mexico, and American folklore in literature. His fieldwork on Cormac McCarthy includes several hundred photographs as evidence of the authenticity of place in McCarthy's Border Trilogy.

SURVEY PARTICIPANTS

Sofia Ahlberg, *La Trobe University*
Iain Bernhoft, *Rhode Island School of Design*
J. Gregory Brister, *Valley City State University*
Jamie Brummer, *Christian Brothers High School (Tennessee)*
Maria Odette Canivell, *Independent Scholar*
Jean W. Cash, *James Madison University*
Will Clemens, *Clark State Community College*
Lydia R. Cooper, *Creighton University*
Matthew Dixon, *Elk Island Public Schools (Alberta, Canada)*
Michael Gibbs, *University of South Carolina, Aiken*
Randall Green, *Oakridge High School*
Morten Hansen, *Bowdoin College*
Lauren Harmon, *Cornell University*
Dustin Hellberg, *Yonsei University*
Christina Bieber Lake, *Wheaton College*
David J. Leigh, *Seattle University*
Marcia B. Littenberg, *Farmingdale State University of New York*
Benjamin Mangrum, *University of Michigan*
Lauren Rule Maxwell, *The Citadel, The Military College of South Carolina*
Matthew McEver, *University of North Georgia*
Nicholas Monk, *University of Warwick*
Rafael Acosta Morales, *University of Kansas*
Jacob P. Pride, *University of Denver*
Matthew Raese, *Kent State University, Stark*
Rebecca Reeder-Hunt, *The Meadows School*
Wallis Sanborn, *Our Lady of the Lake University*
Eric Schaefer, *Independent Scholar*
John D. Schwetman, *University of Minnesota, Duluth*
Mac Snodgrass, *TDS Consulting*
Delys W. Snyder, *Brigham Young University*
Phillip A. Snyder, *Brigham Young University*
James Speese, *Drew University*
Nell Sullivan, *University of Houston, Downtown Campus*
Christy Tidwell, *South Dakota School of Mines and Technology*
Benjamin West, *State University of New York, Delhi*
Kristy Wilson, *Ellenville High School, New York*
Michael Zeitlin, *University of British Columbia*

WORKS CITED

Abbey, Edward. *Desert Solitaire: A Season in the Wilderness*. Ballantine Books, 1968.

———. *Desert Solitaire: A Season in the Wilderness*. Touchstone, 1990.

Adams, Ansel. "Mount McKinley and Wonder Lake, Denali National Park, Alaska." 1947. *National Gallery of Art*, www.nga.gov/collection/art-object-page.66715.html.

———. "Mount Williamson, the Sierra Nevada, from Manzanar, California." 1944. *National Gallery of Art*, www.nga.gov/collection/art-object-page.66682.html.

Ahmed, Sara. *Willful Subjects*. Duke UP, 2014.

Alarcón, Daniel Cooper. "All the Pretty Mexicos: Cormac McCarthy's Mexican Representations." *Southwestern American Literature*, vol. 25, no. 1, 1999, pp. 58–66.

Alberto, José. "Cultura Mexicana." *YouTube*, www.youtube.com/culturamexicana.

Los Alegres de Terán. *10 Corridos norteños*. Vol. 1, Los Alegres de Terán, 2017.

Allison, Dorothy. *Bastard out of Carolina*. Dutton, 1992.

All the Pretty Horses. Directed by Billy Bob Thornton, written by Cormac McCarthy, performances by Matt Damon, Penélope Cruz, Henry Thomas, and Rubén Blades, Miramax, 2000.

Anderson, Leon, and Bonnie Glass-Coffin. "I Learn by Going: Autoethnographic Modes of Inquiry." *Handbook of Autoethnography*, edited by Stacy Holman Jones et al., Left Coast Press, 2013, pp. 57–83.

Anthony, James L., and John A. Downing. "Exploitation Trajectory of a Declining Fauna: A Century of Freshwater Mussel Fisheries in North America." *Canadian Journal of Fisheries and Aquatic Sciences*, vol. 58, no. 10, Oct. 2001, pp. 2071–90.

The Apocryphal New Testament. Translated by M. R. James, Clarendon Press, 2004.

Arnold, Edwin T. "Cormac McCarthy's *The Stonemason*: The Unmaking of a Play." Wallach, *Myth*, pp. 141–53.

———. "McCarthy and the Sacred: A Reading of *The Crossing*." Lilley, pp. 215–38.

———. "Naming, Knowing and Nothingness: McCarthy's Moral Parables." Arnold and Luce, *Perspectives*, pp. 45–70.

Arnold, Edwin T., and Dianne C. Luce. Introduction. Arnold and Luce, *Perspectives*, pp. 1–16.

———, editors. *Perspectives on Cormac McCarthy*. 1993. Revised ed., UP of Mississippi, 1999.

Atwood, Margaret. *MaddAddam*. Anchor Books, 2014.

———. *Oryx and Crake*. Anchor Books, 2004.

———. *The Year of the Flood*. Anchor Books, 2010.

Augustine. *The Augustine Catechism: The Enchiridion on Faith, Hope and Charity*. Edited by Boniface Ramsey, translated by Bruce Harbert, New City Press, 2008.

Bacigalupi, Paolo. *The Water Knife*. Alfred A. Knopf, 2015.

———. *The Windup Girl*. Night Shade Books, 2009.

Baker, W. Oliver. "'Words Are Things': The Settler Colonial Politics of Post-humanist Materialism in Cormac McCarthy's *Blood Meridian*." *Mediations*, vol. 31, no. 1, 2016, pp. 1–24.

The Ballad of Gregorio Cortez. Directed by Robert M. Young, performances by Edward James Olmos, James Gammon, and Barry Corbin, Embassy Pictures, 1982.

Bartlett, Andrew. "From Voyeurism to Archaeology: Cormac McCarthy's *Child of God*." *The Southern Literary Journal*, vol. 24, no. 1, 1991, pp. 3–15.

Bates, John M. "The Impact of Impoundment on the Mussel Fauna of Kentucky Reservoir, Tennessee River." *The American Midland Naturalist*, vol. 68, no. 1, July 1962, pp. 232–36.

The Battle at Elderbush Gulch. Directed by D. W. Griffith, Biograph, 1913. *YouTube*, uploaded by Inter-Pathé, 19 Mar. 2015, www.youtube.com/watch?v=uGe-v-2dkTA.

Baym, Nina, editor. *The Norton Anthology of American Literature*. Shorter 8th ed., vol. 1, W. W. Norton, 2012.

Bazin, André. *What Is Cinema?* Vol. 2, translated by Hugh Gray, U of California P, 2005.

Bell, Vereen M. *The Achievement of Cormac McCarthy*. Louisiana State UP, 1988.

Benjamin, Walter. *Illuminations*. Edited by Hannah Arendt, Schocken Books, 1985.

Bibby, Michael. "'Where Is Vietnam?' Antiwar Poetry and the Canon." *College English*, vol. 55, no. 2, 1993, pp. 158–78.

Bloom, Harold. Introduction. *Blood Meridian; or, The Evening Redness in the West*, by Cormac McCarthy, Modern Library, 2001, pp. v–xiii.

Bone, Martyn. *The Postsouthern Sense of Place in Contemporary Fiction*. 2005. Louisiana State UP, 2014.

Botting, Fred. *Gothic (the New Critical Idiom)*. 2nd ed., Routledge, 2014.

Bowles, Paul. *The Stories of Paul Bowles*. HarperCollins Publishers, 2006.

———. *Their Heads Are Green and Their Hands Are Blue*. Hauraki Publishing, 2016.

Bragard, Véronique. "Sparing Words in the Wasted Land: Garbage, Texture, and Écriture Blanche in Auster's *In the Country of Last Things* and McCarthy's *The Road*." *ISLE*, vol. 20, no. 3, 2013, pp. 479–93.

"Brailing for Mussels in America." *YouTube*, uploaded by The Pearl Girls, 30 Dec. 2013, www.youtube.com/watch?v=zSAtvViPnno&feature=youtu.be.

Braune, Sean. "A Chaotic and Dark Vitalism: A Case Study of Cormac McCarthy's Psychopaths amid a Geology of Immorals." *Western American Literature*, vol. 50, no. 1, 2015, pp. 1–24.

Brewton, Vince. "The Changing Landscape of Violence in Cormac McCarthy's Early Novels and the Border Trilogy." *The Southern Literary Journal*, vol. 37, no. 1, 2004, pp. 121–43. *JSTOR*, www.jstor.org/stable/20078400.

Brinkmeyer, Robert H., Jr. *The Fourth Ghost: White Southern Writers and European Fascism, 1930–1950*. Louisiana State UP, 2009.

———. *Remapping Southern Literature: Contemporary Southern Writers and the West*. Revised ed., U of Georgia P, 2007.

Brown, Larry. *Big Bad Love*. Vintage Books, 1991.

Buell, Frederick. "A Short History of Environmental Apocalypse." *Future Ethics: Climate Change and Apocalyptic Imagination*, edited by Stefan Skrimshire, Continuum Books, 2010, pp. 13–36.

Bullard, Robert D. "Confronting Environmental Racism in the Twenty-First Century." *The Colors of Nature: Culture, Identity, and the Natural World*, edited by Alison H. Deming and Lauret E. Savoy, Milkweed Editions, 2002, pp. 90–97.

———. *Dumping in Dixie: Race, Class, and Environmental Quality*. Westview Press, 1990.

Butler, Judith. *Gender Trouble*. Routledge, 1990.

———. *Undoing Gender*. Routledge, 2004.

Cable, George Washington. "Literature in the Southern States." 1882. *The Negro Question: A Selection of Writings on Civil Rights in the South*, edited by Arlin Turner, Doubleday, 1958, pp. 40–50.

Camus, Albert. *The Myth of Sisyphus*. Vintage Books, 2018.

Canfield, J. Douglas. "Oedipal Complexities in Cormac McCarthy's *The Stonemason* and *The Gardener's Son*." *The Cormac McCarthy Journal*, vol. 2, no. 1, Spring 2002, pp. 12–22.

Cant, John. *Cormac McCarthy and the Myth of American Exceptionalism*. Routledge, 2008.

"Canyon de Chelly National Monument." *American Southwest: A National Register of Historic Places Travel Itinerary*, US Department of the Interior, National Park Service, www.nps.gov/nr/travel/amsw/sw22.htm.

Carson, Rachel. *Silent Spring*. Houghton Mifflin, 1962.

"Catamite." *Oxford English Dictionary*, Oxford UP, 2018, oed.com/view/Entry/28731?redirectedFrom=catamite#eid.

Cather, Willa. *Death Comes for the Archbishop*. 1927. Virago, 1981.

Chabon, Michael. "After the Apocalypse." *The New York Review of Books*, 15 Feb. 2007, www.nybooks.com/articles/2007/02/15/after-the-apocalypse/.

Chamberlain, Samuel E. *My Confession: Recollections of a Rogue*. Harper and Brothers, 1956. *Internet Archive*, archive.org/details/in.ernet.dli.2015.226260/page/n173/mode/2up.

Chesnutt, Charles. *The House behind the Cedars*. Houghton, Mifflin, 1900. *Documenting the American South*, U of North Carolina at Chapel Hill, 1997, docsouth.unc.edu/southlit/chesnutthouse/cheshouse.html.

Child of God. Directed by James Franco, written by Cormac McCarthy, performances by Scott Haze and Tim Blake Nelson, RabbitBandini Productions, 2013.

Christensen, Nels Anchor. "Facing the Weather in James Galvin's *The Meadow* and Cormac McCarthy's *The Road*." *ISLE*, vol. 21, no. 1, 2014, pp. 192–204.

Cixous, Hélène. "The Laugh of the Medusa." *Signs*, vol. 1, no. 4, Summer 1976, pp. 875–93.

Cobb, James C. *Away Down South: A History of Southern Identity*. Oxford UP, 2005.

Coen, Joel, and Ethan Coen. "We've Killed a Lot of Animals." Interview by John Patterson. *The Guardian*, 21 Dec. 2007, www.theguardian.com/film/2007/dec/21/coenbrothers.

Collins, John J. *The Apocalyptic Imagination: An Introduction to Jewish Apocalyptic Literature*. 3rd ed., Eerdmans, 2016.

Colton, Craig E. "Reintroducing Nature to the City: Wetlands in New Orleans." Sutter and Manganiello, pp. 432–57.

"Communion, *N*." *Oxford English Dictionary*, Oxford UP, 2018, oed.com/view/Entry/37318?redirectedFrom=communion#eid.

Connell, R. W. *Gender and Power: Society, the Person and Sexual Politics*. Stanford UP, 1987.

Cooper, Lydia R. "Cormac McCarthy's *The Road* as Apocalyptic Grail Narrative." *Studies in the Novel*, vol. 43, no. 2, Summer 2011, pp. 218–36.

———. "'A Howling Void': Beckett's Influence in Cormac McCarthy's *The Sunset Limited*." *The Cormac McCarthy Journal*, vol. 10, no. 1, 2012, pp. 1–15.

———. *Masculinities in Literature of the American West*. Palgrave Macmillan, 2016.

———. *No More Heroes: Narrative Perspective and Morality in Cormac McCarthy*. Louisiana State UP, 2011.

Cooper, Paul. "See Eerie Pictures inside a Namibian Ghost Town." *National Geographic*, 5 Nov. 2020, www.nationalgeographic.com/travel/destinations/africa/namibia/eerie-fascinating-pictures-kolmanskop-desert-diamond-ghost-town/.

The Counselor. Directed by Ridley Scott, written by Cormac McCarthy, performances by Michael Fassbender, Javier Bardem, and Cameron Diaz, Fox 2000 Pictures, 2014.

Crews, Michael Lynn. *Books Are Made out of Books: A Guide to Cormac McCarthy's Literary Influences*. U of Texas P, 2017.

Cronon, William. "The Trouble with Wilderness; or, Getting Back to the Wrong Nature." *Uncommon Ground: Rethinking the Human Place in Nature*, edited by Cronon, W. W. Norton, 1995, pp. 69–90.

Crutzen, Paul J., and Eugene F. Stoermer. "The 'Anthropocene.'" *Global Change Newsletter*, no. 41, May 2000, pp. 17–18.

Cutchins, Dennis. "Grace and Moss's End in *No Country for Old Men*." King et al., pp. 155–72.

Daugherty, Leo. "Gravers False and True: *Blood Meridian* as Gnostic Tragedy." Arnold and Luce, *Perspectives*, pp. 159–74.

Davidson, Donald. *The Tennessee: Rivers of America*. 2 vols., Rinehart, 1946–48.

Davis, Donald E. "Metropolis: Paradise Lost." *Southern United States: An Environmental History*, edited by Davis et al., ABC-CLIO, 2006, pp. 159–82.

DeCoste, Marcel D. "'A Thing That Even Death Cannot Undo': The Operation of the Theological Virtues in Cormac McCarthy's *The Road*." *Religion and Literature*, vol. 22, no. 2, 2012, pp. 67–91.

Deleuze, Gilles, and Félix Guattari. *A Thousand Plateaus: Capitalism and Schizophrenia*. Translated by Brian Massumi, Continuum, 1987.

DeLillo, Don. *Falling Man*. Picador, 2007.

Derrida, Jacques. "The Law of Genre." *Modern Genre Theory*, edited by David Duff, Longman, 2000, pp. 219–31.

Dimock, Wai Chee. "A Theory of Resonance." *PMLA*, vol. 112, no. 5, 1997, pp. 1060–71.

DiTommaso, Lorenzo. "Apocalypticism and Popular Culture." *Oxford Handbook of Apocalyptic Literature*, edited by John J. Collins, Oxford UP, 2014, pp. 473–509.

Dixon, Thomas. *The Clansman: An Historical Romance of the Ku Klux Klan*. Doubleday, Page, 1905. *Documenting the American South*, U of North Carolina at Chapel Hill, 1997, docsouth.unc.edu/southlit/dixonclan/dixon.html.

Doane, Mary Anne. *The Emergence of Cinematic Time: Modernity, Contingency, the Archive*. Harvard UP, 2002.

Dominy, Jordan J. "Cannibalism, Consumerism, and Profanation: Cormac McCarthy's *The Road* and the End of Capitalism." *The Cormac McCarthy Journal*, vol. 13, no. 1, 2015, pp. 143–58.

Donnelly, Brian. "'Coke Is It!': Placing Coca-Cola in McCarthy's *The Road*." *The Explicator*, vol. 68, no. 1, 2010, pp. 70–73.

Dostoevksy, Fyodor. *The Brothers Karamazov*. 1880. Translated by Richard Pevear and Larissa Volokhonsky, Farrar, Straus and Giroux, 2002.

Douglass, Frederick. "Narrative of the Life of Frederick Douglass." Baym, pp. 938–1002.

Drinnon, Richard. *Facing West: The Metaphysics of Indian-Hating and Empire Building*. U of Minnesota P, 1980.

Drive-By Truckers. "A World of Hurt." *A Blessing and a Curse*, New West, 2006.

Duhm, Ulrike. "One Reporter's Account of SFI's 'Genius and Madness' Event in August." *Santa Fe Institute*, 9 Nov. 2015, www.santafe.edu/news-center/news/genius-and-madness-sz-trans-english.

Eaton, Mark A. "Dis(re)membered Bodies: Cormac McCarty's Border Fiction." *MFS*, vol. 49, no. 1, 2003, pp. 155–80.

Ehrlich, Paul R. *The Population Bomb*. Ballantine Books, 1968.

Eliot, T. S. "The Love Song of J. Alfred Prufrock." McMichael, pp. 1137–40.

———. "Tradition and the Individual Talent." McMichael, pp. 1169–74.

Ellis, Jay. *No Place for Home: Spatial Constraint and Character Flight in the Novels of Cormac McCarthy*. Routledge, 2006.

———. "*The Road* beyond Zombies of the New South." *Critical Insights: Southern Gothic Literature*, edited by Ellis, Salem Press, 2013, pp. 49–72.

Eusebius. *The Church History of Eusebius*. Translated by Arthur Cushman McGiffert. *A Select Library of the Nicene and Post-Nicene Fathers of the Christian Church*, edited by Philip Schaff and Henry Wace, series 2, vol. 1, Eerdmans Publishing, 1963. *Christian Classics Ethereal Library*, www.ccel.org/ccel/schaff/npnf201.iii.xii.xxvi.html.

Faulkner, William. *Absalom, Absalom!* 1936. Vintage Books, 1990.

———. *Go Down, Moses*. Garland Publishing, 1994.

———. *If I Forget Thee, Jerusalem*. 1939. Vintage Books, 1990.

———. *Light in August*. 1932. Vintage Books, 1990.

———. *Selected Short Stories*. Penguin, 1993.

Fiedler, Leslie. *Love and Death in the American Novel*. Dalkey Archive Press, 1997.

Fitzgerald, F. Scott. *The Great Gatsby*. 1925. Charles Scribner's Sons, 2009.

Foer, Jonathan Safran. *Extremely Loud and Incredibly Close*. Houghton Mifflin, 2005.

Forbis, Christopher, et al. "Words Cormac McCarthy Uses in His Novels." 2007, www.johnsepich.com/documents/words_cormac_mccarthy_uses_in_his_novels.pdf.

Fowler, Alastair. *Kinds of Literature: An Introduction to the Theory of Genres and Modes*. Harvard UP, 1982.

Franco, James. "James Franco's *Blood Meridian* Test." *Vice*, 21 July 2014, www.vice.com/en_us/article/5gkad3/james-francos-blood-meridian-test-656.

Franklin, Benjamin. "The Autobiography." Baym, pp. 248–308.

Frye, Steven. "*Blood Meridian* and the Poetics of Violence." Frye, *Cambridge Companion*, pp. 107–20.

———, editor. *The Cambridge Companion to Cormac McCarthy*. Cambridge UP, 2013.

———, editor. *Cormac McCarthy in Context*. Cambridge UP, 2020.

———. "Cormac McCarthy's Life and Career." Frye, *Cormac*, pp. 3–12.

———. "Prospects for the Study of Cormac McCarthy." *Resources for American Literary Study*, vol. 39, 2017, pp. 1–26.

———. *Understanding Cormac McCarthy*. U of South Carolina P, 2009.

Gadamer, Hans-Georg. *Truth and Method*. 2nd ed., Continuum Books, 2004.

Galbraith, John Kenneth. *The Affluent Society*. 1958. Houghton Mifflin, 1998.

Gallón, Natalie. "Another Journalist Found Dead in Mexico, One of the Most Dangerous Countries for Reporters." *CNN*, 11 Sept. 2020, www.cnn.com/2020/09/11/americas/julio-valdivia-mexico-murder-intl/index.html.

The Gardener's Son. Directed by Richard Pearce, written by Cormac McCarthy, performances by Brad Dourif and Ned Beatty, PBS, 1977.

Gast, John. *American Progress*. "John Gast, American Progress, 1872," by Martha A. Sandweiss. *Picturing United States History*, 2021, picturinghistory.gc.cuny.edu/john-gast-american-progress-1872/.

Gersdorf, Catrin. *The Poetics and Politics of the Desert*. Rodopi, 2009.

Giemza, Bryan. "Toward a Catholic Understanding of Cormac McCarthy's Oeuvre." *You Would Not Believe What Watches:* Suttree *and Cormac McCarthy's Knoxville*, edited by Rick Wallach, Cormac McCarthy Society, pp. 154–72.

Glotfelty, Cheryll, and Harold Fromm, editors. *The Ecocriticism Reader: Landmarks in Literary Ecology*. U of Georgia P, 1996.

Grammer, John. "'A Thing against Which Time Will Not Prevail': Pastoral and History in Cormac McCarthy's South." Arnold and Luce, *Perspectives*, pp. 29–44.

Greenwood, Willard P. *Reading Cormac McCarthy*. ABC-CLIO, 2009.

Greeson, Jennifer Rae. *Our South: Geographical Fantasy and the Rise of National Literature*. Harvard UP, 2010.

Greve, Julius. *Shreds of Matter: Cormac McCarthy and the Concept of Nature*. Dartmouth College Press, 2018.

Grey, Zane. *Riders of the Purple Sage*. Edited by Lee Clark Mitchell, Oxford UP, 1998.

Guillemin, Georg. "Cormac McCarthy: A Bibliography of German Translations, Reviews, and Essays." Apr. 1997, cormacmccarthy.com/wp-content/uploads/GermanBib.pdf.

———. *The Pastoral Vision of Cormac McCarthy*. Texas A&M UP, 2004.

Guinn, Matthew. *After Southern Modernism: Fiction of the Contemporary South*. UP of Mississippi, 2000.

Haag, Wendell R. "Past and Future Patterns of Freshwater Mussel Extinctions in North America during the Holocene." *Holocene Extinctions*, edited by Samuel T. Turvey, Oxford UP, 2009, pp. 107–28.

Haddox, Thomas F. "Elizabeth Spencer, the White Civil Rights Novel, and the Post-southern." *MLQ*, vol. 65, no. 4, 2004, pp. 561–81.

Hall, Wade, and Rick Wallach, editors. *Sacred Violence*. 1995. Revised and expanded ed., Texas Western Press, 2002.

Halpern, Daniel. "The Last Existentialist." *The New York Times*, 19 Dec. 1999, www.nytimes.com/1999/12/19/books/bookend-the-last-existentialist.html.

Harman, Graham. *Tool-Being*. Open Court, 2002.

HarperCollins Study Bible. Revised ed., HarperCollins Publishers, 2006.

Hawkins, Ty. *Cormac McCarthy's Philosophy*. Palgrave Macmillan, 2017.

Hegel, Georg Wilhelm Friedrich. *Phenomenology of Mind*. 1807. *Marxists Internet Archive*, www.marxists.org/reference/archive/hegel/phindex.htm.

Hemingway, Ernest. "Big Two-Hearted River, Part 1." Hemingway, *In Our Time*, pp. 177–94.

———. "Big Two-Hearted River, Part 2." Hemingway, *In Our Time*, pp. 195–214.

———. "Hills Like White Elephants." *A Practical Introduction to Literary Study*, edited by James S. Brown and Scott Yarbrough, Pearson, 2005, pp. 296–99.

———. *In Our Time*. Boni and Liveright, 1925.

———. *The Sun Also Rises*. Scribner, 2003.

Hillier, Russell M. "'In a Dark Parody' of John Bunyan's *The Pilgrim's Progress*: The Presence of Subversive Allegory in Cormac McCarthy's *Outer Dark*." *ANQ*, vol. 19, no. 4, 2006, pp. 52–58.

———. *Morality in Cormac McCarthy's Fiction: Souls at Hazard*. Palgrave Macmillan, 2017.

Hobson, Fred. *The Southern Writer in the Postmodern World*. U of Georgia P, 1991.

Holloway, David. *The Late Modernism of Cormac McCarthy*. Greenwood Press, 2002.

The Holy Bible. English Standard Version, Crossway, 2001.

Houser, Heather. *Ecosickness in Contemporary U.S. Fiction: Environment and Affect*. Columbia UP, 2014.

How the West Was Won. Directed by John Ford, performances by Henry Fonda, Gregory Peck, MGM, 1963.

Hungerford, Amy. *Postmodern Belief: American Literature and Religion since 1960*. Princeton UP, 2010.

Hunter, Megan. *The End We Start From*. Picador, 2017.

I Am Legend. Directed by Francis Lawrence, Village Roadshow, 2007.

An Inconvenient Truth. Directed by Davis Guggenheim, performance by Al Gore, Paramount Classics, 2006.

Inge, M. Thomas. Review of *Suttree*, by Cormac McCarthy. *American Humor*, vol. 6, no. 1, Spring 1979, pp. 17–18.

Jackson, Joshua Ryan. "This Too Shall Pass: Distant Reading in a Future of Ruins in Cormac McCarthy's Postsouthern Novels." *The Cormac McCarthy Journal*, vol. 15, no. 2, 2017, pp. 107–27.

Jacobs, Harriet. *Incidents in the Life of a Slave Girl*. Baym, pp. 938–1002.

James, Caryn. "Is Everybody Dead around Here?" *The New York Times Book Review*, 28 Apr. 1985, www.nytimes.com/1985/04/28/books/is-everybody-dead-around-here.html.

Jameson, Fredric. *The Geopolitical Aesthetic: Cinema and Space in the World System*. Indiana UP, 1992.

———. *Postmodernism; or, The Cultural Logic of Late Capitalism*. Duke UP, 1991.

Jarrett, Robert L. *Cormac McCarthy*. Twayne Publishers, 1997.

———. "Cormac McCarthy's Sense of an Ending: Serialized Narrative and Revision in *Cities of the Plain*." Lilley, pp. 313–42.

Jefferson, Thomas. "From Thomas Jefferson to Chastellux, with Enclosure, 2 September 1785." *National Archives*, founders.archives.gov/documents/Jefferson/01-08-02-0362.

Jergenson, Casey. "'In What Direction Did Lost Men Veer?': Late Capitalism and Utopia in *The Road*." *The Cormac McCarthy Journal*, vol. 14, no. 1, 2016, pp. 117–32.

Jianran, Zhang. "Cormac McCarthy: A Bibliography of Criticism in Chinese." 9 Mar. 2013, cormacmccarthy.com/wp-content/uploads/ChineseBib.pdf.

Jonas, Hans. *The Gnostic Religion*. Beacon Press, 1963.

Jones, Edward P. *The Known World*. Amistad, 2003.

Josephs, Allen. "The Quest for God in *The Road*." Frye, *Cambridge Companion*, pp. 133–45.

Joyce, James. *Ulysses*. 1922. Penguin Books, 1992.

Kenan, Randall. *Let the Dead Bury the Dead*. Harcourt, 1993.

Keneally, Thomas. *The Place Where Souls Are Born: A Journey into the American Southwest*. Hodder and Stoughton, 1992.

Kermode, Frank. *The Sense of an Ending: Studies in the Theory of Fiction with a New Epilogue*. Oxford UP, 2000.

King, Lynnea Chapman, et al., editors. No Country for Old Men*: From Novel to Film*, Scarecrow Press, 2009.

Koch, Klaus. *Ratlos vor der Apocaklyptik*. Mohn, 1970.

Kollin, Susan. "Genre and the Geographies of Violence: Cormac McCarthy and the Contemporary Western." *Contemporary Literature*, vol. 42, no. 3, 2001, pp. 557–88.

Kreml, Nancy. "Implicatures of Styleshifting in the Narrative Voice of Cormac McCarthy's *All the Pretty Horses*." *Codes and Consequences: Choosing Linguistic Varieties*, edited by Carol Myers-Scotton, Oxford UP, 1998, pp. 41–61.

Kreyling, Michael. *Inventing Southern Literature*. UP of Mississippi, 1998.

———. *The South That Wasn't There: Postsouthern Memory and History*. Louisiana UP, 2010.

Lang, James M. *Small Teaching: Everyday Lessons from the Science of Learning*. Jossey-Bass, 2016.

Leech, Geoffrey, and Mick Short. *Style in Fiction: A Linguistic Introduction to English Fictional Prose*. 2nd ed., Pearson, 2007.

Le Guin, Ursula K. *The Unreal and the Real: The Selected Short Stories*. Saga Press, 2014.

Lenihan, John H. "Teaching the Western." *OAH Magazine of History*, vol. 16, no. 4, 2002, pp. 27–30.

Levine, Caroline. *Forms: Whole, Rhythm, Hierarchy, Network*. Princeton UP, 2017.

Lilienfeld, Scott O., and Hal Arkowitz. "What 'Psychopath' Means." *Scientific American*, 1 Dec. 2007, www.scientificamerican.com/article/what-psychopath-means/.

Lilley, James, editor. *Cormac McCarthy: New Directions*. U of New Mexico P, 2002.

Lopez, Barry. *Of Wolves and Men*. Scribner, 1978.

Love, Glen A. "Revaluing Nature: Toward an Ecological Criticism." *The Ecocriticism Reader: Landmarks in Literary Ecology*, edited by Cheryll Glotfelty and Harold Fromm, U of Georgia P, 1996, pp. 225–40.

Luce, Dianne C. "Ballard Rising in *Outer Dark*: The Genesis and Early Composition of *Child of God*." *The Cormac McCarthy Journal*, vol. 17, no. 2, 2019, pp. 88–115.

———. "Cormac McCarthy and Albert Erskine: Evolution of a Working Relationship." *Resources for American Literary Study*, vol. 35, 2010, pp. 303–38.

———. "Cormac McCarthy in High School: 1951." *The Cormac McCarthy Journal*, vol. 7, no. 1, 2009, pp. 1–6.

———. "Projecting Interiority: Psychogenesis and the Composition of *Outer Dark*." *The Cormac McCarthy Journal*, vol. 16, no. 1, 2018, pp. 1–35.

———. *Reading the World: Cormac McCarthy's Tennessee Period*. U of South Carolina P, 2011.

———. "Tall Tales and Raw Realities: Late-Stage Deletions from Cormac McCarthy's *Suttree*." *Resources for American Literary Study*, vol. 38, 2015, pp. 213–56.

Lyotard, Jean-François. *The Postmodern Condition: A Report on Knowledge*. Translated by Geoff Bennington and Brian Massumi, U Minnesota P, 1984.

Mad Max: Fury Road. Directed by George Miller, Kennedy Miller Mitchell, 2015.

Malewitz, Raymond. "Regeneration through Misuse: Rugged Consumerism in Contemporary American Culture." *PMLA*, vol. 127, no. 3, 2012, pp. 526–41.

Manganiello, Christopher J. *Southern Water, Southern Power: How the Politics of Cheap Energy and Water Scarcity Shaped a Region*. U of North Carolina P, 2015.

Marx, Leo. 1964. *The Machine in the Garden*. Oxford UP, 2000.

Matthews, John T. "The Moveable South: Plantation Memory in Cormac McCarthy's *The Road*." *Unsteadily Marching On: The U.S. South in Motion*, edited by Constante González Groba, Publicacions de la Universitat de València, 2013, pp. 67–73.

———. *William Faulkner: Seeing through the South*. Blackwell Publishing, 2009.

Maxwell, Lauren Rule. "Hemingway, His Contemporaries, and the South Carolina Corps of Cadets: Exploring Veterans' Inner Worlds." *Teaching Hemingway and Modernism*, edited by Joseph Fruscione, Kent State UP, 2015, pp. 128–36.

McCarthy, Cormac. *All the Pretty Horses*. Alfred A. Knopf, 1992.

———. "Author Lives in Blount." *News-Sentinel* [Knoxville, TN], 6 Oct. 1968, p. F5.

———. "Autumn's Magic." *The Gold and Blue*, Knoxville Catholic High School, 22 Nov. 1950, p. 2.

———. *Blood Meridian*. Random House, 1985.

———. *Blood Meridian*. Vintage Books, 2010. E-book.

———. *Child of God*. 1973. Vintage Books, 1993.

———. *Cities of the Plain*. 1984. Cormac McCarthy Papers, box 70, folder 3, Southwestern Writers Collection, Wittliff Collections, Texas State University, San Marcos. Shooting script.

———. *Cities of the Plain*. 1998. Vintage Books, 1999.

———. "Cormac Country." Interview by Richard B. Woodward. *Vanity Fair*, Aug. 2005, pp. 98, 100, 103–04.

———. "Cormac McCarthy's Apocalypse." Interview by David Kushner. *Rolling Stone*, 27 Dec. 2007, www.davidkushner.com/article/cormac-mccarthys-apocalypse/.

———. "Cormac McCarthy's Venomous Fiction." Interview by Richard B. Woodward. *The New York Times*, 19 Apr. 1992, www.nytimes.com/1992/04/19/magazine/cormac-mccarthy-s-venomous-fiction.html.

———. *The Counselor: A Screenplay*. Vintage Books, 2013.

———. *The Crossing*. 1994. Cormac McCarthy Papers, box 58, folder 1, Southwestern Writers Collection, Wittliff Collections, Texas State University, San Marcos. Draft.

———. *The Crossing*. 1994. Vintage Books, 1995.

———. *The Gardener's Son*. 1996. Ecco Press, 2015.

———. "Hollywood's Favorite Cowboy." Interview by John Jurgensen. *The Wall Street Journal*, 13 Nov. 2009, www.wsj.com/articles/SB10001424052748704576204574529703577274572.

———. Interview by Oprah Winfrey. *The Oprah Winfrey Show*, CBS, 5 June 2007. *Oprah.com*, www.oprah.com/oprahsbookclub/oprahs-exclusive-interview-with-cormac-mccarthy-video.

———. "'Just Write' Says Successful Author." Interview by Richard Jordan. *Daily Beacon* [U of Tennessee], 28 Jan. 1969, p. 6.

———. "The Kekulé Problem." *Nautilus*, vol. 19, nos. 46–47, Mar.-Apr. 2017, pp. 22–31.

———. "Knox Native McCarthy's 'Outer Dark' Second Novel Gets Good Reviews." Interview by Pat Fields. *Knoxville Journal*, 7 Oct. 1968, p. A8.

———. Letter to Albert Erskine. Mar. 1984. Albert Erskine Papers, box 28, folder 8, Albert and Shirley Small Special Collections Library, University of Virginia.

———. "McCarthy Is One of Nation's Most Remarked Young Authors." Interview by Mark Owen. *Maryville-Alcoa Times* [TN], 26 Feb. 1971, p. 4B.

———. *No Country for Old Men*. Alfred A. Knopf, 2005.

———. *No Country for Old Men*. Cormac McCarthy Papers, box 79, folder 5, Southwestern Writers Collection, Wittliff Collections, Texas State University, San Marcos. Screenplay.

———. *The Orchard Keeper*. 1965. Vintage Books, 1993.

———. *Outer Dark*. 1968. Vintage Books, 1993.

———. *The Road*. Vintage Books, 2006.

———. "Sportsman's Wish." *The Gold and Blue*, Knoxville Catholic High School, Nov. 1948, p. 2.

———. *The Stonemason*. 1994. Vintage Books, 1995.

———. *The Sunset Limited: A Novel in Dramatic Form*. Vintage Books, 2006.

———. *Suttree*. Vintage Books, 1979.

———. *Suttree*. Vintage Books, 2010. E-book.

———. "Two Hour Scholar Loses His Dollar." *The Gold and Blue*, Knoxville Catholic High School, 29 Sept. 1950.

———. *Whales and Men*. Cormac McCarthy Papers, box 97, folder 5, Southwestern Writers Collection, Wittliff Collections, Texas State University, San Marcos. Uncorrected screenplay.

McCarthy, Cormac, et al. "Connecting Science and Art." Interview by Ira Flatow. *Science Friday*, 8 Apr. 2011, www.sciencefriday.com/segments/connecting-science-and-art/.

McCarthy, Cormac, et al. "A Conversation between Author Cormac McCarthy and the Coen Brothers, about the New Movie *No Country for Old Men*." Interview by Lev Grossman. *Time Magazine*, 18 Oct. 2007, content.time.com/time/magazine/article/0,9171,1673269,00.html.

McCarthy, Cormac, et al. "'Tis Nobler to Dive in Front of a Train? Discuss: A Word with Tommy Lee Jones, Samuel L. Jackson and Cormac McCarthy." Interview by David Carr. *The New York Times*, 11 Feb. 2011, p. C4.

McCoy, Kariss. "Whiteness and the 'Subject' of Waste: The Art of Slumming in *Suttree*." *The Cormac McCarthy Journal*, vol. 4, no. 1, 2004, pp. 85–99.

McFague, Sallie. *Speaking in Parables*. Augsburg Fortress Publishers, 2000.

McGilchrist, Megan Riley. *The Western Landscape in Cormac McCarthy and Wallace Stegner: Myths of the Frontier*. Routledge, 2010.

McGill, Mary McEntee. "Have You Seen a Burning Bush Lately?" *Catechist*, 21 June 2013, www.catechist.com/have-you-seen-a-burning-bush-lately/.

McKibben, Bill. *The End of Nature*. Anchor Books, 1989.

McLuhan, Marshal. *Understanding Media: The Extensions of Man*. Routledge, 2001.

McMichael, George, editor. *Realism to the Present*. 1993. *Anthology of American Literature*, vol. 2, Prentice Hall, 1985–93.

Melville, Herman. *Moby-Dick; or, The Whale*. 1851. W. W. Norton, 2002.

Metress, Christopher. "Via Negativa: The Way of Unknowing in Cormac McCarthy's *Outer Dark*." *Southern Review*, vol. 37, no. 1, Winter 2001, pp. 147–54.

Metz, Christian. *Film Language: A Semiotics of Cinema*. Translated by Michael Taylor, Oxford UP, 1974.

The Mexican Revolution: Corridos about the Heroes and Events, 1910–1920 and Beyond. Arhoolie Records, 1996.

The Mishnah: A New Translation. Translated by Jacob Neusner, Yale UP, 1988.

Monk, Nicholas. *A True and Living Prophet of Destruction: Cormac McCarthy and Modernity*. U of New Mexico P, 2016.

Monk, Nicholas, et al. *Open-Space Learning: A Study in Transdisciplinary Pedagogy*. Bloomsbury, 2011.

Montague, Kate. "Baroque Meridians: Between Myth and Actuality on the American Frontier." *Cormac McCarthy's Borders and Landscapes*, edited by Louise Jillett, Bloomsbury, 2016, pp. 95–106.

Moretti, Franco. *Atlas of the European Novel, 1800–1900*. Verso, 1999.

Morgan, Wesley. "Cormac McCarthy and *The Yearling*." *The Cormac McCarthy Journal*, vol. 17, no. 1, 2019, pp. 70–72.

———. "The 'Government Tank' in *The Orchard Keeper*." *The Cormac McCarthy Journal*, vol. 10, no. 1, 2012, pp. 93–96.

———. "McCarthy's High School Years." *The Cormac McCarthy Journal*, vol. 3, no. 1, 2003, pp. 6–9.

———. "Red Callahan: The Actual and the Fictitious." *The Cormac McCarthy Journal*, vol. 4, no. 1, 2005, pp. 210–19.

———. "The Route and Roots of *The Road*." *The Cormac McCarthy Journal*, vol. 6, no. 1, 2008, pp. 39–47.

———. "Suttree's Dead Acquaintances and McCarthy's Dead Friends." *The Cormac McCarthy Journal*, vol. 11, no. 1, 2013, pp. 96–104.

Morgenstern, Naomi. "Postapocalyptic Responsibility: Patriarchy at the End of the World in Cormac McCarthy's *The Road*." *Differences*, vol. 25, no. 2, Summer 2014, pp. 33–61.

Morrison, Gail Moore. "*All the Pretty Horses*: John Grady Cole's Expulsion from Paradise." Arnold and Luce, *Perspectives*, pp. 175–94.

Morrison, Toni. *Beloved*. 1987. Vintage Books, 2004.

Morton, Timothy. *Ecology without Nature: Rethinking Environmental Aesthetics*. Harvard UP, 2007.

Mugerauer, Robert. *Responding to Loss: Heideggerian Reflections on Literature*. Oxford UP, 2015.

Mulvey, Laura. "Visual Pleasure and Narrative Cinema." *Screen*, vol. 16, no. 3, 1975, pp. 6–18.

Mundik, Petra. *A Bloody and Barbarous God: The Metaphysics of Cormac McCarthy*. U of New Mexico P, 2016.

Murphy, Kelly J., and Justin Jeffcoat Schedtler, editors. *Apocalypses in Context: Apocalyptic Currents throughout History*. Fortress Press, 2016.

Nasi, Irene, and Manuela Fioretto. "Cormac McCarthy: A Bibliography of Criticism in Italian." 18 Mar. 2013, cormacmccarthy.com/wp-content/uploads/ItalianBib.pdf.

The New Oxford Annotated Bible. New Revised Standard Version, Oxford UP, 2018.

No Country for Old Men. Directed by Ethan Coen and Joel Coen, written by Cormac McCarthy, performances by Tommy Lee Jones, Javier Bardem, and Josh Brolin, Paramount Vantage / Miramax Films, 2007.

Norris, Frank. *The Complete Works of Frank Norris*. P. F. Collier.

O'Connor, Flannery. *The Complete Stories*. Farrar, Straus and Giroux, 1971.

———. "The Grotesque in Southern Fiction." *Mystery and Manners: Occasional Prose*, edited by Sally Fitzgerald and Robert Fitzgerald, Farrar, Strauss and Giroux, 1969, pp. 36–50.

O'Gorman, Farrell. "Joyce and Contesting Priesthoods in *Suttree* and *Blood Meridian*." *The Cormac McCarthy Journal*, vol. 4, no. 1, 2004, pp. 123–44.

"On Location with Ben Rivers' The Two Eyes Are Not Brothers." *BFI*, 29 Apr. 2016, www2.bfi.org.uk/news-opinion/sight-sound-magazine/features/pictures/location-ben-rivers-two-eyes-are-not-brothers.

O'Sullivan, John Louis. "Annexation." *United States Magazine and Democratic Review*, 1845, pp. 5–10.

Owens, Barcley. *Cormac McCarthy's Western Novels*. U of Arizona P, 2000.

Page, Thomas Nelson. *Ole Virginia; or, "Marse Chan" and Other Stories*, Charles Scribner's Sons, 1895. *Documenting the American South*, U of North Carolina at Chapel Hill, 2003, docsouth.unc.edu/southlit/pageolevir/page.html.

Palmer, Louis H., III. "Southern Gothic and Appalachian Gothic: A Comparative Look at Flannery O'Connor and Cormac McCarthy." *The Journal of the Appalachian Studies Association*, vol. 3, 1991, pp. 166–76.

Papineau, David. "Naturalism." *Stanford Encyclopedia of Philosophy*, 31 Mar. 2020, plato.stanford.edu/entries/naturalism/.

Paredes, Americo. *With His Pistol in His Hand: A Border Ballad and Its Hero*. U of Texas P, 1958.

Parrish, Tim. "History and the Problem of Evil in McCarthy's Western Novels." Frye, *Cambridge Companion*, pp. 67–78.

Peebles, Stacey. "Cormac McCarthy: A Critical History." Frye, *Cormac*, pp. 316–25.

———. *Cormac McCarthy and Performance: Page, Stage, Screen*. U of Texas P, 2017.

———. "McCarthy and Film." Frye, *Cambridge Companion*, pp. 162–74.

Phillips, Dana. "History and the Ugly Facts of Cormac McCarthy's *Blood Meridian*." *American Literature*, vol. 68, no. 2, 1996, pp. 433–60.

Pinsker, Sanford. "Post-war Civilization and Its Existential Discontents: Paul Bowles's *The Sheltering Sky*." *Critique*, vol. 27, no. 1, 1985, pp. 3–14.

Pitts, Jonathan. "*Blood Meridian* as Devisionary Western." *Western American Literature*, vol. 33, no. 1, 1998, pp. 6–25.

Poe, Edgar Allan. "Ligeia." 1838. *The Norton Anthology of American Literature*, edited by Robert S. Levine, shorter 9th ed., vol. 1, W. W. Norton, 2017, pp. 739–49.

Polk, Noel. *Children of the Dark House: Text and Context in Faulkner*. UP of Mississippi, 1998.

Potts, Matthew L. *Cormac McCarthy and the Signs of Sacrament: Literature, Theology, and the Moral of Stories*. Bloomsbury, 2015.

Prather, William. "'The Color of This Life Is Water': History, Stones and the River in *Suttree*." *The Cormac McCarthy Journal*, vol. 4, no. 1, 2004, pp. 39–73.

Psycho. Directed by Alfred Hitchcock, Paramount, 1960.

Purcell, Aaron D. *White Collar Radicals: TVA's Knoxville Fifteen, the New Deal, and the McCarthy Era*. U of Tennessee P, 2009.

Remedial Investigation / Feasibility Study for the David Witherspoon, Inc., 901 Site, Knoxville, Tennessee. Vol. 1, United States Department of Energy, 1996, doi:10.2172/436387.

The Revenant. Directed by Alejandro Iñárritu, performances by Leonardo DiCaprio and Tom Hardy, Twentieth Century Fox, 2015.

Rich, Nathaniel. *Odds against Tomorrow*. Farrar, Straus and Giroux, 2013.

Rivkin, Julie, and Michael Ryan. "The Class of 1968: Post-structuralism par Lui-Même." *Literary Theory: An Anthology*, edited by Rivkin and Ryan, Wiley-Blackwell, 2017, pp. 445–65.

The Road. Directed by John Hillcoat, written by Cormac McCarthy, performances by Viggo Mortensen, Kodi Smit-McPhee, Dimension Films / 2929 Productions, 2009.

"The Road—Trailer." *YouTube*, uploaded by Movies at Cinemas, 15 Jan. 2010, www.youtube.com/watch?v=M8RuQrhVBvo.

Rodríguez Marcos, Javier. "Más cerca de Texas que del DF." *El País*, 3 Dec. 2015, elpais.com/cultura/2015/12/02/actualidad/1449087419_272487.html.

Romine, Scott. "Where Is Southern Literature? The Practice of Place in a Postsouthern Age." *South to a New Place: Region, Literature, Culture*, edited by Suzanne W. Jones and Sharon Monteith, Louisiana UP, 2002, pp. 23–43.

Rubin, Louis D., Jr. "The American South: The Continuity of Self-Definition." *The American South*, edited by Rubin, Louisiana State UP, 1980, pp. 3–23.

Sanborn, Wallis R. *Animals in the Fiction of Cormac McCarthy*. McFarland, 2006.

Scarry, Elaine. *The Body in Pain: The Making and Unmaking of the World*. Oxford UP, 1985.

Scruggs, George D. *Status of Fresh-Water Mussel Stocks in the Tennessee River*. Fish and Wildlife Service, United States Department of Interior, 1960.

The Searchers. Directed by John Ford, performances by John Wayne and Claire Trevor, Warner Brothers, 1956.

Sepich, John. "All Cormac McCarthy's Words, by Book." *JohnSepich.com*, 2021, johnsepich.com/category/mccarthy-resources/.

———. *Notes on* Blood Meridian. U of Texas P, 2008.

Sepich, John, and Christopher Forbis. "A Concordance to *The Road* by Cormac McCarthy." 15 Mar. 2010, www.johnsepich.com/documents/a_concordance_to_the_road_287.pdf.

Shane. Directed by George Stevens, performances by Alan Ladd and Jean Arthur, Paramount, 1953.

Shaviro, Steven. "'The Very Life of the Darkness': A Reading of *Blood Meridian*." Arnold and Luce, *Perspectives*, pp. 145–56.

Sheinfeld, Shayna. "Scenes from the End of the World in American Popular Culture." *The Oxford Handbook of the Bible and Popular Culture*, edited by Dan W. Clanton, Jr., and Terry Ray Clark, Oxford UP, 2020, pp. 201–18.

Simpson, Helen. "Diary of an Interesting Year." *The New Yorker*, 21 Dec. 2009, www.newyorker.com/magazine/2009/12/21/diary-of-an-interesting-year.

Simpson, Lewis P. *The Brazen Face of History: Studies in the Literary Consciousness in America*. Louisiana State UP, 1980.

Sinykin, Dan. "Evening in America: *Blood Meridian* and the Origins and Ends of Imperial Capitalism." *American Literary History*, vol. 28, no. 2, 2016, pp. 362–80.

Slotkin, Richard. *Gunfighter Nation: The Myth of the Frontier in Twentieth-Century America*. Atheneum, 1992.

Smith, John. "A Description of New England." Baym, pp. 69–72.

Snyder, Phillip A., and Delys W. Snyder. "Modernism, Postmodernism, and Language: McCarthy's Style." Frye, *Cambridge Companion*, pp. 27–38.

Snyder, Phillip A., et al. *Cormac McCarthy Corpus Project*. Brigham Young University, 27 Feb. 2018, cmcp.byu.edu.

Spencer, William C. "Cormac McCarthy's Unholy Trinity: Biblical Parody in *Outer Dark*." Hall and Wallach, *Sacred Violence*, pp. 83–91.

Spiegelman, Art. *In the Shadow of No Towers*. Pantheon, 2004.

Stewart, Mart. "If John Muir Had Been an Agrarian: American Environmental History West and South." Sutter and Manganiello, pp. 196–219.

Sullivan, Nell. "Boys Will Be Boys and Girls Will Be Gone: The Circuit of Male Desire in Cormac McCarthy's Border Trilogy." *A Cormac McCarthy Companion: The Border Trilogy*, edited by Edwin T. Arnold and Dianne C. Luce, UP of Mississippi, 2001, pp. 228–55.

———. "The Evolution of the Dead Girlfriend Motif in *Outer Dark* and *Child of God*." Wallach, *Myth*, pp. 68–77.

———. "The Good Guys: McCarthy's *The Road* as Post-9/11 Male Sentimental Novel." *Genre*, vol. 46, no. 1, 2013, pp. 79–101.

Sullivan, Walter. *A Requiem for the Renascence: The State of Fiction in the Modern South*. U of Georgia P, 1976.

The Sunset Limited. Directed by Tommy Lee Jones, written by Cormac McCarthy, performances by Tommy Lee Jones and Samuel L. Jackson, HBO Films, 2011.

Sutter, Paul S., and Christopher J. Manganiello. *Environmental History and the American South: A Reader*. U of Georgia P, 2009.

Swift, Jonathan. "A Modest Proposal." *Project Gutenberg E-book*, 17 Oct. 2019, www.gutenberg.org/files/1080/1080-h/1080-h.htm.

Tate, Allen. *The Literature of the American South*. Edited by William L. Andrews, W. W. Norton, 1998.

Tatum, Stephen. "'Mercantile Ethics': *No Country for Old Men* and the Narcocorrido." *Cormac McCarthy:* All the Pretty Horses, No Country for Old Men, The Road, edited by Sara Spurgeon, Continuum Books, 2011, pp. 77–93.

Thiess, Derek J. "On *The Road* to Santa Fe: Complexity in Cormac McCarthy and Climate Change." *ISLE*, vol. 20, no. 3, 2013, pp. 532–52.

This Is the End. Directed by Seth Rogan and Evan Goldberg, Columbia Pictures, 2013.

Thoreau, Henry David. "Resistance to Civil Government." Baym, pp. 843–58.

Timrod, Henry. *The Poems of Henry Timrod*. Hale and Son, 1872. *Documenting the American South*, U of North Carolina at Chapel Hill, 1998, docsouth.unc.edu/southlit/timrod/timrod.html.

"La toma de Zacatecas—Revolución mexicana." *YouTube*, uploaded by José Alberto, 29 Oct. 2009, www.youtube.com/watch?v=-8k9aaE1rI0.

Topolnisky, Sonya. "'For Every Tatter in Its Mortal Dress': Costume and Character in *No Country for Old Men*." King et al., pp. 110–23.

"Transcript of the Monroe Doctrine (1823)." *Ourdocuments.gov*, www.ourdocuments.gov/print_friendly.php?flash=false&page=transcript&doc=23&title=Transcript+of+Monroe+Doctrine+%281823%29.

"Travel Advisory: Mexico—Level 2: (Exercise Increased Caution)." *OSAC*, United States Overseas Security Advisory Council, 17 June 2020, www.osac.gov/Content/Report/ad699d44-81aa-4e94-9834-18f444eb5266.

Trotignon, Béatrice. "A Bibliography of Cormac McCarthy's Works in Translation." *The Cormac McCarthy Journal*, vol. 17, no. 1, 2019, pp. 43–63.

———. "Cormac McCarthy: A Bibliography of French Translations, Reviews, and Essays." Dec. 1997, cormacmccarthy.com/wp-content/uploads/FrenchBib.pdf.

Turner, Frederick Jackson. "The Significance of the Frontier in American History." 1893. nationalhumanitiescenter.org/pds/gilded/empire/text1/turner.pdf.

Twain, Mark. *The Adventures of Huckleberry Finn*. Penguin, 2003.

Veblen, Thorstein. *The Theory of the Leisure Class*. 1899. Edited by Martha Banta, Oxford UP, 2007. *ProQuest*, ebookcentral.proquest.com/lib/csuniv/detail.action?docID=415975.

Vescio, Bryan. "Strangers in Everyland: Suttree, Huckleberry Finn, and Tragic Humanism." *The Cormac McCarthy Journal*, vol. 4, no. 1, 2004, pp. 74–88.

Walcutt, Charles Child. "Frank Norris on Realism and Naturalism." *American Literature*, vol. 13, no. 1, 1941, pp. 61–63.

Wallace, Garry. "Meeting McCarthy." *Southern Quarterly*, vol. 30, Summer 1992, pp. 134–39.

Wallach, Rick. "From *Beowulf* to *Blood Meridian*: Cormac McCarthy's Demystification of the Martial Code." *Southern Quarterly*, vol. 36, no. 4, 1998, pp. 113–20.

———. "Judge Holden, *Blood Meridian*'s Evil Archon." Hall and Wallach, *Sacred Violence*, pp. 125–36.

———, editor. *Myth, Legend, Dust: Critical Responses to Cormac McCarthy*. Manchester UP, 2000.

Walsh, Chris. "The Post-southern Sense of Place in *The Road*." *The Cormac McCarthy Journal*, vol. 6, 2008, pp. 48–53.

Wegner, John. "'Mexico para los mexicanos': Revolution, Mexico, and Cormac McCarthy's Border Trilogy." *Southwestern American Literature*, vol. 25, no. 1, Fall 1999, pp. 67–73.

Wheeler, Michael. "Martin Heidegger." *Stanford Encyclopedia of Philosophy*, 12 Oct. 2011, plato.stanford.edu/entries/heidegger/.

Wielenberg, Eric. "God, Morality, and Meaning in Cormac McCarthy's *The Road*." *The Cormac McCarthy Journal*, vol. 8, no. 1, 2010, pp. 1–16.

The Wild Bunch. Directed by Sam Peckinpah, performances by William Holden and Ernest Borgnine, Warner Brothers, 1969.

Willbern, David. "Dialogic Frontiers: History and Psychology in *Lonesome Dove* and *Blood Meridian*." *Arizona Quarterly*, vol. 70, no. 1, 2014, pp. 81–108.

Williams, Raymond. *Marxism and Literature*. Oxford UP, 1977.

Witek, Terri. "Reeds and Hides: Cormac McCarthy's Domestic Spaces." *The Southern Review*, vol. 30, 1994, pp. 136–42.

Witness. Produced by Michael Mann, performance by Eros Hoagland, season 1, episode 1, HBO, 2012.

Wood, Daniel Davis. *Frontier Justice in the Novels of James Fenimore Cooper and Cormac McCarthy*. Cambridge Scholars Publishing, 2016.

Woodson, Linda. "Mapping *The Road* in Post-postmodernism." *The Cormac McCarthy Journal*, vol. 6, 2008, pp. 87–97.

Woodward, C. Vann. *The Burden of Southern History*. Louisiana State UP, 1960.

Woolf, Virginia. *Selected Essays*. Edited by David Bradshaw, Oxford UP, 2009.

Wordsworth, William. "My Heart Leaps Up." *Poets.org*, Academy of American Poets, 2020, poets.org/poem/my-heart-leaps.

Wright, Laura. "Vegans, Zombies, and Eco-apocalypse: McCarthy's *The Road* and Atwood's *Year of the Flood*." *ISLE*, vol. 22, no. 3, 2015, pp. 507–24.

Yeats, W. B. "The Second Coming." *The Norton Anthology of English Literature*, edited by M. H. Abrams, 5th ed., vol. 2, W. W. Norton, 1986, p. 1948.